CAMBRIDGE STUDIES IN PHILOSOPHY

Assertion and Conditionals

CAMBRIDGE STUDIES IN PHILOSOPHY

General editor SYDNEY SHOEMAKER

Advisory editors J. E. J. ALTHAM, SIMON BLACKBURN,
GILBERT HARMAN, MARTIN HOLLIS, FRANK JACKSON,
JONATHAN LEAR, JOHN PERRY, T. J. SMILEY, BARRY STROUD

Assertion and Conditionals

Anthony Appiah

Assistant Professor of Philosophy and Afro-American Studies,
Yale University

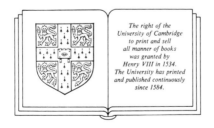

The right of the
University of Cambridge
to print and sell
all manner of books
was granted by
Henry VIII in 1534.
The University has printed
and published continuously
since 1584.

Cambridge University Press

Cambridge

London   New York   New Rochelle
Melbourne   Sydney

Published by the Press Syndicate of the University of Cambridge
The Pitt Building, Trumpington Street, Cambridge CB2 1RP
32 East 57th Street, New York, NY 10022, USA
10 Stamford Road, Oakleigh, Melbourne 3166, Australia

First published 1985

Printed in Great Britain at the University Press, Cambridge

Library of Congress catalogue card number: 85–4738

British Library cataloguing in publication data
Appiah, Anthony
Assertion and conditionals. – (Cambridge
studies in philosophy)
1. Conditionals (Logic)
I. Title
160   BC199.C56

ISBN 0 521 30411 3

AN

For M.: Quod spiro et placeo, si placeo, tuum est.

Horace, 'Quem, tu, Melpomene...'

Contents

Acknowledgements

Hugh Mellor knows that it is literally true that without him this book would not have been written. Without him I might have written another one, but it would certainly have been worse. He guided me through the doctoral work on which this book is based, and I have had many fruitful conversations with him since, especially in a seminar we organised in Cambridge in the autumn of 1983. That this book is not better is despite his many patient corrections, fruitful questions and kind encouragements.

Terry Moore, and the other members of a lunchtime seminar in the Cambridge Department of Linguistics in 1980–81 helped to make me aware of how wide a gap there is between what I have said about conditionals and a proper account of their linguistic behaviour; and I should have written a better book, if I had known how to use more of what I learnt from them. Terry also helped clarify my views with his questions at my 1981 lectures on the 'background to meaning'; as did David Papineau in the same course of lectures and Hugh Mellor, Jonathan Lear and Isaac Levi at my lectures on conditionals the year before. Isaac Levi's famous vigour in argument was more stimulating than I think he realised; but I do not want to give the misleading impression that he agrees with me: on every central claim in this book, I think he holds a view at odds with mine!

I am grateful too to Tim Smiley for much helpful discussion since he examined my dissertation; to Dorothy Edgington for making many helpful suggestions as the other examiner of my dissertation, and for discussions of the matter of this book since; to Robert Stalnaker who also read my dissertation carefully and made many helpful and encouraging remarks, even though he thinks my view of conditionals neither correct nor plausible (I concentrated on the encouragement); to Frank Jackson for discussing conditionals with me whilst busy packing to go home to Australia; to Nick Jardine for introducing me to Adams' work in the first place; to David Lewis for a brief but helpful discussion of beliefs in 1981 and longer discussion of conditionals in 1983; to Brian Ellis, for sending me many useful ideas on conditionals in unpublished papers; and to Ruth Marcus for many discussions and much kindness both while I was first at Yale and since. I owe much to many students at Cambridge and at Yale: but especially to Alasdair Palmer.

Part of Chapter 5 are from 'A Causal Theory of Truth Conditions', a paper I gave at the Thyssen seminar in April 1984, and which was helpfully criticised there, most extensively by Michael Ayers, Jeremy Butterfield, Hide Ishiguro, Hugh Mellor, John Perry and John Skorupski. I am grateful to them especially; and also to the Thyssen Group and the Thyssen Foundation, who made, between them, an extremely enjoyable meeting possible.

Portions of this book have appeared before in journals, and I am grateful to their editors and publishers, both for permission to republish, and for commenting or arranging comments on earlier versions of the arguments.

In particular, parts of Chapter 8 are from 'Conversation and Conditionals', which appeared in the *Philosophical Quarterly* in 1982, and was based on a paper which was improved by criticism it received at a Keele conference on philosophy of language and logic, in 1981; and from 'Jackson on the Material Conditional', which appeared in the *Australasian Journal Of Philosophy* in 1984, and owes much to Professor Brian Ellis, its editor, and to Phil Bricker. Chapter 9 owes a good deal to my paper 'Generalising the Probabilistic Semantics of Conditionals', which appeared in the *Journal Of Philosophical Logic* in 1984, to which Professor Thomason, the editor, and an anonymous referee made important contributions. This paper is © D. Reidel publishing company, Dordrecht, Holland.

Since I wrote my dissertation I have been at Yale; and the collegiality of my fellows in the departments of Afro-American Studies and Philosophy has been a constant pleasure. If I pick out Phil Bricker for special mention here, it is because Phil has helped me to clarify the triviality proofs and the dispute, reported in Chapter 9, about implicatures and conditionals.

But I owe Yale also the Morse Fellowship which allowed me to spend a year at Clare College in Cambridge. As many of you will know, it is one thing to write a dissertation, another to write a book. Without the Morse I should not have had the opportunity to learn this for myself. Having mentioned Clare several times already, I cannot end without acknowledging the friendship and stimulation of the Fellows of the college, where I have been for much of the last decade; more especially during my two years as a Research Fellow, and this year while I have had all the pleasures and priveleges of Fellowship, but, as a visiting Fellow, none of the responsibilities. No circumstances could have been more conducive to happy and productive labour.

A. A.

Notation

A few notes on notation and other conventions may prove helpful: I use '→', '⊃', '≡', '□→', for the indicative conditional, the material conditional, material equivalence and the subjunctive conditional respectively. '⟨S_1, S_2, ... S_n⟩' denotes an ordered set with n members, S_1 to S_n. '⊢' is the consequence relation (classical entailment or probabilistic consequences as context requires); and '⊣' is its converse.

I use 'P', 'Q', 'R', 'S', 'U', as variables for sentences, beliefs or other representations; and 'T' for a sentence, which is logically true, except where it is used, with 'F' for 'false', for the truth-value 'true' in the truth-tables of Chapter 8. 'i', 'k', 'm', 'n' are used as numerical variables. Other letters are used less systematically. Brackets are dropped wherever they are not necessary to avoid ambiguity.

In general, indented expressions or sentences are named (usually with a mnemonic label) where they will be referred to again in other sections or remote parts of the same section; numbered if they will be referred to again immediately and then not again (the numbering beginning anew in each section); and unlabelled if they do not need to be referred back to. But these principles are not strictly applied.

1

Cartesianism, behaviourism, and the philosophical context

I had even intended to ask your attention a little while on trust, and (as sometimes one contrives, in taking a friend to see a favourite piece of scenery) to hide what I wanted most to show with such imperfect cunning as I might, until we had unexpectedly reached the best point of view by winding paths. But . . . since I have heard it said by men practised in public address, that hearers are never so much fatigued as by the endeavour to follow a speaker who gives them no clue to his purposes – I will take off the slight mask at once.

(John Ruskin, 1865)

1.1 AFTER BEHAVIOURISM

In the sixth of the *Meditations on First Philosophy*, which he published in 1641, Descartes expresses the core of the dominant philosophy of mind of the last three centuries:

from the mere fact that I know for certain that I exist and that I cannot see anything else that belongs necessarily to my nature or essence, except that I am a thinking thing, I rightly conclude that my essence consists in this alone: that I am a thinking thing, a substance whose whole nature or essence is to think . . . it is certain that this *I*, that is to say my soul, which makes me what I am, is entirely and truly distinct from my body, and can be or exist without it. (1968: 156, translation slightly altered)

For a Cartesian, therefore, the mind is the private domain of a single consciousness, and it is possible, at least in principle, that there should be disembodied minds, unable, however hard they tried, to become aware of each other. Descartes knew, of course, that the way we do in fact come to know what is happening in other minds is by way of observing the speech and actions of 'other bodies'. But for Descartes it was always a serious conceptual possibility[1] that the evidence we normally take as adequate for supposing that other bodies are inhabited by minds should be produced by automata. Minds and bodies are quite distinct sorts of things – 'substances' – whose causal relations are obscure; and there is a serious epistemological worry about how one mind should know anything about another.

I have said this was the dominant view: and so it was. So dominant, in fact,

---

1. Ruled out, in fact, only by the guarantee of a God, who is 'no deceiver'.

I

that by the post-war era the central problems of the philosophy of mind were reduced, in effect to two. First, the 'problem of other minds':[2] 'What justifies our belief that other minds exist at all?' And secondly, 'the mind–body question':[3] 'How are we to explain the relations of a mind and its body?'

The very evident fact that we *do* know that other people have minds has lead some philosophers and psychologists in our own century to behaviourism. Faced with these problems for the Cartesian view of mind as different in substance from the body, they have identified the mind with certain bodily dispositions. In particular, they have sought to characterise belief, which for Descartes (and for the British empiricists who followed him) was a paradigmatically private matter, in terms of dispositions to produce and respond to language. On such a view, which we can find, for example, in Quine, believing that, say, grass is green, is simply being disposed, in certain circumstances, to assent to the sentence 'Grass is green.'[4] Since bodily dispositions seem to be less epistemologically puzzling than the states of a mental substance, this solution to the second question also solves the first.

This behaviourist view may solve some problems, but it leaves others. It makes it impossible, for example, to give a straightforward account of the beliefs of non-speaking creatures (including infants), and has led some philosophers to deny that such creatures can have beliefs at all.[5] The behaviourist also has to deny what is, I think, the natural view of language. In a Cartesian framework, of the sort adopted by Descartes' contemporaries Arnauld and Hobbes,[6] language can be seen as simply the expression of our thought; or, as Hobbes puts it, with characteristic directness:

Words so connected as that they become signs of our thoughts, are called SPEECH, of which every part is a name. (Hobbes, 1839)

The behaviourist objection to this account is rooted in a scepticism as to the existence of the private states – Hobbes' 'thoughts' – which Cartesianism regards as the one sort of thing 'that I know for certain.' Blaming the defects of the Cartesian view on its commitment to the existence of private mental states, they have placed their confidence in the certain existence of the public sphere of utterance.

2. See, for example, John Wisdom's well-known *Other Minds* (1952).
3. See, for example, H. Feigl's *The Mental and the Physical* (1967).
4. Quine's reflective view is more subtle than this; but there are passages where he commits himself to what looks like just this position; see (Quine, 1960: 217; 1975). This view, which seems to me one that common sense should find faintly bizarre, is nevertheless, held also by, for example, Donald Davidson and Michael Dummett; see Davidson's 'Thought and Talk' (1975), and Drummett's *Frege, The Philosophy of Language* (1973), *passim*. This unanimity is especially striking as they agree about almost nothing else.
5. Davidson, Dummett, Quine, see previous footnote.
6. See Hacking (1975a), which influences this whole (brisk!) account.

And, in my view, it has been a significant part of the appeal which language has had for many recent philosophers, as an object of philosophical study, that it is public. Spoken and written language, unlike the intentions and beliefs of its speakers, is open to the inspection of all. In short, a critique of the Cartesian view of the mind as a pure consciousness, privately available to itself, led many philosophers in the analytic tradition to embrace language as something empirically accessible, and to reject an account of language, therefore, as the expression of interior states.

Now though there is something rather unsatisfactory about the privacy of the Cartesian mind, there is something absurd about the publicity of the behaviourist one. 'Hello; you're fine. How am I?' says the behaviourist in the cartoon; and the cartoonist has a point. What was needed was somewhere in a gap which most philosophers could not discover between the Cartesian Scylla and the behaviourist Charybdis: and this book is an attempt to see what we can do in the philosophy of language, now that what we call 'functionalism' has shown us how to chart a course between them.

1.2 THE BACKGROUND

Functionalism, therefore, is the key thought behind the account I offer in this book of language and its relation to the mind and to reality; and a large portion of Part I of this book is devoted to explaining and defending a functionalist account of the mental. But I can best explain the detailed structure of the book by saying how it came to be written. The story I shall tell is, like most accounts of the origin of an intellectual project, a kind of friction. But it is, I hope, an explanatory fiction, in the sense that it helps to make intelligible the project whose origins it purports to describe.

I had been concerned, when I started research for my doctoral dissertation, with what then (in 1975) seemed to me the most important question in philosophical semantics: the issue between realism and antirealism, which Dummett had made central to his discussion of Frege; see Dummett (1973). Dummett's view was that semantic realism, the thesis that the meaning of declarative sentences was given by their truth conditions, was irremediably flawed; and that we should do better if we tried to explain meaning in terms of conditions which provided epistemic warrant for assertion; in terms, in other words, of what have been called 'assertibility conditions'. My initial feeling was that Dummett's arguments against realist semantics were challenging, perhaps even unanswerable; but that their conclusion – that our grasp of the meaning of most sentences could not issue from knowledge of their truth conditions – was very hard to accept. If Dummett was wrong in his arguments against realism, there was no compulsion to do assertibility condition semantics. I felt he *was* wrong. But in philosophy we are supposed to follow reason, even where it conflicts with our hunches; so I thought it was necessary to examine the question: 'What would a semantics in terms of assertibility conditions look like?'

In casting about for ways to approach this question, I came across some work on the logic of conditionals which offered a promising starting place. For, just in this case, it seemed, there was overwhelming evidence that a truth-conditional account – which Dummett claimed was the essence of realism – could not be provided. This, I thought, was the message of David Lewis' triviality proofs, which were finally published in Lewis (1976). Ernest Adams had suggested, in two papers (1965, 1966) and, finally, in his book *The Logic of Conditionals* (1975), that the indicative conditional's semantics should be given not by way of truth conditions, but by way of a rule of assertibility. That rule was that conditionals were assertible when the conditional probability of the consequent, given the antecedent, was high. I call this Adams' Hypothesis.

In examining this view I came to two conclusions, first, that if Adams was right, there was a good sense in which indicative conditionals do not have truth conditions; and secondly, that the relevant notion of assertibility was one that needed further examination.

There was an obvious place to look for an account, both of the sense in which conditionals do not have truth conditions and of the notion of assertibility. And that was in an examination of the nature of the subjective probabilities in terms of which the assertibility rule was couched: and of their relation to the speech-act of assertion. So I began the work which takes up the first two parts of this book.

I set out, then, to explain subjective probabilities in a way which could plausibly ground the kind of assertibility rule that Adams had proposed. In doing so I became dissatisfied with the standard accounts of the status of subjective probabilities. The source of my dissatisfaction was the simple fact that nothing adequate had been said about the way subjective probability theory could form part of a descriptive account of agents and the sources of their behaviour. Plainly, people's degrees of belief are not coherent in the way that standard decision theory requires, and the question why that was seemed to lack an answer I could believe.

In finding the answer I was lucky in two things: first, I had read some time in the mid-1970s Ian Hacking's paper on 'slightly more realistic personal probability' (1967*b*); second, while spending a year at work in the Yale Graduate School, I had attended a seminar of Jerry Fodor's on the philosophy of psychology. What Fodor provided me with was the notion of computational structure, which I shall use to explain the relation between decision theory and the actual behaviour of agents. What Hacking gave me was the only paper I know of in which what is, in essence, a computational approach had been applied to subjective probability. Classical decision theory cannot explain how people can come to give assent to sentences which ought, because they are logically impossible, to have zero probability in every probability function; or how they can fail to give assent to sentences which follow from sentences they believe. Given the theory of computational structure, which is outlined in Chapter 4, this can now be explained.

In coming to see how to deal with these questions I became more convinced that decision theory, in its descriptive guise, is best seen as part of the functionalist theory of representational states.

What I also came to see was that the notion of assertibility was not needed only for structures like the conditional which do not determine truth conditions; rather it was a central explanatory concept in the philosophy of language. For truth-conditional sentences, the account of assertibility is rather straightforward: what is assertible is what you believe to be very probably true. But though it is straightforward it is not unimportant. For without this much theory, we cannot connect work in logic with the actual linguistic behaviour of speakers. It is this connection between probability and assertion that is at the core of what has come to be called 'probabilistic semantics'. And this book is an attempt to set out (one way of looking at) the foundations of this new, and, in my view, important departure in semantic theory. I say 'one way' because the particular way in which I develop probabilistic semantics within a functionalist framework is not one that will appeal to all philosophical tastes: however, I think it is at present the best way.

Though assertibility now seems to me a crucial notion, the issue of antirealism has faded somewhat into the background; I now think it is a diversion. For, for the large class of truth-conditional sentences, the assertibility rule makes explicit reference to the truth conditions. We do not need to chose between truth and assertibility: we have to have them both. For this and other reasons, which are set out in my forthcoming book *For Truth In Semantics*, I think that Dummett's global antirealism is ill advised: but I do argue in this book for a modest local antirealism about indicative conditionals.

1.3 THE STRUCTURE OF THE BOOK

This book is intended, therefore, as an introduction to this new approach to semantic theorising, whose outlines I have discerned in the recent writings of a number of philosophers. What is new in it is not just the technical apparatus of probability theory; for it also offers the possibility of reconciling the view that language is the expression of interior states, on the one hand, with the legitimate rejection both of the Cartesian view of the inner and of the behaviourist over-reaction to Cartesianism, on the other. Much of the argument in the literature in this area is extremely technically demanding; and, like most new work, its philosophical underpinnings are often glossed over in the urgent desire to communicate the latest insight. In consequence many assumptions are not spelled out in sufficient detail to be accessible to the generally interested reader; indeed, so far as I know, some of these assumptions have never been examined in a detailed way before the work of my own dissertation. They require detailed philosophical exploration and defence.

So Part I begins with a discussion of the nature of beliefs. I have already sketched the central features of the Cartesian tradition – 'our' tradition, one is bound to say – and criticised its notion of privacy; and that critique is a crucial element in the motivation for the first chapter, where I argue for functionalism in the philosophy of mind. The new few chapters elaborate a picture of beliefs as a kind of functional representation, in a theory with two interlocking parts. Chapter 3 discusses the first part, which focusses on the role of beliefs, in concert with desires, in producing action; Chapter 4, the second part, which looks to the role of belief in thought. It is argued that we can capture this latter role by way of a notion of *computational structure*, which is a way of saying how beliefs interact with each other, and with desires, to produce other desires and beliefs. 'Computational' because I think that there is a good analogy here with the way the information-bearing states of computers interact; 'structure', because the patterns of interaction depend on features analogous to the syntactic structure of strings in a natural or artificial language. Chapter 5 shows how, once the central role of belief in thought, prior to action, is understood, truth conditions can be assigned to beliefs along with their computational structures. And truth conditions and computational structure are major features, I claim, of beliefs (and, as it happens, of desires). Each of these kinds of state has other features also: notably degrees or strengths, which, for beliefs are called *subjective probabilities* and for desires are called *desirabilities*.

Part II, which begins at Chapter 6, is about the theory of meaning. I think that the core of the theory of meaning can be given by the simple thought that assertion expresses belief. But Chapter 6 looks first at a way of thinking about meaning in terms of truth not in terms of the expression of inner states, but in terms of the outer states sentences set out to describe. That theory is that the meanings of assertions are their truth conditions – conditions which hold when and only when they are true; and I discuss briefly Donald Davidson's way of setting such a theory up. My interest here is not in Davidson's theory in itself, but in two things that it allows us to see clearly: first, how we can use the structure of a truth-theory to set up a picture of the relations between the truth conditions of sentences; second, how important is the subjunctive dependency of a sentence's meaning on the way the world is. The first of these things is successfully captured in the structure of Davidson's theory; the second is not. But both Davidson's successes and his failures are instructive.

These lessons learnt, I can say, in Chapter 7, how I think a theory of meaning should work. Since I take it that sentences express beliefs, the job is to say for each sentence what belief it expresses in a given context; and since Part I gives a canonical representation for beliefs, I claim that the right mapping is from sentences into those canonical representations. It will emerge that Davidson is half right. Sentences do have truth conditions and they partly fix their meaning. But the reason they have truth conditions is that beliefs do; and truth conditions won't do on their own to individuate beliefs.

Part III then takes up the problem I began with a decade ago: how do we fix the meanings of indicative conditionals? And I try to show how the theory of meaning of Part II allows us to solve this old question. I think the semantics of conditionals is an intrinsically interesting question; but you do not have to believe that to read Part III. For the fact that we can solve some previously intractable problems about conditionals is part of the evidence for the view that the theory of meaning is right. And if you are not interested in the theory of meaning – in the relation of language, mind and world – you should not be reading a philosophy book.

1.4 NEGLECTED TOPICS

There are two conspicuous absences in this book, absences which will worry those familiar with recent work in the philosophy of language. First, I have not discussed the general issue of psychologism in semantics; which Dummett has on one occasion defined as the 'invasion of the theory of meaning by notions concerned with mental processes' (1975: 240). What may appear worse is that I have actually assumed the opposite of what is now widely believed, since my position is unabashedly psychologistic. I had originally written a chapter in defence of my psychologism. But it seems to me, in the end, that most of the arguments against the kind of psychologism that I espouse were just bad arguments; and that the best defence of my position was just to show that I could proceed on psychologistic assumptions without getting into trouble. My psychologism amounts to this: I hold that we can give an account of the contents of the beliefs of agents, independent of any account of their languages, and then go on to explain linguistic acts as the expression of those beliefs. Dummett (1973, *passim*) and Davidson (1975) both deny this. I hope that as my argument proceeds my position will at least remain plausible. I have argued against Dummett in the last part of *For Truth In Semantics* (forthcoming); Jonathan Bennett has ably pursued the same conclusion in his *Linguistic Behaviour* (1976); and Jerry Fodor has also done so, in a different way, in *The Language Of Thought* (1976). Between them, I think these defences alone – and there are, of course, others – make the absence of an elaborate discussion of psychologism excusable. All the work of the first five chapters is meant to apply to agents whether or not they have languages: and granted that the account works, I see no reason to accept Dummett's position.

What is also conspicuously absent is any detailed discussion of possible world approaches to meaning and to the conditional. I have one general and one particular reason for avoiding possible worlds. The general reason is this: my account of the mind is functionalist and thus fundamentally causal. Possible worlds do not, of course, enter into causal relations with each other, and so, in particular, there are no causal interactions 'across' worlds. The question of how possible worlds relate to causation is not yet at all clear. Until an account of the causal facts entailed by an ascription to a belief of a class of worlds in which it is true is available, it is difficult to see how possible worlds can be of use to functionalism. When it is available, I conjecture, it will be clear that, *pace* David Lewis (1973), they play no essential explanatory role. That accounts for my general suspicion of possible world accounts.

But my specific objection is, in the context of what I am doing, quite decisive. Possible world semantics assigns to sentences truth conditions: it tells us which sentences are true in the actual world in virtue of truths about other worlds. But I believe, and I argue, that the conditionals I am concerned with do not have truth conditions; and, if I am right, there cannot therefore be a possible world semantics for them.

This argument is, I have no doubt, too brisk to satisfy everyone. There are non-realist ways of construing possible world semantics: seeing possible worlds as maximal consistent sets of sentences, for example, is one, provided the relevant notion of consistency is not defined in terms of truth. But such interpretations require a restructuring of the way possible world semantics is usually done, certainly for conditionals: and I do not feel obliged to do that restructuring. If we can do conditional semantics without possible worlds, I see nothing to be gained by doing it with them.

Part I   *Belief*

2

A theory of the mind

The concept of a mental state is primarily the concept of a state of the person apt for bringing about a certain sort of behaviour.

(Armstrong, 1968: 82)

2.1 OVERVIEW

The central claim of this book is that the meaning of an asserted sentence is, in a certain sense, the content of the belief that it expresses. So I must begin with a story about beliefs and their contents. In fact, as I have said, my story is functionalism, the story encapsulated in the remark of Armstrong's which provides my epigraph. I need to give the outlines of functionalism's picture of the mental because the general account of belief and of the contents of beliefs is needed if I am to make good my central claim. Since my interest is mainly in assertion, and in beliefs as what assertions express, I concentrate mainly on giving an account of the mental state of believing; but because, as I shall argue, that account can only be given in the context of a theory that also takes account of desires, I am obliged also to say something about desire.

The theory I hold is functionalist: for it claims that we can state sufficient *a priori* truths about the causal roles of mental states in interaction with each other and with events outside the mind, to be able to individuate those mental states by their causal roles. For the states of belief and desire the relevant events outside the mind fall into two classes: those events which lead to changes in the sensory and perceptual states of agents, on the one hand; and those events which are caused in the agent's actions, on the other. The next section elaborates some of the features of functionalism, but the general idea is easily grasped, by way of a simpler case. Take, then, by way of example, an account of the workings of a thermostat.

Consider some particular thermostat. We can give a complete physical account of its workings, by saying what its parts are made of, and what physical laws govern those parts. It will follow from such an account that if a certain part of the thermostat – the heat-sensor – is heated, the result will be to open a switch; and that if it is cooled, the result will be to close that switch. It will also follow that the opening of the switch turns off a heater; and that the closing of the switch turns it on. Thus, from the full physical description we shall be able to predict how the thermostat will function: as a device which turns a heater on and off in ways which depend on the temperature around the heat-sensor. But suppose we were not interested in a particular thermostat, but in thermostats in general. Then we could, of course, find no general physical description of the constitution of a thermostat and the laws which govern the working of its parts. For we can make a thermostat in an indefinite number of different ways. And if we want to say what all these different systems have in common, what it is that makes them all thermostats, we will have to describe not their physical constitution — what they are made of and what laws govern their parts — but their functioning. So, for example, we will have to say that a thermostat must contain

(a) some physical part, the heat-sensor, whose behaviour depends upon the temperature

(b) another part, the switch, which has two states, ON and OFF,

(c) a third part, the heater, which also has two states, ON and OFF,

and that

(d) when the heat-sensor has its temperature raised above some temperature T, the changes thus caused in it, cause the switch to go OFF, and

(e) when the heat-sensor has its temperature fall below T, the changes thus caused lead to the switch's going ON, and

(f) when the switch goes ON, the heater goes ON; and when the switch goes OFF, the heater goes OFF, and

(g) when the heater is ON, it gives out heat; and when it is OFF, it does not.

This description of a thermostat is functionalist: for it characterises a thermostat by saying what the causal roles of its parts are in mediating between changes in (the temperature of) the thermostat's environment and changes (in heat output) caused by events within the thermostat; and it does this partly by characterising the causal interactions of the parts with each other.

What this theory does not tell us is almost as important as what it does. It says nothing about the mass or the size or the shape or the colour of the thermostat: it only tells us what we need to know to get its *function* in temperature-regulation right.

We can generalise the idea.

What we need for a functionalist characterisation of a system generally is a specification of

(a) a set of inputs, changes in the environment which produce changes in the system,

(b) a set of outputs, changes in the environment produced by changes in the system,

and

(c) a model of the internal structure of the system in terms of the causal roles of its parts, in interaction with each other and with inputs and outputs.

Given a set of inputs and outputs, a functionalist model can then be indifferent between different systems whose physical structure is such as to guarantee that they have states with just the causal roles specified in the model of the internal structure. And, again generally, this is all we get. In the case of the thermostat, it does not matter whether the heat-sensor is a bi-metallic strip or a cylinder of gas; all that matters is that, given a change in the temperature of the environment, the heat sensor should change in such a way as to turn the switch ON and OFF as the model requires. All that matters, so far as the specification of the parts is concerned, is their causal role; their *function*.

In 2.2 of this chapter I outline the appeal of functionalism about minds. But I do not intend to say much to defend the general strategy of functionalism. That has been well done in many places: starting at least as far back as Ramsey (1978), and going on through, for example, Braithwaite (1932/3), Armstrong (1968, 1973), Lewis (1966, 1972*a*), Field (1977, 1978), and Loar (1980). For the moment bear in mind just this: I want to defend a functionalist account of beliefs and desires, for which the inputs are events in the sensory environments of agents, and the outputs are actions; a theory in which the function of minds is fixed by the way action depends upon states of minds, and states of mind depend on each other and on experiences of the world.

Functionalist theories characterise states by assigning them causal roles. In the kind of theory I envisage, which is what Shoemaker calls an 'analytical functionalist' theory, our project is one of conceptual analysis. 'The analytical functionalist seeks to extract his definition [of a mental state] from a 'theory' consisting of analytic or conceptual truths about the relations of mental states to inputs, outputs and other mental states' (1982: 104). So the relevant aspects of the causal roles of mental states are the *a priori* truths about their causal roles in the life of the agent; and I call such a set of truths a functional role.[1]

1. A word of warning is in order about the way an analytical functionalist theory is *a priori*. It is not, of course, *a priori* that an organism has any beliefs and desires at all. The *a priori* claims are claims about what an organism has to be like if it is to have any beliefs, desires and other mental states, not claims to the effect that it is *a priori* that they do have mental states. It is a theory of what organisms with minds must be like; not a theory that says that organisms must have minds.

My theory is not, however, just functionalist; it is also computational. For it holds that the mental states which correspond to the propositional attitudes — states, which, like belief and desire, are characterised by verbs in English which take a sentential complement with a 'that . . . ' clause — are what I, following Field (1978) and Fodor (1976), call 'representational'; and that computations with these representations make up at least part of the inner life of the mind. I spend 2.3 trying to make this claim plausible; but, once again, the general idea is easily grasped. For the language of representations draws on an analogy between the objects of belief, desire and the rest, and sentences, first of natural, then of artificial languages.

Natural language sentences are regarded in traditional grammar as having two distinct kinds of characteristics: namely, syntactic characteristics and semantic ones. It is taken for granted that sentences of identical semantics, sentences which 'mean the same', need not have identical syntax. Thus, for example,

(1) John loves Mary

and

(2) Mary is loved by John

are naturally regarded, at least *prima facie*, as meaning the same even though they differ in syntax. They contain some of the same minimal syntactic units (roughly, words): 'John', 'love', 'Mary'. But (2) differs from (1) in being in the passive, and thus requiring a different form of the verb 'love' and completion by 'by' to mark 'John' as the subject term. Yet despite these syntactic differences, they seem to make the same claim: certainly, it seems, (1) is true iff (2) is.

Now (1) and (2) are both 'representations': they are sentences which represent the fact that John loves Mary. It is natural to say that (1) and (2) have the same content, at least as far as truth is concerned, just because one is true iff the other is. And having hit upon the idea of 'content' it is natural to describe the respects in which (1) and (2) differ as questions of form; natural, that is, to see differences of syntax as differences of form.

So to talk of beliefs and desires as representations[2] is to suggest that beliefs and desires, like sentences, have both form and content: and, as I argue, the form of beliefs is in fact closely analogous to the syntax of sentences, though

---

2. I say beliefs *are* token representations not that they are relations to token representations. My beliefs represent the way the world is, my desires the way I would like it to be: it is reasonable to call them representations. When I *do* say that something *has* a relation to a representation, it is a believer, who has it to a type of representation. The relation is just 'believing a token of that type'.

the mapping from the syntax of a sentence to the form of the belief it expresses is not, in my view, one-to-one in either direction. Because our theory is basically functionalist we have to try to characterise both the form and the content of mental states in terms of their causal roles. And it is here that computation comes in. For I argue in 2.3, and in more detail in Chapter 4, that the features of beliefs which determine their form — what corresponds to the syntax of sentences — show up in aspects of their behaviour, which are like the behaviour of (some of the) internal states of computers. That, as I said in Chapter 1, is why I call the form of beliefs their 'computational structure'.

Computation is, I admit, another metaphor, yet to be made good. But it is an attractive metaphor which sees the processes that occur in minds as being like the processes which occur in computers: for computers are, after all, the physical systems which are intended to be most like minds. The processes that go on in computers are usually known to most users only under functional descriptions, just as, as I claim, mental states in others are known to us largely under functional descriptions. Thus, we write a program which will take numerals as input and produce the numeral which denotes the sum of the numbers the input numerals denote as output; and we say this program 'adds'. We do not manipulate the physical parts of the machine directly in order to get it to print out the numeral that denotes the sum. The program specifies what output the machine will produce, in terms of features of the input, and the previous states of the machine. And it does this in terms of the formal properties of the machine's representational states. So, we tell the machine to print out, say, 'S', whenever we input 'S & R'; and this operation is charac- terised solely in terms of the syntax of the representations. It is only when the 'S' gets printed out that the semantics gets put in; and it gets put in by us, when we interpret the printed symbols.

My theory claims that we can characterise some mental processes as being in this way like computations in a machine: they take a set of mental states with a certain form, analogous to the syntax of a formula of a programming language, and produce another mental state with a form that depends on that of the members of the original set. I call such processes 'computations', because in that respect they are like the computations of machines. A computation, then, is an operation of the functional system of the mind, which takes states with structures as inputs, and produces, as outputs, states whose structures are a function of the input structures. And I claim, as I say, that we can characterise the form of beliefs, that feature of them which corresponds to the syntax of sentences, in terms of how they behave under such computations.

These then are the two main tasks of this chapter: to say why functionalism is attractive and to characterise the sense in which the theory I am developing is representational. In 2.4, 2.5 and 2.6 some further general features of the theory I rely on in the chapters that follow are discussed, and 2.7 is a summary of the main results.

Functionalism's appeal begins simply with the fact that it is intuitive. Most people judge that the best test of a person's real beliefs is what they do and not, for instance, just what they say. If Mary tells us she thinks the bridge is safe but refuses to walk across it, or does so only tentatively, we are inclined to believe that she is either self-deceived or insincere. And this sort of view follows naturally from the functionalist account of the mental state of believing. For a belief is, on a functionalist view, a state which disposes an agent, against the background of other beliefs and desires, to certain actions. It is not enough that someone be disposed simply to say that she thinks that the bridge is safe; she must also act as if she thinks it, if we are to believe her.

Other functionalist claims, which I will make in the next few chapters, are also deeply rooted in our common-sense conception of ourselves as agents. Thus, for example, it seems hardly worth questioning the claim that normally sighted individuals placed before large red objects in normal lighting, when conscious, will normally believe that those objects are red. Yet this claim, and many others like it, play a crucial part in a functionalist account of beliefs and desires.

But I want to offer two more theoretical sorts of consideration in favour of functionalism: the first epistemological and the second ontological.

Mental states share with theoretical entities a certain epistemological problem: they are not accessible directly to the evidence of the senses. Recent work in the philosophy of science may have led us to question the value of the traditional distinction between observation and theory; but there is a rough and ready line to be drawn between those sentences whose truth we can discover simply by looking (listening, or otherwise directing our senses) in the right place, and those which cannot. And, if sentences reporting the colour of middle-sized objects fall on the observational side of this line (for most of us), sentences reporting the beliefs of others or the presence of electrons seem to fall pretty clearly on the non-observational side. Beliefs, so it seems, are at least as epistemically inaccessible as electrons.

As I said in 1.1, the inaccessibility of other people's minds to observation is at the centre of the twentieth-century discussion of the 'problem of other minds'. For, granted that we cannot observe other minds, how can we find out about them; indeed, how do we know that anyone else has a mind at all?

Part of the appeal of functionalist theories is that they offer answers to these last two questions. The causal role of a belief, for example, is given by saying how it will be changed by sensations, perceptions, and changes in other beliefs, on the one hand; and by how it helps to determine causally, in concert with other beliefs and desires, which actions the agent performs. Actions and perceptions are pretty public. If it is *a priori* true that beliefs do interact causally in these specific ways with such public phenomena as actions and the perceiving of objects, then it is *a priori* true that we can gain evidence, from their actions in the presence of perceived objects, as to the nature of agents' beliefs. If, for example, the theory says *a priori* that agents will do A, when stimulated by having a certain kind of visible (or audible) object before their eyes (or ears), only if they are in one of a certain set of mental states, then, if they do A when so stimulated, that is decisive evidence that they are in one of those states. Provided the action A and the stimulation are observable, we shall here have evidence, rooted in observation, for the ascription of mental states.

A functionalist theory will not, of course, deny the underdetermination of mental state ascription by the agent's actual behaviour; it will have to leave open the very evident possibility that, in any case, we may have got it wrong. But since a functionalist theory associates mental states with causal roles in the production of behaviour when the agent is subject to sensory and other input, the ascription of mental states will have, for functionalists, consequences about what the results would be of any such input: and it will thus entail subjunctive conditionals about behaviour. It thus characterises mental states not simply by the actual behaviour of agents but by way of a whole range of possible behavioural responses to stimuli.

Suppose, then, we ascribe to an agent a set of beliefs and desires. That ascription will entail, on a functionalist theory, conditionals about the consequences of stimulation in the behaviour of the agent. Where stimulation produces the predicted result, the ascription is confirmed, or, at least, not refuted.

There is a useful analogy here, which I shall be developing later, with those states that philosophers have called dispositional. (I say 'analogy' for reasons discussed in 2.4). Take the standard case: fragility. The breaking of a glass when it is dropped is evidence of its having been fragile. But with glasses, as with agents, one can be misled. Perhaps the glass was not at all fragile, but was shattered by a high energy laser beam at the moment of impact. Perhaps any one of an indefinite number of alternative explanations is correct. Still, in the absence of support for these alternatives, the breaking on the stone floor is grounds for ascribing fragility; just as, according to functionalism, particular actions in particular circumstances are grounds for ascribing, say, beliefs.

Functionalism thus entails that the ascription of mental states is responsive in certain specific ways to the evidence of behaviour, thus showing that, and how, it is possible for us to come to know about other minds. That way we escape the puzzling privacy of Cartesianism.

But we escape the implausible publicity of behaviourism also; for there are important differences between a functionalist theory and a behaviourist one. As Fodor has argued recently (1981), a key difference lies in the way that a functionalist theory, unlike a behaviourist one, specifies the causal role of a mental state, not only by way of the effects it has on agents' dispositions to respond to stimuli, but also by way of that state's interactions with other mental states. For behaviourism, mental states are dispositions, elicited by stimuli and producing responses. For functionalism, though mental states do indeed interact causally with stimuli − as when, for example, sensory stimulation gives rise to belief; and do give rise to action − as when an intention produces (against a certain background) an action; they also interact causally with each other − as when the production of one belief leads to the production of another, for which the agent takes it to be evidence. Functionalism, in other words, takes the internal states of an agent's mind seriously as connecting causally with each other, while behaviourism does not.

But functionalism not only takes inner states seriously, it allows also that these real states can be present without anyone − even the agent − knowing about them. Their presence has consequences for what would happen if certain things happened to the agent. But if those things don't happen, the states may never manifest themselves to anybody; and that is another way in which functionalism avoids the crazy publicity of the behaviourist mind.

2.3 COMPUTATION AND REPRESENTATION

For reasons discussed now and elaborated later, I do not see how an adequate theory of the propositional attitudes of human agents could fail to be representational. In this section I begin by showing that beliefs must be representational and by making it clear what this means. And I then go on to show what the connection is between representational theories and what I have called computation.

The cases which force upon us the computational view are cases where what someone does depends not simply on the truth conditions of their beliefs about a situation but also upon how they represent it to themselves. Take an artificial but illuminating example.

In two cases, which I call A and B, I offer you an empty cup. In case A I told you first, a minute ago,

A: 'I am going to give you a cup. And it will not be both empty and mine.'

When the cup arrives you judge quickly that it is not mine; for you see that it is empty. In case B I told you first, also a minute earlier

B: 'I am going to give you a cup. And it will be either not empty or not mine.'

You judge less quickly that it is not mine. Further if I ask you in case A to make your mind up in five seconds; and if I ask you to do the same in case B; you get the answer right for A but not for B.

I have tried to make this case a natural one. I think that it is quite realistic to expect that in this case such a thing might happen with a particular subject. But even if it did not happen this way ever; if, for example, the answer came quicker in case B, and was more prone to error in case B also; even if all agents always performed identically in the two set-ups; the point would still be made. For it must surely be admitted that it is at least conceivable that someone should behave as they are supposed to do in set-ups A and B. And that is all I require. For I am an analytical functionalist: if it is *a priori* possible it is part of our concept of the mental. Since it is possible, analytical functionalism must show how it is possible. And, so far as I can see, there is only one natural way of explaining the fact that the response takes longer in case B than in case A, and is more prone to error. And it is that you have stored in each case a representation of the state of affairs which each of my utterances identically represents: but that the processing time for the representation of the form $\neg(\text{EMPTY} \& \text{MINE})$ is shorter than for the representation of the form $(\neg\text{EMPTY} \vee \neg\text{MINE})$. Granted that this is a possibility it follows that there must be a difference between the functional roles of the two different states; and this, despite the fact that, since they are logically equivalent, they have the same truth conditions. Since this case is conceivable, it follows that it is consistent with our *a priori* theory that two beliefs, with identical truth conditions should have different causal roles. Thus any theory which treats logically equivalent beliefs identically cannot fully characterise the functional roles of beliefs.

At this point it would be natural to ask why I say that what is stored is a representation and not a sentence. Plausibly, the difference in the two cases is that in one case the belief is somehow stored in a state isomorphic to the sentence

'The cup will not be both empty and his';

and in the other case in a state isomorphic to the sentence

'The cup will be either not empty or not his.'

I object to attempts to explain the representational features of beliefs by supposing them to be in some obvious sense isomorphic to sentences; and I want now to say why.

To begin with, we must be clear what we are thinking about. If beliefs are stored as sentences, they must be stored as sentence tokens, and not as sentence types; tokens of the same sentence type are isomorphic. So that if beliefs are stored as sentences they must be stored as states which have the same structure as sentences, in a sense yet to be elucidated. This much said, I have four lines of objection to saying that beliefs are stored as (something isomorphic with) sentences.

First, I believe, though this is not a thesis which I shall defend, that animals such as dogs and chimpanzees quite plainly have beliefs. It is unnatural to refer to sentences when discussing the beliefs of non-speaking animals. That it is unnatural does not, of course, rule it out. It is *our* talk about animals, so we might understand the beliefs that undergird their behaviour as structured in ways that are reflected in the structures of the sentences we use to talk about them.

This consideration, then, certainly is not decisive. But my second line of objection *does* show decisively that natural language sentences will not do on their own as the objects of belief, and it is just this: there simply are not enough sentences to do the job. There are many topics about which I have beliefs but for which there are no sentences in English, or, so far as I know, in any language. I believe, for example, of the walls of my room that they are a certain shade of blue. There is no name in English that I know of that picks out just the shade of blue that I believe my wall to be. That is because there are not, in English, words for every shade of colour I am able to discriminate. So too, as I look at the sky I have certain quite specific beliefs about the shapes of the clouds and their spatial distribution, which are, so to speak, much more fine grained than any sentences in English I might use to describe them. Still, someone committed to sentences might want to say we can use the structure of English to model beliefs, extending it, where necessary, to give the extra material we need. Beliefs have the same form as sentences, but a richer vocabulary, then: that is the theory.

Perhaps there is something to this proposal. But it seems open, *prima facie*, to the third line of objection, which follows.

Think, for the moment, about translation. Plausibly, what Pierre believes when he says sincerely 'Il n'est pas ici' is that someone or other (the referent of 'il') is not here. If what he believes is what I believe when I say sincerely 'He is not here' in the same set-up, then, presumably, if my belief is isomorphic with the English sentence 'He is not here' so is his. So then the English sentence is isomorphic, presumably, with the French sentence. For, presumably, isomorphism is transitive. And presumably English has no especial privilege in the language of thought, so that this belief is isomorphic with the French sentence which expresses it, as it is with the English one. Now the trouble is that if these two sentences are in the relevant sense isomorphic, this is certainly not something that is plain to the eye or ear. The isomorphism is not one of linear structure in time. For the negation is achieved in French by a device that is plainly distributed in two places in the sentence. And at some theoretical level of 'semantic representation', at which both sentences receive the reading 'NOT (HE IS HERE)', we are no longer talking about sentences of natural language at all.

I place little rhetorical weight on this argument, since those who are disposed to take sentences as in some sense the objects of thought are not, usually, very happy about arguments which make assumptions about translation. But unless we can find a way of mapping sentences from one language to another, there seems to be the possibility that these theorists will end up denying that anyone outside their own linguistic group has beliefs at all. That would be in a long tradition of anglophone chauvinism, but it does not look well in philosophy.

These are considerations which suggest that talk of beliefs having the structure of sentences would be misleading at best. But I think there is reason to think that it would generally be simply wrong.

Remember we are trying to capture the *a priori* features of belief. If it is consistent with our *a priori* theory that beliefs should be structured in ways very unlike sentences, then the proposal I am discussing would just be wrong. But it *is* consistent with our theory. It is not only possible but actually plausible that our beliefs about the visible world, the beliefs generated by seeing, are structured more like three-dimensional images than like sentences. I sit here gazing across the garden of the college, my consciousness filled with beliefs about the spatial distribution of flowers and birds, river and sky. I can produce sentences about all this: in an extended language, enriched to cope with shades and shapes we do not talk about normally, I might even be able to say *everything* that I believe about this scene. But what reason is there to think that that is how my beliefs are structured – in strings like sentences – now?

I think the answer is: None. And if that is right, it is better to speak of representations than of sentences in the language of the mind. Perhaps one day cognitive psychologists will show that all the thoughts we have are best modelled by structures like sentences. If they do, that will be an interesting discovery. It will mean that our pre-scientific conception of beliefs has here (as it certainly will have *some*where) space for an unactualised possibility. We might even revise our concepts in response; but, frankly, I find this suggestion amazing. And until some such evidence comes in, I will stick to talk of representations.

It is essential not to go from one extreme – 'all structural features of beliefs are sentence-like' – to the other – 'none are'. What I have said does not exclude the possibility that *some* of our beliefs have structural features that are sentence-like. That *none* did would be an equally amazing possibility. Certainly, the beliefs we express in sentences must have some abstract features that are like the syntax of sentences, otherwise the internal structure of phrases of the form 'the belief that *S*' could play no role in fixing the contents of the belief that '*S*' expresses. But if *that* were true, the only feature left to fix the content would seem to be the truth condition: and that is a consequence that talk of representations was precisely meant to allow us to avoid. But notice that this does not mean that beliefs do not have aspects of their structure which are *not* sentence-like. Suppose the belief that the cat is on the mat is 'encoded' as a three-dimensional image. Then the belief that it is not the case that the cat is on the mat might be stored as the same image of the same scene with a cross through it. Provided the image of the cross *functions* in the right way, then this latter belief has a structural feature which makes it a negative belief: it has, as we might say, a 'NOT' in its computational structure. For this reason, when I come, in Chapter 4, to provide ways of characterising the computational structures of beliefs we actually do express in English, the model will give them sentence-like structural features. In English, the standard way of referring to beliefs trades on the structure of sentences, and on nothing else save their truth conditions.

Not that the form of every belief is exactly isomorphic with the syntax of the sentence which expresses it, indeed the mapping from the syntax of sentences to the form of beliefs is not going, in general, to be one-to-one in either direction; see the end of 2.3. The same sentence can express two different beliefs: which is why sentences can be ambiguous. And two sentences, of different form, can plainly express the same belief: active sentences and their passive tranformations frequently do this. But all this shows is that not *every* structural feature of a sentence helps to individuate the belief it expresses, and that the same computational structure can be captured in different ways. So sentences which express the same belief can be held to be identical in meaning, even where they differ in their syntax; and if a sentence can express two different beliefs then, plausibly, it has (at least) two meanings. Provided we find for each unambiguous sentence a belief, individuated by more than truth conditions, for it to express, then we have a good chance of saying what it means; see Chapter 7.

This diversion from the main argument began when I observed that the only way I knew of which would explain the difference between the behaviour of an agent in set-up *A* and set-up *B* was to suppose that, though the agent's beliefs in the two set-ups had identical truth conditions, they were differently represented; and the two representations had (amongst other differences) different processing times. Though the example I have given is trivial, in the case of the empty cup, Fodor's (1976) book is full of interesting experiments which we can explain if we assume that subjects store representations, and which are mysterious otherwise. The theory I am advocating is one that holds that at least some mental states – beliefs and desires – are representations, and that some mental processes are carried out by computations with these representations.

If we put together the functionalist and the computational streams of the theory, we can say both how simple, and yet how important, the contribution of the computational component is. For the combined theory amounts to this: the propositional attitudes are states whose causal roles are functions not only of their truth conditions, but also of another feature as well. I shall call that feature computational structure.

We need the notion of computational structure in order to deal with the fact that beliefs with the same truth conditions may have different causal roles. Let us say that two beliefs have the same truth-content iff they have the same truth conditions; where they have the same truth conditions iff it is logically necessary that if one of them is true the other one is also. Consider now two beliefs with the same truth-content, B_1 and B_2. They are beliefs of the same agent at the same time, yet they differ in causal role. The notion of computational structure provides us with what we need to distinguish these beliefs. Provided there are beliefs with the same truth conditions and different causal roles, according to our *a priori* theory, then beliefs are bound to have computational structure.

It is time now to say more about the kind of way in which computational structure determines functional role. And the place to begin is with the analogy with computers that gave us the 'computational' in 'computational structure'.

Such features of a program as how long it takes to run depend not on the truth conditions of the sentences the program contains, but simply on their syntactic structure. If for every '4' in some program I write '1 + 2 + 3 − 1 − 1', then, on reasonable assumptions, it will take longer to run. But I shall not have changed the truth-content, in the sense recently defined, of any of its sentences: for '4' and '1 + 2 + 3 − 1 − 1' denote the same number. In a programming language the structure of sentences – representations – is given by saying what component symbols they are made up of, how many of these symbols there are, and in what order. The programming time will be (roughly) a function of the structure, thus defined, of the sentences of the program, along with other features of the overall state of the machine. If we want to make use of the notion of the structure of representations in a functionalist theory of agents, then the structure of representations will have to make a difference of this sort in the way representations are processed. For in a functionalist theory it is causal role that individuates mental states, so the structure of representations must determine features of their causal role, if the theory is to be functionalist.

By combining functionalism with a computational view of the mind we shall be able to treat beliefs and desires and the rest of the propositional attitudes as relations between agents and representations, while at the same time insisting that the relation be realised in states of agents individuated by their causal roles. On the view I have outlined, when agents are in the relation to a representation, which makes it true that they believe something, they are in a state with a certain causal role; a causal role which is individuated, in part, by the structure of the representation. There is no reason to expect this last claim to entail a vicious circularity in the theory. For we can have a theory that first specifies that aspect of causal role which does depend on truth conditions – in fact by way of decision-theory in Chapter 3 – and then assigns different computational structures to beliefs with the same causal role, from the point of view of decision theory, using causal properties other than those which decision theory takes into account. That the strategy is successful will only be clear when, at the end of Chapter 5, we have more of the theory before us.

Before moving on, let me make some notational remarks. Sentences in quotation marks name English sentences in the usual way; token or type as the context requires. Thus:

'Snow is white.'

Bracketed sentences are used to name type representations; thus:

(Snow is white.)

And beliefs are named in the normal way by using a 'that . . .' clause. Thus:

The belief that snow is white.

Representations, like sentences and beliefs, can be type or token, and I shall try to keep clear which is at issue when. A token belief *is* a token representation and the believer has a relation to a type representation. Tokens of the same type representation have the same computational structure. I call the state of desiring to some degree that snow is white 'the desire that snow be white'; and this state too I speak of as existing where an agent has a certain relation to a type representation, the relation being, of course, having a desire of that type. Someone who has the desire that snow be white has a token representation of the type (Snow is white).

Some might think this notation question-begging, particularly since I have objected to the view that beliefs are isomorphic with sentences. For this way of putting the matter suggests, perhaps, that we know more about the structure of representations than we actually do. It suggests, for example, that tokens of the type of (Snow is white) are isomorphic with the sentence 'Snow is white.' And even granting that we can make sense of this, it is not obvious that it is true.

But the notation does not beg as many questions as it might seem to. To begin with, as I have insisted, it does not commit us to this strong notion of isomorphism. All that is required is that if the belief that S and the belief that R are different beliefs, and if 'S' and 'R' have the same truth conditions, then the representations S and R should have different computational structure. It is quite consistent with this notation that John's belief that Mary hit James and his belief that James was hit by Mary should be the very same state, even though the surface structures of the sentences

'Mary hit James'

and

'James was hit by Mary'

are not isomorphic.

Further, as I also insisted above, we do, in fact, individuate beliefs by sentences in 'that . . .' clauses. If it is true at t that John believes that snow is white and true also at t_1, then, at those times, he has at least one type belief that is the same. The notation is not committed to the converse implication: that if John believes at t that snow is white and believes at t_1 that snow has the property of being white, these two beliefs must be of distinct types. Identity in the 'that . . .' clause entails identity of beliefs; but identity of beliefs does not entail identity in the 'that . . .' clause.

2.4 STATES AND DISPOSITIONS

Functionalism about beliefs grows out of pragmatism; and at least one important source is Ramsey's 'Facts and Propositions' (1978: Chapter 2). As Brian Loar has put the matter recently:

'An analysis of belief for Ramsey would be an account of what it is about z's having a certain attitude towards a sentence of z's that constitutes z thereby as believing that p. Ramsey's proposal is this: it is a matter of z's state, his attitude towards that sentence, having certain causal properties' (Loar, 1980: 55).

If for 'sentence' we put 'representation' we have the kind of functionalism

I am defending for beliefs. If we put the name of any other propositional attitude for 'belief' we get the general thesis for all such mental states.[3]

The theory Ramsey proposed, and variants of it and their developments – see Braithwaite (1932/3), Armstrong (1968, 1973) – are often called dispositional theories of belief. This term has its advantages, but it is sometimes a source of confusion. One reason for this is that any plausible functionalist theory will give an account of beliefs that makes them unlike standard dispositions in one important respect.

The difference is that beliefs, unlike many of the dispositions standardly discussed, do not have anything which uniquely displays their presence. I want now to say a little about standard dispositions in order to examine this difference; and to prepare the way for the discussion of the next section.

Let us take as our examplar, the state of antigenicity. It is, roughly speaking, the state of being disposed to cause antibody production in a species of organism. Some molecules are sometimes in this state. Adding functional groups may cause them to cease to be in it; and, likewise, molecules can be made antigenic by adding functional groups. (Doing it this way involves individuating molecules by something that does not entail identity of molecular structure: organic chemists may be shocked, but this is a standard way of talking in biochemistry.)

A molecule, then, is antigenic iff there is a kind of organism such that if you place the molecule in its tissues the organism will produce antibodies; see Nossal (1978). We can dress this up a little more formally. Taking a quantifier which ranges over molecules, '$( )_m$' we get:

CD: $(x)_m$ (x is antigenic iff $Ey(z)$ (y is a species of organism and if z is a member of y, and x is or were placed in z, then z is or would be caused to produce antibodies.))

There is a large number of such dispositional states which are studied in biology. If, for example, we substituted 'pathogenic' for 'antigenic' and 'become diseased' for 'produce antibodies', we should get another approximate truth. ('$( )_m$' will now have to range over micro-organisms.)

Let us call sentences of the form of CD 'causal definitions'.

In the cases of antigenicity and pathogenicity the truth of the relevant causal definition is a consequence of facts about the meaning of the dispositional

---

3. For some states, e.g. knowledge, we may have to give an account which separates out the subjective factor, e.g. the belief, for which the account will be functionalist, and the objective factor, e.g. the truth of the belief and its having been reliably acquired, which will not; see Grandy (1980). So, for some mental states, functionalism applies only to their subjective part. Others can be sufficiently individuated by their causal properties alone, and thus can be given an account that makes no reference to any objective factors.

term. It is *a priori* true that antigens are disposed to bring about antibody-production; and *a priori* true that pathogens are disposed to produce disease. Not only is it *a priori* true, the causal definition provides conditions necessary and sufficient for something (organism or molecule) to be in the relevant state. Thus, when someone knows that the introduction of a molecule will always cause antibody-production, then they know that the molecule is antigenic. And where they know that the introduction of a micro-organism will cause disease, they know it is pathogenic. Let us call the production of antibodies in an organism, caused by the introduction of an antigen, a display of antigenicity. Similarly, the onset of disease in an organism caused by the introduction of a pathogen is a display of pathogenicity. We could speak of displays of other states whose holding can be defined by way of a causal definition.

In these cases, just as, according to functionalism, it is *a priori* true that mental states have certain causal properties, so it is *a priori* true that anything satisfying a causal definition has the disposition it defines. Similarly, as I argue later, mental states only give rise to actions when the agent is suitably stimulated, just as antigenicity, say, only shows up when the molecule is suitably introduced into an organism. So much, then, for similarities. Now for some differences.

Ramsey (1978) suggested, in effect, that we might begin to say what beliefs were by characterising their role in the causation of actions. But, familiarly enough, there is a problem with this. For what actions a belief will lead to depend fundamentally on what else the agent believes and on what the agent desires. In the simplest explanation of an action in terms of a belief, we may say, for example, that John left the room because he thought Mary was coming. But this will only provide an adequate explanation if we suppose that John wishes to avoid Mary.

The phenomenon is absolutely general. If someone believes that S, this will only lead them to perform an action A, if they also believe, for some R,

If S and I do A, R

and they desire that R.

We may lose sight of this general dependence of explanations of action in terms of beliefs on assumptions about desires, because in many cases where we mention beliefs to explain actions, the relevant desires and the relevant conditional are completely obvious. But reflection on cases makes clear that it is always possible to challenge the explanation of an action by a belief by pointing to the absence of a relevant supporting desire.

This is by no means the end of the complexity; indeed we might say (gritting our teeth for what is to come) that it is not the beginning of the end nor even the end of the beginning. For, though it is necessary for the intentional performance of an action A, that I believe it will achieve some desire of mine, it is not sufficient that this should be so. Desires compete; and their competition is mediated by beliefs. I desire tea, and believe that if I go into the kitchen and boil a kettle I shall have some. But I also believe that my family is asleep, and think that if I boil a kettle I may wake them. But perhaps I will wake them anyway. For perhaps the noise in the hall downstairs is a burglar. If there is a burglar downstairs and I wake my family, then we shall stand a better chance of avoiding the loss of the family silver. Unless, of course, arousing the burglar puts our lives at risk.

Such a sequence of thoughts might 'pass through one's head' in suitable circumstances as the background to action. And such thoughts may all be causally relevant to the outcome.

This essential interdependence of beliefs and desires in the causation of action has important consequences. It means that a functionalist theory of belief and desire must differ in form from the kind of account given in a causal definition. For while causal definitions characterise something directly by way of what it is disposed to cause, a functionalist theory will, it seems, have to characterise a belief not by the actions to which it would give rise, *simpliciter*, but by the actions to which it would give rise in conjunction with an indefinitely large set of other beliefs and desires. The reason for this can be simply put: there is no way of characterising the actions to which a belief that S will give rise; against appropriately varied backgrounds of other beliefs and desires, it can give rise to any action at all.

What follows from this is that, though a causal definition standardly links a state with only one kind of display, a functionalist theory cannot do so. Rather it will connect beliefs with other mental states in such a way as then to entail some display for total mental states. That there must be some display, though not necessarily a highly specific one, follows from the claim of functionalism to be able to individuate mental states; and I shall now try to say what constraints functionalism places on the way total mental states are displayed.

The functionalist theory thus allows us to ascribe to every agent a great number of states. It characterises how they must change in relation to inputs (see 2.6) and what outputs these changes produce. The inputs will be causal – they will be events producing physical changes in the agent (though, of course, not every such cause of change will end up counting as input). The outputs will be actions, so far as beliefs and desires are concerned; but they might include, for example, physical agitation, for states like rage which are neither beliefs nor desires. Since I am largely concerned with belief it will be actions that concern us; and in fact I shall be discussing the antecedents of 'trying-to-act' (except briefly in 4.4), though there is some hope of an *a priori* account of the constraints on relations between trying-to-act and action; see Hornsby (1980).

We need now to say what it would be for this theory to specify a display for a total mental state. For dispositional states which have causal definitions, there is (in general) some particular event – dropping on the floor, for fragility; introduction into the tissues of an organism, for pathogenicity – which elicits a response – breaking, for fragility; the onset of disease for pathogenicity – in the thing whose state it is. Let us call the eliciting event E and the response R. Then a display occurs when E causes R. We cannot write a causal definition for total mental states, because there is not, for any total mental state M, just one E whose causation of some R is necessary and sufficient for it to be true that the agent is in the state M. Given my present total mental state, I shall get up and go to the door if I hear a knock; go to the kitchen if I hear a kettle boil; wave if my friend Caroline passes the window. But what we can do for total mental states, which we cannot do for beliefs and desires singly, is to specify what I shall call a display function: a function from inputs to outputs, whose domain is the set of possible sequences of experience, and whose range is the set of possible sequences of actions.

Now there must be a unique function for every distinct type of total mental state. For consider what would happen if we had a theory which allowed that there could be two mental states of distinct types, which had the same display function. In such a theory it would be true that the response, O, to any possible sequence of input, I, would be the same for both of two total states M_1 and M_2. But then functionalism would be false. For it would not be possible to distinguish states by *a priori* facts about their causal roles in the production of output. I am not, as I say, defending the general strategy of functionalism; only developing a form of it. But I find this consequence quite plausible. For, as said in 2.2, if it were false that mental states could be individuated by *a priori* facts about their causal roles in the production of output in response to input, there would be the possibility of essentially private states.

Thus, though analytical functionalism does not entail a unique display for such states as beliefs, it does entail a unique display function for any total mental state. Given a full specification of Peter's beliefs, desires and other mental states, a functionalist theory will entail that he reacts in certain ways to certain stimuli. If it were possible for him to be in some other total state, with different beliefs or desires or other mental states, and nevertheless to be disposed to react identically to all stimuli, then the theory would not be functionalist, in the sense I have defined. So the theory will characterise a set of functions from inputs to outputs, one function per total mental state.

The difference between 'believing that S' as applied to agents and 'being antigenic' as applied to molecules, should not, however, be exaggerated. For though antigenicity is only linked conceptually to one kind of display, it is causally linked, as immunologists know, to many other kinds of event, and many other states. There are many truths of the form of a causal definition about antigens, but they are not *a priori*. That, of course, is part of the reason why antigenicity is an interesting theoretical concept; compare Mellor (1971: 114 *et seq*.). And, correspondingly, though the belief that S, for specific S, is conceptually tied to an indefinite number of actions in whose causation it might play a part, and thus *a priori* true that its presence will show up in many different ways in many different circumstances, it is purely *a posteriori* that there are any states with all the causal powers of a particular belief; for it is *a posteriori* that there are any beliefs at all. Thus, the state of belief that S, for some S, and the state of being antigenic, are both involved in complex networks of causal laws: our functionalist theory is *a priori* committed to large numbers of these laws in the case of belief, while our concept of antigenicity is committed rather less widely. There are thus differences in the way we identify the states, but no differences in principle in the states thus identified.

I have suggested that specific beliefs are

(a) states which are *a priori* possessed of certain causal properties, which

(b) dispose an agent to certain kinds of action against a background of other mental states, and that

(c) they are not conceptually tied to any particular display.

It is (c) that might be misunderstood if we called the theory a dispositional theory of belief: for the dispositions standardly discussed – fragility, irascibility, for example – are strongly conceptually tied to but one kind of display – breaking, being angry. This is why I did not say that this was a dispositional theory of belief.

2.5 STATES, EVENTS AND CAUSES

Ramsey's suggestion – see Loar (1980) – was that we could analyse belief as a state with certain causal powers; and in particular the power of causing certain actions. I have modified this claim by arguing that beliefs are states which play a part in the causation of action against a background of other mental states, in particular, of desires. But actions are events and beliefs are states; and though it is possible to speak of causation in cases where it is not obviously a relation between events, this one will not do. For states cannot cause events. States do, of course, play a part, as we have several times noticed, in the causation of events. But pathogenicity does not cause disease, nor does antigenicity cause antibody production. We do say that pathogens cause disease or that antigens cause immune responses. We do say, putting the matter generally, that the bearers of states cause events. And this is true in the case of agents; for we speak of John's causing a rumpus, or Mary causing me to revolutionise my ideas about women. But it is reasonable to suppose in general that where an object O (including an agent) causes an event E, there is some change in O which event-causes E.

In the particular case of agents this has sometimes been denied: it has been argued (for example by von Wright (1971)) that there is a relation of agent-causation which is explanatorily prior to event-causation. But Jennifer Hornsby has recently disposed of this view (1980: Chapter 7), and I follow her in holding that there is no 'special relation of causation particularly operative when people do things' (1980: 90). It follows that the causal role of beliefs must be cashed in terms of event-causation. Since beliefs and other propositional attitudes are not events it follows that they cannot event-cause actions. So a functionalist theory cannot characterise beliefs, as Ramsey suggested, as causes of actions. Fortunately this does not mean there cannot be a functionalist theory of mental states. For though states cannot cause events, they play important parts in the causation of events; and all functionalism is committed to is an account of mental states in terms of causal roles. Still, if beliefs and desires do not cause actions, what, according to functionalism, does? The obvious answer is that what causes action is not mental states but changes of mental state. And that is exactly what I want to argue.

Let us consider two cases where we explain an action by its mental antecedents. First a case where someone acts on a settled intention; and second a case where someone takes a quick decision.

Suppose Mary has decided to go swimming tomorrow; and suppose that she has decided to leave at three in the afternoon. Then, as she sets off at three, it may be true that she is leaving because she decided to do so yesterday. In all the intervening period she has been in the state of intending to go swimming. That state cannot explain why she leaves when she does. What does explain it, surely, is that at some time she comes to believe that it is now three; the time at which she intended to carry out this intention. So here is an event – namely coming to believe that it is *now* three p.m. – which causes the action. Not that the intention plays no causal role. Far from it. For what makes it true that she had the intention is just that, provided she did not change her mind in the interval, when she came to judge that it was three, she got up and went. Notice that it is possible to provide something like a causal definition (2.3) of that intention:

I: a state of the person is the intention to do A at t iff the person is in that state and comes to believe that it is now t (and that they can now do A), they will try to do A.

But it would be misleading to describe trying to do A as a display of the intention; because, with a little curare, we could put Mary in a state in which trying to do A produced no overt signs. It would be more natural to describe doing A as a display of the intention to A; and for the relations between trying to do A and doing A there may be no simple truths; see Hornsby (1980: Chapter 3).

Now consider a swift decision. I drive along a city street. A child runs off the pavement ahead of me, across my path. I brake sharply. I do so because I believe I will hit the child if I do not brake. But what causes my braking is, plausibly, not that I believe this, but that I come to believe it.

There are, then, reasons for thinking that functionalism can accommodate the truth that only events cause events, while still characterising mental states by their causal roles.

2.6 INPUT, OUTPUT AND THROUGHPUT

The fact that we have to explain actions by way of changes of mental state draws attention to two rather important things. First, that there will have to be token-referential states, such as the state of believing that it is now three, if we are to explain any actions at all. For it is in general the belief that they will *now* achieve one of their desires that causes people to act. I look at token-reference for sentences in Chapter 6 and beliefs in Chapter 7.

But the second fact that the importance of changes of mental state draws attention to will be discussed now. It is that if functionalism gives an account of action in terms of changes of mental state, we may wonder if the *a priori* theory tells us about the causes of those changes. I want now to argue that it must; and that it must also tell us something about the causal relations of mental states with each other.

There are certainly some *a priori* truths about the events which cause changes of mental state. I mentioned one earlier (2.2: paragraph 2). More precisely expressed (though still not precisely enough) it might go:

B: If normally sighted people with colour concepts are placed in normal lighting before a large red surface, when conscious, they will come, if they notice its colour, to believe that it is red, unless they believe that they are sensorily deceived.

This claim is neither very strong – what does 'normal' mean, here? – nor very exciting. (For comment on 'normal', however, see 4.1.) But it, or something very like it, is true. We know *a priori* that, *ceteris paribus*, visual exposure to red things produces beliefs about redness.

But functionalism claims not just that there are *a priori* truths about the mental and its causal role, but that they are sufficient to individuate mental states. What I want now to argue is that unless our theory entails some theses about non-mental events which cause changes of belief, it cannot be strong enough to individuate beliefs. I call sentences characterising the events which cause changes of belief (desire, or other mental states) from outside the mind input claims.

The easiest way to see that a functionalist theory must entail input claims is to see what would happen if we tried to do without them. To do this, we should have to have a theory which said what changes of belief and desire caused action, but which said nothing about changes of beliefs brought about otherwise than by either

(a) changes of other beliefs, or

(b) changes of desires or

(c) changes in other mental states.

Suppose we had such a theory and call it θ. Suppose, that is, that θ entailed every *a priori* truth about how changes of belief and desire cause changes of belief and desire (and other mental states) and actions. And suppose that according to θ, two agents, A and B, were in the same overall mental state; so that, according to θ, they had all the same beliefs and desires. Since it is part of the present hypothesis that θ contains enough truths about every belief to individuate it, it would follow that A and B had the same beliefs. And this would follow because, if θ were true, nothing that had the properties by which θ individuated 'the belief that snow is white' could fail to be the belief that snow is white. The constraints θ lays on any belief (or other mental state) would have to be such that their satisfaction is both necessary and sufficient for being that belief (or that other state.)

Consider A and B, then. Since θ contains, *ex hypothesi*, no input claims, it does not constrain the way their beliefs are caused. In particular it will be consistent with θ, that A, when placed before a large red surface should come to believe that it was red, and B, while identically placed, should come to believe that it was green.

Now it is perfectly possible for someone who looks at a red thing to believe that it is green. But if they *do*, there must be some explanation of why this is. Since A and B are in the same mental state according to θ, and θ is our theory of the mental, there cannot be any *mental* explanation. There cannot, that is, be an account of the difference in the contents of their new beliefs which relies on differences in their original ones; for, *ex hypothesi*, there is no such original difference. It follows that if θ is true we cannot explain the acquisition of a false belief in the face of sensory evidence by the beliefs of the agent at the time of sensory simulation. But that consequence of θ is absurd. If I look at a red thing, believing that the lighting is peculiar in ways that make

33

green things look red, then (*ceteris paribus*) I shall believe that it is green; and this is part of our *a priori* theory. It follows that θ fails to capture an essential part of our concept of belief. So a theory of the mind adequate to our conception of beliefs has to make input claims.[4]

I have also promised to show that functionalism must lay constraints on the way changes of belief affect other beliefs. In one sense, this is obvious. No theory that did not entail that the belief that S and the belief that it is not the case that S change only in ways that mean the production of the one leads to the loss of the other would be at all plausible. When I come later to look at degrees of belief, I make this point more precisely by arguing that the total belief state can change only in ways that preserve certain probability relations. This is not the place for those details, but the general strategy is fairly simple. If a sentence S entails a sentence R, then, *ceteris paribus*, every agent (who both believes that S and believes that R to some degree) should believe that R at least as strongly as they believe that S. But, of course, this *ceteris paribus* has a lot to do. It does not seem at all plausible to hold that anyone who believes that 2 and 2 is 4 must believe that 2 raised to the power of 10 is 1,024; many people who are certain of the first of these things doubt the second. Yet one of these is, necessarily, true iff the other is. Still there are some entailments, the 'obvious' ones, which it is difficult to imagine someone failing to observe. I show in the next chapters how we can capture some facts about entailments in a functionalist theory.

What I want to point out finally, however, is that, *prima facie* at least, capturing the facts about entailments will not be enough. Take the belief that a surface before me seems to be red. A theory which did not show that this state normally leads to the formation of the belief that a surface before me is red would have no hope of success. In general, people believe their senses unless they have reason not to; and this seems to be *a priori* true. As Smart (1959) argued a long time ago and Armstrong (1973) has done more recently, it is of the essence of states of this kind that they normally cause the corresponding belief. If, as I shall suppose, following Armstrong, this is indeed so, then entailments will not be enough to structure our account of beliefs, since, plainly, the perceptual belief that it looks as though U, does not entail the corresponding belief that U.

It might seem that if we looked further afield, we might find other beliefs which, together with the perceptual belief entail the corresponding belief about the world. Thus, if the perceptual belief is

---

4. I have not claimed – nor do I believe – that we can *always* explain mistakes in belief in terms of the believer's prior mental state. All the argument requires is that we sometimes can: and that, I think, is uncontroversial.

S: It seems to me to be red

and the corresponding judgement is

R: It is red

it may seem that an agent will often have other beliefs which entail[5] 'If *S, R*'. Call this the validating conditional. Then, in the case of visual appearances, it might seem to some to be plausible to suppose that agents with the concept of redness. normally believe, when they are presented with a red surface in daylight, that the light is normal and their eyes are working as they should; and that it follows from this that if the surface looks red to them, it is red. But we cannot require that agents always believe that the light is normal and their eyes are working iff the light is normal and their eyes are working, since this would require anyone with the concept of redness to be infallible in his perceptual judgements.

How, then, are we to proceed? We cannot treat the validating conditional as something every speaker must believe: that would be to treat it as an entailment, which it is not. And we cannot require that the agent believes it only when it is true, since that would be to treat speakers as infallible. But it will not do either to require that someone believes the validating conditional unless they believe that either the light is wrong or their eyes are not working properly; for then it would be consistent with our *a priori* theory that some agents never believed their senses, because they always believed their senses unreliable. And this will not do because, as I have said, it is *a priori* true that agents with the concepts of visual appearance and the perceptual apparatus required for vision, normally *do* believe their senses.

The way to proceed, I believe, is to require that agents disbelieve their senses when they are caused in certain specific ways to do so; and a proper account of perception will have to say in more detail what this means. But however this is done, it cannot be done by capturing the constraints on the structure of an agent's beliefs which derive from the relations of entailment between them alone. For the truth of a statement to the effect that I have grounds for disbelieving my senses does not entail that my senses are indeed deceiving me; any more than the truth of a statement to the effect that I have grounds for believing my senses entails that what I seem to see is actually so.

The reason for this is the now familiar fact that the truth-values of our beliefs are underdetermined by the perceptual evidence we have for them.

---

5. A belief that *S* entails a belief that *R* iff it is not possible that the truth conditions of an agent's belief that *S* should hold at *t* and the truth conditions of an agent's belief that *R* should not hold at *t*. This allows us to have entailments between token-referential beliefs: between the belief that I am a bachelor and the belief that I am a man.

Because of this no amount of perceptual evidence entails the truth of the judgements about the world we may make on the basis of that evidence. In possessing the concept of redness people are committed to believing that what is before them is red if it looks to be so, in the absence of prior evidence for doubting their senses, even though it is logically possible that what looks to someone to be red is not red, even when they have no reason to doubt their eyes.

This is not an empty commitment. For a colour-blind organism visually insensitive to the distinction between, say, red and green, classifying them both under the concept 'gred', will not regard objects which change from red to green as having changed (at least on the basis of what it sees). And this will have consequences for its behaviour. Thus, for example, such a creature will, if it desires a gred environment, be indifferent between environments that are red and environments that are green. And such a creature need not revise its beliefs about the world if, on a certain occasion, all the emeralds in the world change from green to red. Of course, if this were to happen, the change in colour would presumably be accompanied by other changes, and this organism might be sensitive to these other changes. But if they were changes that did not produce differences in the reactions of the organism's 'visual' organs, when operating at a distance, then only contact with emeralds *via* other senses would produce the appropriate change of the agent's beliefs; would produce, that is, the belief that emeralds have changed.

So we need to keep in mind the fact that our theory must say more about the relations between beliefs than that, where *S* entails *T*, certain specific changes in the belief that *S* will produce specific changes in the belief that *T*. What is required here is a proper functionalist account of perception. Many important questions do not get answered in this book: I'm afraid I answer none of the important questions about perception. But Chapter 5 says a little more about some constraints on how a functionalist account of perception would proceed.

2.7 SUMMARY

(1) In 2.2 I outlined the kind of functionalism I espouse and suggested some of its virtues. I claimed that there could be a theory of the mental states of an agent which

(a) characterised the causal role of mental states, by

(b) stating *a priori* truths about the mind which were

(c) sufficient to identify each mental state as the state with such and such causal powers; sufficient, that is, to individuate each state by its causal powers.

I have called these *a priori* features of causal role, 'functional role'. That is, if it is true *a priori* that two states with causal role C are the same mental state(–type) M, then C is the functional role of M. I call (c) the individuation claim.

A functionalist theory clearly says, for every mental state M, what the concept of M is. For it states conditions *a priori* necessary and sufficient for falling under that concept. If the belief that snow is white is *a priori* the state with causal role C, then nothing with those causal powers could fail to be that belief; and nothing without them could succeed.

(2) I went on to argue in 2.3 that, because beliefs with identical truth conditions could have different functional roles, the theory must be

(d) representational, individuating beliefs and desires partly by their computational structure.

(3) Then, in 2.4, I made a comparison between mental states, on the one hand, on a functionalist view, and some dispositions. I pointed out that

(e) though mental states, unlike many dispositions, are not conceptually linked to a unique display, a functionalist theory will entail that every total mental state has a unique display function.

(4) In 2.5 I argued that, since we are characterising states, and states cannot be causes, the functionalist theory must

(f) characterise the causal consequences, in action and other output, of changes of mental state, and not, *per impossibile*, the causal consequences of the states themselves.

I shall call consequences of the functionalist theory which state that certain changes of mental state will produce certain output, 'output claims'.

(5) In 2.6 I argued finally that the theory must

(g) ascribe token-referential beliefs,

(h) make input class – that is, must entail *a priori* truths about the events which bring about changes of mental state from outside the mind, and

(i) lay certain constraints on the way changes of belief lead to changes in other beliefs. I shall call claims made by the theory about the interactions of mental states with each other 'throughput claims'.

I also argue that

(k) some throughput claims will reflect entailment relations between beliefs, but some will reflect other weaker relations, of a kind yet to be specified.

I think all of these claims must be true of a functionalist theory of any agents at all. They must be true of bats and cats if they are agents. But in fact we are only in a position to state anything at all adequate by way of a functionalist theory for human beings; and human beings with our concepts at that. Though we know that bats and cats have beliefs, we do not know much about those beliefs. They have some beliefs that we do not: those that go with their perceptual systems, for example. They lack some we possess: beliefs about electrons, for example, or beliefs about the solar system. But we know very little about the detail. In coming to do their psychology we should have, for example, to develop the concepts necessary for describing those sensory states of bats which are causally affected by their 'radar' system.

It might be thought that truths about these states, unlike the truths that characterise our own, would be *a posteriori*. But this would be wrong. Suppose that we came to believe for example that bats had a concept of 'sonar density'. Then it would have to be true, *a priori*, that if a bat has the concept of sonar density, it will normally arrive in the state of sensing that something is sonar dense only when that thing is sonar dense and the bat has the appropriate stimulation of its sonar organs. If that were not true, we should have no good reason for thinking that that state was a sensory state, or that sonar density was the proper object of the sensations produced in the sonar organs. Still even if there would have to be some *a priori* truths about these states, they are *a priori* truths constitutive of concepts we do not yet have. It would be idle for me to speculate about them. But it is not idle speculation that the concepts we needed would have to satisfy (a) to (k) above. For only a theory of this form, I claim, would be a theory of a kind of mind.

Because we know relatively little about other kinds of mind, I shall be talking from now on largely about the concepts and capacities of human agents. And, of course, everything I say should be read as being consistent with the fact that people differ in having different concepts. If I say it is a truth about redness that the state of sensing that something is red is elicited normally by red things, it should be understood that I mean it is so elicited in agents who are capable of having beliefs about redness at all. In fact the whole theory is, in this sense, conditional. It says of those physical systems which are, in fact, agents, that if they have a state with such and such causal powers, then they are in such and such a mental state. It is not *a priori* that anyone has the capacity to form any particular beliefs. And I do not see much hope for fruitful discussion as to which beliefs you have to have to be an agent at all.

3

Belief and decision

In order therefore to construct a theory of quantities of belief . . . I propose to take as a basis a general psychological theory . . . I mean the theory that we act in the way we think most likely to realise the objects of our desires.

(Ramsey, 1978:75)

3.1 OVERVIEW

The last chapter ended by listing 11 of the principal demands I claim functionalism makes of a theory of the mind. In this chapter I set about developing an account of belief that has grown up with functionalism, trying, as I go, to adjust it to those demands.

We can begin with a simple observation: belief comes by degrees. I believe more strongly that it will rain tomorrow than that President Carter will win the United States Presidential election in 1988. Our language is full of idioms that allow us to express the relative strengths of our beliefs. We say we think one thing more likely than another; or that we have more confidence that one thing will happen than another; or that we think something extremely likely or are highly confident that it will happen. And such differences in the strengths of our beliefs show up not only in what we say, but in what we do. People who believe only fairly strongly that aeroplanes are safe need a stronger motive for flying than they would if they had more confidence in them.

I have already said that beliefs play their role in the causation of actions only in the context of desires. And correlative with the observation that beliefs come by degrees is the observation that desires do also. I would rather it was dry tomorrow and wet tonight than that it should be dry tonight and rain tomorrow. Once again there are many ways of expressing the strengths (and relative strengths) of our desires. We speak of preferring this to that, wanting this more, or that very much, and of desiring one thing more than another. And once again, these differences will affect what we do also. How much we want a thing will affect how hard we try to get it.

I begin, therefore, with a theory that sets out to explain how degrees of belief and strengths of desire interact to produce action. That theory is decision

39

theory: the theory that degrees of belief obey the laws of probability and degrees of desire have the measure of a utility function; and that action consists in trying to maximise expected utility. My project is functionalist: so that I take the theory in the form which claims that degrees of belief do conform to probability laws and strengths of desire are utilities, not in the form which claims merely that they should.[1] Hugh Mellor has recently dealt with some bad reasons for thinking that degrees of belief are not subjective probabilities; and to that extent has defended the view that decision theory can be descriptive rather than merely normative (1980c: Part II). He has allowed, however, that the theory is descriptively inadequate in ways that depend upon the fact that it requires that beliefs with the same truth conditions have the same probability. This is a serious inadequacy – at least on the standard account – and it is one that I intend to remedy; thus reducing further the plausibility of the case of those who see decision theory normatively but not descriptively.

Despite the fact that some of its proponents have wanted to treat decision theory normatively, their account grew up with a functionalist theory of belief. It was Ramsey who was one of the fathers of modern functionalism about beliefs; and it was Ramsey too who showed how we might make operational sense of degrees of belief conforming to the laws of probability. He argued, as is now well known, that we could see degrees of belief manifested in the behaviour of gamblers in suitably constrained circumstances (Mellor, 1971: Chapter 2). I claim that Ramsey's basic account, suitably generalised and refined, can allow us to see subjective probability theory descriptively, and thus return it to its functionalist origins.

Since beliefs only give rise to action in concert with desires (see 2.4), Ramsey's account of the betting situation had to make assumptions about the desirability of money. In the simplest version of the argument from betting we can assume that the desirability of the outcome of a bet is measured adequately by the amount of money gained on that outcome. As it happens, this seems, in a range of cases, to be not far from the truth (Edwards, 1960). But it is not, in general, a sound assumption and we can avoid it in a realistic theory. For, as decision theorists from Ramsey on have shown, there are ways of recovering agents' probabilities and desirabilities from their preferences; from their rankings of all available options (Jeffrey, 1965). My interest is in beliefs, so I shall concentrate on argument about the p-function. I shall say, therefore, only the minimum amount about the measure of the desirabilities of outcomes consistent with giving an intelligible picture of the general form of decision theories. I assume that every agent's preferences are well behaved: transitive, complete and so on (Luce and Raiffa, 1957). This is controversial

1. Hereafter I use 'desirability' instead of 'utility', until 3.3, where the reason for doing this is made clear.

among decision theorists: but, for reasons I shall be able to give at the end of 4.2, that does not concern me. (For objections, however, see, e.g. Edwards, (1960), Kyburg (1978).)

3.2 DECISION THEORY: THE GENERAL FORM

We suppose that the agent's degrees of belief and strengths of desire are characterised by a p-function, p, and a desirability function, d. These functions are defined over the agent's system of representations, which, for simplicity, I suppose to be of the form of the sentential calculus. The agent's representations thus consist of a finite set of atomic representations, and the recursively enumerable set of conjunctions, disjunctions and negations of these. Thus we specify an initial class of atomic representations, $[A]$, and require that, for any members of $[A]$, S and R, (not-S), (S & R), ($S \vee R$) are also representations. The probability and desirability functions are complete: every representation has both a p- and a d-value. There are a number of ways of characterising these functions, but I follow Jeffrey (1965) in the general form of the theory. I do not defend the general form of Jeffrey's theory, I only adapt it in response to the arguments I offer. What I *do* rely on is the existence of representation theorems: theorems which show that probability and desirability functions exist for any system of representations over which a preference ordering of sufficiently rich structure is defined; see Eells (1982: 9–11). It will turn out that the representation theorems for Jeffrey's decision theory will not quite do the job: but it is a *desideratum* for any account of the foundations of a decision theory that representation theorems are found.[2]

To begin, then, with probability. I call a probability function a p-function; we could qualify this, as in the 'p_{John}-function', to indicate whose degrees of belief are in question. But no ambiguity arises from the absence of such subscripting in what I have to say. Still, it is as well to keep in mind from the very beginning that particular p-functions belong to particular agents: we are dealing with subjective probabilities, which are the degrees of belief of subjects.

Any function over the representations in an agent's system of representations of the following form is a p-function. Where S, R are any representations, and T is a representation whose truth conditions hold necessarily:

---

2. It would be a major distraction to discuss the comparative merits of differing decision theories. The strategy I adopt would be able to be adapted to different forms of the theory.

I show in the next section how to rework Jeffrey's theory, in the way suggested by David Lewis (1981a), to cope with so-called 'Newcomb' problems; for which see Eells (1982: *passim*.) Eells, however, denies the reworking is necessary. I say why I think he is wrong in 3.3.

1: $p(S) \geqslant 0$

2: $p(T) = 1$

3: If $(S \ \& \ R)$ entails (not-T) then $p(S \lor R) = p(S) + p(R)$

4: $p(S) = 1 - p(\neg S)$

Probabilities clearly lie in the interval from 0 to 1. And I say that S is certain iff $p(S) = 1$. There is also a notion of conditional probability which will be of great interest in later portions of this book.

COND: $p(S/R) = p(S \ \& \ R)/p(R)$

if $p(R) \neq 0$; otherwise $p(S/R)$ is undefined.

I call $p(S/R)$ the conditional probability of S on R. A p-function which satisfies the further condition

5: If $p(S) = 1$, then S has truth-conditions which hold *a priori*

is called a regular p-function. In 4.5 I defend the claim that the p-functions we need are regular.

We can now define the class of desirability functions. Call these d-functions, where the desirability of S is $d(S)$. (We could qualify d-functions, with respect to agents as we can p-functions: but, once more, this will not generally be necessary.) We define the class of d-functions by adding an axiom which relates desirabilities to probabilities. Any distribution of desirabilities which conforms to all these axioms is then a d-function.

DES: $d(S \lor R) = (d(S)p(S) + d(R)p(R))/(p(S) + p(R))$

provided (a) $p(S \ \& \ R) = 0$

and (b) $p(S \lor R) \neq 0$

I am concerned with belief and it would be a complex and distracting task to say a great deal about d-functions. But the intuitive idea is simple. If John's $d(S)$ is greater than his $d(R)$, then he desires that S more than that R. If d-values are the same, the agent is indifferent. Desirabilities are real-valued, positive or negative, and the relation $\geqslant$ is transitive over desirabilities: if $d(S) \geqslant d(R)$ and $d(R) \geqslant d(U)$, then $d(S) \geqslant d(U)$.

Since desirabilities and probabilities are intended simply to allow us to calculate preferences, and since, given probabilities, the d-function is only unique up to a fractional linear transformation, with positive determinant, of the desirabilities, we require some arbitrary reference points to fix the numerical scale for d-values. It simplifies matters if we take $d(T)$, where T is certain – see the definition above – to be 0; and the simplification is purely algebraic. We must also leave the desirability of $(\neg T)$, where T is certain, undefined, so that the d-function is defined over all representations except those with probability 0. Further, having fixed the d-value of representations that are certain at 0, then it will be true for all S, that if $d(S) \neq 0$, and $d(\neg S) \neq 0$, then $d(S)$ and $d(\neg S)$ have opposite signs. It turns out that we need to fix two further points; and the methods available for solving this measurement problem are set out Jeffrey (1965: Chapter 9). This is not, as I say, the only way of setting up p-functions and d-functions, but nothing germane to my purposes hangs on the difference between Jeffrey's methods and the classical theory of, say, von Neumann and Morgenstern (1947).

Consider a class of representations, $[C_1, C_2, \ldots, C_n]$, all of which are in the agent's system of representations, and which are pairwise inconsistent and exhaustive collectively in disjunction. For any pair, $\langle C_i, C_k \rangle$, which are members of this class, $p(C_i \& C_k)$ will be 0; for if they are pairwise inconsistent then $(C_i \& C_k)$ will be necessarily false, for any $\langle i,k \rangle$. And the disjunction of all the n members of the set will be necessarily true – they are exhaustive in disjunction – so that the probability of that disjunction will be 1. We suppose that for all the C_i, for all i, between 1 and n, $d(A \& C_i) \neq d(A \& \neg C_i)$.

Intuitively it is clear that these conditions, which I shall call conditions relevant for A, are matters germane to deciding whether or not to do A. For the desirability of A, will depend, in part, on whether or not C_i, for every i from 1 to n. For any agent with a structure of desirabilities sufficiently rich to apply Jeffrey's account, there is, for every action A, such that $p(A) \neq 0$, 1, a class of pairwise inconsistent conditions which are exhaustive in disjunction which are conditions relevant for A. Any set of pairwise inconsistent and exhaustive conditions is called a partition; and we can say that for all A, such that $p(A) \neq 0, 1$, there exists at least one partition every one of whose members is relevant for A. Call any such partition a relevant partition.

The significance of relevant partitions will become clear later. So far I have said nothing about the way in which the desirability which someone attaches to a state of affairs may depend causally on their view of the desirability of the outcome occurring under relevant conditions and their view of the likelihood of the various relevant conditions occurring. Clearly any adequate theory is going to have to say something about this. I shall leave the discussion of this question until later. But the intuition is obvious: if I am considering whether to go to dinner, my estimation of the desirability of doing so will naturally depend on my views about the desirability of various kinds of food that I may be offered; and on the likelihood that I will be offered food I like.

Now let us take a relevant partition for A; call it $C(A)$ and its members $[C(A)_1$ to $C(A)_n]$; and take, likewise, a relevant partition for B, $C(B)$, with members $[C(B)_1$ to $C(B)_m]$. Then our theory now says that:

$$d(A) = \sum_{i=1}^{i=n} p(C(A)_i/A) \cdot d(A \ \& \ C(A)_i)$$

$$d(B) = \sum_{i=1}^{i=m} p(C(B)_i/B) \cdot d(B \ \& \ C(B)_i)$$

So that A is preferred to B iff

$$\sum_{i=1}^{i=n} (C(A)_i/A) \cdot d(A \ \& \ C(A)_i) > \sum_{i=1}^{i=m} p(C(B)_i/B) \cdot d(B \ \& \ C(B)_i).$$

Now in fact this result will hold where $C(A)$ and $C(B)$ are any partitions at all, whether every member is relevant or not. And this is convenient since it allows us to concentrate on the case where $C(A) = C(B)$, without any loss of generality. So let us call

$$\sum_{i=1}^{i=n} p(C_i/S) \cdot d(C_i \ \& \ S)$$

the expected desirability of S on the partition C; where C is the partition whose members are $[C_1, C_2, \ldots, C_n]$. Then two actions are indifferent iff they have the same expected desirability on any partition; and otherwise the one with higher desirability wins.

The notion of a set of relevant conditions plays no essential role in the general theory. For, as I have said, the expected desirability is the same on any partition whatsoever. But relevant conditions will be very important in the use to which I want to put the decision theory. For provided some C is relevant for A, then the partition $[C, \neg C]$ will be a relevant partition. And if we wish to calculate the agent's desirability $d(A)$, then we need only $d(A \ \& C)$, $d(A \ \& \ \neg C)$ and $p(C/A)$ to calculate it. We will in general want to consider cases where the agent does have a conditional probability for some relevant C on A: for these are the cases that look like real decision making. They are cases where someone's preference depends on their evaluation of the probability of a certain outcome if they do some A, where the desirability of the outcome depends on whether or not C. I shall take up this matter again later, both in this chapter and the next.

3.3 CAUSAL DECISION THEORY

I have sketched Jeffrey's account of probabilities and desirabilities and the relation between them. His theory is elegantly set out in Jeffrey (1965), and it is extremely easy to understand. But it is not quite right. The reason has nothing to do with probabilities and desirabilities themselves, but with the relation between them and action.

I have spoken so far as if people decided what to do by deciding what action had highest desirability. And I have nothing to say against their doing this, in a wide range of cases. But it is not always true that an agent will do what is most desirable, in Jeffrey's sense, for a reason I must now explain.

Suppose I believe, what the statistician Ronald Fisher once suggested, see Jeffrey (1983: 25), that the correlation between smoking and cancer is due to a common cause of both. The reason more smokers get cancer is that people who want to smoke have a cancer-producing gene, which also sets them up so they like smoking. The evidence for the gene is statistical evidence based on classical genetics, but there is no known way of identifying it in someone.

It seems to me that if I believed all this then, as Jeffrey would claim, I should find the fact that I smoke undesirable; it should have a low desirability in the technical sense I have just explained. That Jeffrey's theory gets this much right can be seen if we give the case some plausible numbers. So, taking S as 'I smoke' and C as 'I will get cancer', let us fix some desirabilities:

$$d(S \ \& \ \neg C) \ = \ 10$$

$$d(\neg S \ \& \ \neg C) \ = \ 9$$

$$d(S \ \& \ C) \ = \ -100$$

$$d(\neg S \ \& \ \neg C) \ = \ -101$$

Since smoking is positively correlated with cancer,

$$p(C/S) \ > \ p(C/\neg S)$$

so that

$$p(\neg C/S) \ < \ p(\neg C/\neg S)$$

Then,

$$d(S) \ = \ (-100) \cdot p(C/S) \ + \ 10 \cdot p(\neg C/S)$$

$$d(\neg S) \ = \ (-101) \cdot p(C/\neg S) \ + \ 9 \cdot p(\neg C/\neg S)$$

And, with a little algebra, that gives us that

$$d(S) \ < \ d(\neg S)$$

iff

$$p(C/S) \ > \ p(C/\neg S) \ + \ 1/110$$

So that there only has to be this very small increase in the probability of cancer, given that a person smokes, for smoking to be less desirable than not. But smoking plays no role in the causation of cancer – indeed, if we want to make the case really compelling, we can suppose that if someone has got the cancer-gene, smoking, if they can bear to do it, reduces the chance of getting cancer slightly. So, on this story, though my smoking is bad news, that is no reason not to smoke.

This line of reasoning, which you can find in technical detail in the literature on the 'Newcomb'[3] problem (see Eells (1982) for bibliography) seems to me perfectly correct. And, consistently with it, we ought, I think, to give up the idea that expected desirability is what determines whether an agent acts. For the expected desirability of smoking is such as to make not-smoking preferable in this case; and no one who believed Fisher's theory could possibly think this the right response to the evidence.

[Jeffrey's] decision theory endorses the ostrich's policy of managing the news. It tells you to decline the good, though doing so does not at all tend to prevent the evil. If a theory tells you that, it stands refuted. (Lewis, 1981a: 9)

What should we do? Certainly not give up the elegance of Jeffrey's account of desirability and probability. What we have to do is to find some way of getting desirabilities and probabilities to give the right answer. And that, as I now show, can be done.

Gibbard and Harper (1978), Skyrms (1980a), and Lewis (1981a), have all suggested that we need to define something which we can call the utility of an action, writing it $u(A)$, which depends on desirabilities and on probabilities, but which gives an action along with its expected desirability an expected utility as well. And utility, according to them, is what fixes what we do.

The idea follows from a diagnosis of what went wrong when we used Jeffrey's theory under Fisher's hypothesis. What went wrong, they think, is that we used conditional probabilities as the weights of the desirabilities of the various possible combinations of smoking and cancer. But the conditional probabilities only showed that there was a correlation between smoking and cancer, not that there was any sort of causal relation between them. Instead of the conditional probability of cancer, given that you smoke, what you need is the probability of a conditional: the conditional 'If I were to smoke, I would get cancer'. So let us introduce a symbol '□→', which stands in for this conditional, remembering that we read it: 'If it were the case that . . . , it would be the case that . . .' Then, Gibbard and Harper suggest, we should

---

3. So-called because the first problem of this kind was ascribed by Robert Nozick to a mathematician named 'Newcomb'. The original Newcomb problem is highly artificial; so I prefer the Fisher Hypothesis. But this is the standard term for problems of this kind; see Nozick (1969).

decide what to do by calculating the expected utility, which we define thus:[4]

$$u(A) = \sum_{i=1}^{i=n} d(A \ \& \ S_i) \cdot p(A \mathbin{\square\!\!\rightarrow} S_i).$$

How does this help? Let us consider the Fisher Hypothesis again, and take the desirabilities of the combinations of smoking (or not) and cancer (or not) as before. We got into trouble with Jeffrey's view, because $p(C/S) > p(C/\neg S)$. But on the Gibbard and Harper proposal, we use probabilities of conditionals instead. So that

$$u(S) = (-100) \cdot p(S \mathbin{\square\!\!\rightarrow} C) + 10 \cdot p(S \mathbin{\square\!\!\rightarrow} \neg C)$$

$$u(\neg S) = (-101) \cdot p(\neg S \mathbin{\square\!\!\rightarrow} C) + 9 \cdot p(\neg S \mathbin{\square\!\!\rightarrow} \neg C).$$

If we believe Fisher, then

$$p(S \mathbin{\square\!\!\rightarrow} C) = p(\neg S \mathbin{\square\!\!\rightarrow} C)$$

$$p(S \mathbin{\square\!\!\rightarrow} \neg C) = p(\neg S \mathbin{\square\!\!\rightarrow} \neg C)$$

so that $u(S) < u(\neg S)$ iff

$$p(S \mathbin{\square\!\!\rightarrow} C) < -p(S \mathbin{\square\!\!\rightarrow} \neg C)$$

But, of course, since probabilities are positive, this cannot be; so $u(S)$ is not less than $u(\neg S)$, which is just what we needed. I propose, then, to introduce, in addition to the representations of the structure of the sentential calculus, the class of representations of the form '$S \mathbin{\square\!\!\rightarrow} R$', where S and R are representations. (Since this works recursively, as usual, we can get embedded conditionals this way.) Then we can use the expected utility to determine what the agent will do, as a function of desirabilities and probabilities of these conditionals. Since we need the distinction between utility and desirability only for actions, I shall suppose that the utility function is defined only for representations of the form (I bring it about now that A); and I write this as $u(A)$ for short. (Since utilities are only defined over actions, no ambiguity exists between the utility of A and the utility of my doing A.)[5]

Quite how this works in the details, and, in particular, what constraints are needed to introduce on p-functions defined over these conditionals, depends, of course, on the semantics conceived for them. I am sceptical of the existing

4. Henceforward, both utilities and desirabilities will be called 'desires'.
5. As Lewis argues (1981a: 24-28), Gibbard and Harper's account is only adequate for agents who are certain that the world is deterministic. For them conditional excluded middle (see 9.7) holds, so that $(A \mathbin{\square\!\!\rightarrow} C)$ and $(A \mathbin{\square\!\!\rightarrow} \neg C)$ are not just contraries but each other's negations. To get the theory for an agent who (more reasonably) thinks the universe might not be deterministic, you need to use his more general formula (17) in 1981a: 28.

semantic proposals, of which the best seems to me to be Lewis' possible world semantics (1973). So I shall not commit myself here. When the dust has settled in the dispute over these new 'causal' decision theories, we shall have to answer such questions; for the moment, when I need to, I rely, as one always does when developing a logic, on intuitions about inference.

Allowing myself just such an intuition I can make, in one way, the point that Jeffrey's theory without utilities will often not go astray.

If $(A \& (A \mathbin{\square\!\!\rightarrow} C))$ is true then, of course, so is $(A \& C)$. But there are good grounds for holding that the converse implication holds also. If, in any situation, someone says 'If it were the case that A, it would be the case that C', that is confirmed if we find out that A and C; that is the logical intuition I require.[6] If this is so then we have as a theorem

1: $A \& (A \mathbin{\square\!\!\rightarrow} C) \dashv\vdash A \& C$

Now suppose that someone's $p(A \mathbin{\square\!\!\rightarrow} C)$ is statistically independent of $p(A)$, so that

2: $p(A \mathbin{\square\!\!\rightarrow} C / A) \;=\; p(A \mathbin{\square\!\!\rightarrow} C)$.

Then, given 1,

$$p(A \mathbin{\square\!\!\rightarrow} C / A) \;=\; \frac{p(A \& (A \mathbin{\square\!\!\rightarrow} C))}{p(A)} \;=\; \frac{p(A \& C)}{p(A)}$$

so that $p(A \mathbin{\square\!\!\rightarrow} C / A) = p(C/A)$, and so, given 2, $p(A \mathbin{\square\!\!\rightarrow} C) = p(C/A)$. What this means is that where the n $(A \mathbin{\square\!\!\rightarrow} S_i)$, corresponding to some partition $[S_1, \ldots, S_n]$, on which we define the expected utility of an action A, are all statistically independent of $p(A)$, the expected utility and the expected desirability are the same.[7]

Now in many cases, this condition seems likely to hold. In particular, where the partition is of conditions agents believe to be fixed independently of what they chose to do, and where what they chose to do is not a *symptom* of these background conditions (in the way smoking is a sympton of the cancer-gene in the Fisher Hypothesis), it will certainly hold. And often this is how we take

---

6. This is certainly true for someone who satisfies the condition that we have already presupposed, namely that they are certain the world is deterministic, an assumption I make here and later for ease of exposition. That it does follow is obvious enough: for in a deterministic world we have conditional excluded middle, so that it follows at once that

$(A \& C) \dashv\vdash (A \& C \& (A \mathbin{\square\!\!\rightarrow} C)) \lor (A \& C \& (A \mathbin{\square\!\!\rightarrow} \neg C))$

But given that conditionals obey *modus ponens*, the right-hand disjunct here is impossible.
   That $(A \& C)$ and $(A \& (A \mathbin{\square\!\!\rightarrow} C))$ are equivalent is, however, widely accepted by conditional logicians; see, for example, Lewis (1973).

7. The connection between 1, 2 and the claim that $p(A \mathbin{\square\!\!\rightarrow} C) = p(C/A)$ was pointed out to me by Brian Ellis.

decisions: we decide whether to take the umbrella on the basis of beliefs about whether it will rain, and we take it whether it will rain or not is up to us *and* that taking the umbrella is not evidence that it will rain. In all such cases, Jeffrey's theory will give the correct answer, because the conditional probability works as a suitable surrogate for the probability of the subjunctive conditional.

Some people have argued that, where doing A is an action, the probability of the conditional (I do $A \mathrel{\Box\!\!\!\rightarrow} S$) will *always* be statistically independent of p(I do A), provided the agent is rational. Thus, Ellery Eells has offered an elegant argument which shows that an agent who satisfies certain plausible constraints for rationality and self-knowledge cannot have $p(A \mathrel{\Box\!\!\!\rightarrow} C) \neq p(C/A)$, where '$A$' specifies one of the agent's options for action. It would be nice if we could suppose this; for Jeffrey's theory is much neater than causal decision theory. But, sadly, I do not think we can.

Eells' defence is modelled on the so-called 'Tickle Defence'; see Skyrms, (1980a), which I now summarise. It is essential to the situation in a Newcomb problem that choosing something – call it 'the good' – is a symptom, but not a cause, of something else – call it 'the evil'. In the Fisher Hypothesis, the good is smoking and the evil is cancer. Someone defending Jeffrey's theory by way of the Tickle Defence would argue thus:

Supposedly the prior state that tends to cause the evil also tends to cause you to take the good . . . How can it do that? If you are fully rational your choices are governed by your beliefs and desires so nothing can influence your choices except by influencing your beliefs and desires. *But if you are fully rational, you know your own mind* . . . So you won't have to wait until you find yourself [smoking] to get the bad news. You will have it already when you feel that tickle in the tastebuds – or whatever introspectible state it might be – that manifests your desire [to smoke]. Your consequent choice tells you nothing more. By the time you decide whether to [smoke], your [probability] function has been modified by the evidence of the tickle. (Lewis, 1981a: 10, altered where indicated, my italics)

In the smoking case this would mean that $p(C/S)$ was equal to $p(C/\neg S)$, by the time you came to act. Since the evidence that you are going to get cancer is not that you smoke, but that you have a set of beliefs and desires that make you want to smoke, the actual smoking is not evidence at all.

Eells' actual line of reasoning is much more subtle and complex than this, since he make much weaker assumptions than that we always 'know our own mind'. But Eells does require that agents be relatively well informed about the desirabilities and probabilities of their representations; and his rationale for this is that agents must be aware of their degrees of belief and the strengths of their desires, since an awareness of them plays a role in decision.

Now I am sure that this rationale is not satisfactory, at least for my purposes. For I am trying to develop this decision theory in the context of a functionalism that aims to escape the worst excesses both of Cartesianism and of behaviourism; and it seems to me that Eells is here required to sail perilously close to the Cartesian rocks. In my view it is not an awareness of degrees of belief and desire that is important in action: it is degrees of belief and desire themselves. Their role in decision has nothing to do with our awareness of them. Of course, since I am not a behaviourist, I agree that sometimes we *are* aware of these states; and I, like Eells, follow Mellor in thinking that when we are aware of them, that *is* our believing that we have them; see Mellor (1980c). But the role of 'second-order' belief, like the role of all belief, is in action in relation to the things it is about. And, on Mellor's theory, what second-order beliefs are about is current first-order beliefs of one's own. Beliefs about my current first-order beliefs – say, about my not having any strong degree of belief about what o'clock it is – play a role in determining actions directed at affecting my own beliefs – say, looking to see what the clock says. It is primarily first-order beliefs that determine actions whose objects are states of the outside world: and these we can – and often do – act on, whether we are conscious or not.

So that, even though Eells' assumptions about self-knowledge are weaker than the Tickle Defence, they are too strong for my purposes in building decision theory into an account of the functioning of the mind. Eells has shown that someone whose awareness of their degrees of belief amounted to a fairly high degree of self-knowledge, would always act to maximise expected desirability. But if beliefs and desires work the way I have suggested, we could be totally wrong about our own minds; and that makes Jeffrey's decision theory inappropriate as a general model.

Part of Eells' motivation seems to be that if it is possible to keep Jeffrey's theory and the related representation theorems, a neat account of the relations between probability, desirability and preference is the result. I share his sense that this would be nice, since the representation theorems play – as we shall see – a crucial role in the way I want to make decision theory functional.

But this seems to me no good reason for avoiding the introduction of the connective '$\square\!\!\rightarrow$' and p-functions defined over them, since we have independent reasons for wanting to have our language defined over subjunctive conditionals. Since we have to find ways of fitting such conditionals in anyway, there is no obvious saving in dodging them in the setting up of decision theory: and once we have them, utilities are, as we have seen, easily defined in terms of conditionals and of desirabilities. It will then be a side consequence of the full theory it avoids Newcomb's problems for agents who do not know their own minds; and that, in my view, is a good thing, since the class of such agents includes everyone I know.

So much, then, for the formal outlines of the theory. Let us now ask how it might work in the very simplest kind of case. As is standard, we can use two matrices to characterise the relevant values of the probability and desirability functions; see, e.g. Jeffrey (1965, *passim*). Thus, in the probability matrix, we label the rows with possible actions and the columns with members of some partition of conditions. The value in the row for action A and condition C, is just $p(A \mathrel{\square\!\rightarrow} C)$. In the desirability matrix, the entry in the row for A and the column for C is $d(C \mathbin{\&} A)$. If we multiply the corresponding values in each matrix and sum across rows, we get a new matrix: it has one column and as many rows as there are actions contemplated. And the values in the rows are the expected utilities of the actions on that partition of conditions.

Suppose we wish merely to calculate whether Mary prefers taking to not taking her umbrella; and suppose that we calculate the expected utility on the (presumably relevant!) partition [(It rains), (It does not rain)].

Then we might have (writing 'R' for 'It rains'; 'U' for 'I take my umbrella'):

p	R	$\neg R$
U	0.6	0.4
$\neg U$	0.6	0.4

d	R	$\neg R$
U	2	−1
$\neg U$	−3	1.5

The expected utility of taking the umbrella on the partition $[R, \neg R]$ is thus: $(2 \times 0.6) + (-1 \times 0.4) = 0.8$. And the expected utility of not taking the umbrella is given by $(-3 \times 0.6) + (1.5 \times 0.4) = -1.2$. It is consequently true that Mary prefers to take the umbrella.

It is worth noticing about this case that the two rows of the probability matrix are identical. This reflects the fact that Mary does not believe that the probability of rain depends on whether or not she takes her umbrella. In this case,

$$p(U \mathrel{\Box\!\!\!\rightarrow} R) = p(\neg U \mathrel{\Box\!\!\!\rightarrow} R) = p(R).$$

Now suppose Peter were contemplating whether or not to sit in the front row of the stalls. Suppose too that there is only one other possible seat, high up in the gods. Unfortunately for the simple life, he thinks that sitting in the front row of the stalls may cause a reduction in the quality of the performance: for he is a leading critic, well known to the cast. We might then have a p-matrix and a d-matrix as follows (writing 'S' for 'Sit in stalls'; and 'P' for 'I am seen'; and assuming that sitting in the stalls and in the gods are the only two possibilities):

p	P	$\neg P$
S	0.5	0.5
$\neg S$	0.1	0.9

d	P	$\neg P$
S	-5	4
$\neg S$	-2	0.5

Here, since $u(S) = -0.5$, and $u(\neg S) = 0.25$, Peter will prefer to sit in the gods, where he will enjoy the show, in all probability, though not very much, rather than in the stalls, where he might have a terrible evening or a marvellous one. If the rows of the p-matrix had been identically (0.4, 0.6) then he would have chosen to sit in the stalls.

We now have the bare bones of a theory that allows us to derive the agent's preference ordering for states of affairs in terms of degrees of beliefs and strengths of desires. But what decision theorists have shown, and what is important, is that we can go the other way. Granted that we fix a scale for measuring desirabilities – by fixing the numerical value of $d(S \lor \neg S)$ at 0, for all S, and taking two more reference points – we can reconstruct both probabilities and desirabilities, given only the preference ordering of the agent.[8] And this allows us to make the account functionalist. For if we require that the agent performs that action which has highest expected utilty (or, if a number of them 'tie', one of them), we can characterise a total probability and desirability state in terms of its role in the causation of actions. If we offer someone pairs of choices, they ought always to pick the one whose utility is higher. So, it might seem, we can now say what it is to be in a state which embodies a certain p- and d-function: it is to be in a state which would cause you to choose A out of any pair of options $[A_1, A_2]$, iff $u(A_1)$ is greater than $u(A_2)$; and to be indifferent iff $u(A_1) = u(A_2)$.

The result ought to be surprising. For, as argued in Chapter 2, a functionalist theory needs to make both input and output claims. It needs to fix not only how (changes in) mental states produce action, but also how (changes in) mental states are causally produced. But this result looks as though it shows that we can fix the contents of beliefs and desires purely on the basis of output claims. For all the theory appears to tell us so far is the consequence in action and disposition to action of the strengths of belief and desire. It says nothing about the causation of changes in the degrees of those beliefs or in the strengths of those desires. Since input claims are about the non-mental antecedents of mental events, the theory tells us nothing about input. In the next two sections I shall show that the proper interpretation of the decision-theoretic result – that preference-orderings determine both p- and d-functions – is consistent with the claims of Chapter 2.

8. On Jeffrey's account the p-function is 'unique only up to a certain quantisation' (1965: i): this is not so on the classical Ramsey-style model. But whichever way one decides on this question, we need not worry. The absence of a unique real value for probability should upset us no more than the analogous problem for physical lengths. Talk of lengths is not suspect because there is no clear notion of an absolute molecular boundary for objects (Jeffrey, 1965: 138).

I should also point out that the representation theorems for causal decision theory do not exist yet: we should need a better understanding of the semantics and probability of the '□→' connective, to get them; but there does not look as though there is any reason why we should not have them once we get the semantics straight.

I have offered an account of degrees of belief as probabilities and strengths of desire as desirabilities. And this account is offered as part of a functionalist theory. If I am right, then, we need some reason for thinking not merely that this theory adequately describes the relations between beliefs, desires and preferences of actual agents, but that it must do so. *Prima facie*, this is implausible. I mentioned why in 3.1. It is implausible because the account entails that the degree of someone's belief that R, for any R, will be the same as their degree of belief that S, for any S, provided S and R share truth conditions. This result is proved, in, for example Field (1977), for pairs of sentences which are either tautologically equivalent or equivalent in virtue of their quantificational form. But it is, as a matter of fact, a consequence of the theory that was explicitly stated and endorsed by Ramsey (1978:84). Indeed, Ramsey says, it is because any account of degrees of belief that did not assign them a probability measure would *not* have this consequence, that he thinks any such other account would be 'absurd'. So Ramsey actually represents his famous version of the Dutch Book argument as a *reductio* proof:

If anyone's mental condition violated these laws [of probability] his choice would depend upon the precise form in which the options were offered to him, *which would be absurd*. (1978: 84; my italics)

This is, on the face of it, as I say, rather surprising. For as I showed in 2.3, it is perfectly consistent with our expectations that someone's choice of action should depend upon something other than the truth conditions of their beliefs (and desires); something I have dubbed 'computational structure'. We cannot hold that agents' degrees of belief and desire behave as suggested in 3.2, 3.3, and 3.4, at the same time as holding that they always maximise expected utility. For, if that were so, the situation described in 2.3 would be impossible. It would be impossible because the account of decision theory I have given is committed to logically equivalent representations having the same p- and d-values. If p- and d-values determine a representation's position in the preference ranking, then two logically equivalent representations cannot have different positions in that ranking.

If we want to keep the account of the last section, as it relates to probability, desirability, and utility, then we must allow that what an agent will do is not uniquely determined by the preference ordering that the account generates. And this is what I intend to argue. But in order to do this we shall have to show that the modified account is consistent with functionalism. Ramsey's account was consistent with functionalism because it claimed that if someone had a certain p- and d-function, then that would cause them to act in a way that maximised expected utility. Preference orderings thus had a functionalist character: they reflected people's dispositions to action. But if the preference ordering does not have that functionalist character, then, though we can save the decision theoretic apparatus from actual inconsistency with the facts, we can only do so by disconnecting preference and action.

I proceed in two steps. First, in this section, I suggest an account of the relations between preference and action which is consistent with the decision-theoretic picture and continues to assume that truth-conditionally equivalent beliefs do not differ in their functional roles; then, in the next chapter, I offer an account, in terms of computational structure, of how we are to achieve a functionalist individuation of beliefs which allows truth-conditionally equivalent beliefs to have different causal roles.

Our theory says that, given a particular state of a person's p- and d-functions, we can discover the structure of their preferences. But we still need a fuller account of the relations between the preference ordering and action. Each total probability–desirability state defines a utility ordering for a class of options, which may have only one member at the top. All we have suggested about the relations between the preference ordering and action so far is that people will try to bring about one of the actions at the top of their utility rankings.

This initial proposal is open, however, to a simple and fatal objection. Consider Mary, whose highest ranking utility is u(Everybody in the world is happy). (Remember this is the utility of *Mary's* making everybody happy; utilities are only defined for the agent's own actions.) This altruist values her own next meal lower (much lower, perhaps) than everybody's being happy. And yet, of course, even though (Everybody in the world is happy) tops her preference ranking she does not spend all her time trying to make everybody in the world happy. The reason is simple: Mary has no idea how to make everyone in the world happy. How are we to deal with this fact?

The right intuition to follow, I think, is that what Mary does not know how to do is to perform some basic action, whose occurrence she believes will bring it about that everybody in the world is happy. All of us carry out our actions by way of bodily movements which are under our direct control. Only when a representation is of a state of affairs which someone believes they can bring about by such a basic action, will that representation's having highest utility lead them to try to bring about that state of affairs.

Jennifer Hornsby has characterised actions that are basic in the sense I require as follows:

The kinds of actions in an agent's repertoire that are BASIC for him are those which he knows how to do, and knows how to do other than on the basis of knowing how they are done by him (1980: 84)

To say that an action is BASIC, is not to say that it is a simple bodily movement. For most of us tying one's shoelace is a BASIC action, even though the physical movements involved are complex and articulated. So too, for most of us, uttering the sentence 'Serendipity drinks procrastination' would count as a BASIC act; for it is something we can all do without considering the oral, laryngeal and other muscular processes involved in sentence articulation.

It may seem unsatisfactory in an account of beliefs and desires to have to make use of the notion of an action which the agent knows how to perform without relying on his knowledge of how it is performed by him. And it would, I think, be desirable to do without this. Hornsby makes moves towards a further analysis of this problem in her discussion of the BASIC action which she considers, namely that of trilling with one's right hand. She says:

[S]ome people can trill certain phrases of piano music to a certain standard with their right hand, but not with their left. The difference is presumably not to be accounted for by a contrast between presence and absence of knowledge of how it is done with the right hand and the left. That is not enough to establish that there is no interesting bodily movement description that could figure in any rational explanation of the skill, since it is still possible that the man who trills with his right hand believes he has to make movements of his fingers in some specific complicated serial arrangement, and still possible that we should see such movements as movements that he makes because he believes that this is the way to trill the phrase. But . . . [i]f we thought the triller, though he knows in detail how he trills might just as well have forgotten, then we should have . . . a reason [for thinking the beliefs do not explain the performance]. (1980: 82–3)

The key question to answer in considering which actions are BASIC for some specific person – say, Mary – then, is whether beliefs to the effect that if she does some B she will bring it about that A, play a causal role in her bringing about B. If they do not, the action A is BASIC for her; provided that it is usually the case that Mary's trying to A brings it about that A.

I do not want to say any more than this about BASIC actions. Hornsby's book contains (particularly in Chapter 5) a detailed defence of her account of BASIC actions, with which I concur. There is not scope in this chapter to go further into the philosophy of action, and I hope only that I have made sense of the notion of a BASIC action.

Granted this notion, we can set about remedying the problem that arose with our altruist. She preferred making everyone else happy to anything else; but for her (as for all of us, save, perhaps God) making everybody happy was not a BASIC action. Instead, then, of saying that agents will try to bring about the state of affairs S, whose $u(S)$ has highest value, I shall say that agents will try to perform that BASIC action which has highest utility at any time. Which actions are BASIC for someone is a fact about them, not about agents in general. For you and me, but not for young Peter, aged four, tying shoelaces is a BASIC action; for someone else, perhaps, but certainly not for me, trilling on the flute is a BASIC action.

We have answered the first crucial question about the relations between preference and action. It is the BASIC action with highest utility that the agent will try to perform: this, we may take it, is what is meant by maximising expected utility. If we took maximising expected utility to involve trying to bring about the state of affairs at the top of the preference ranking, we should have to suppose that agents regularly tried to do things which they did not know (and knew they did not know) how to do.

But this is still not nearly enough. For all we are able to determine on this basis is which BASIC action is highest (or one of the highest, but I shall usually leave this consideration aside from now on) in a preference ranking. Granted that agents do have probability and desirability functions and that they determine utility in the way I have described, how can we discover more about an agent's preference ordering than simply which BASIC action ranks highest?

The answer, in broad outlines, is rather simple. All we have to do is to write in constraints on how the agent's probability and desirability functions will change with input. For given such constraints we can say what options will come to the top of the ranking in the new d-function produced by the new input. The preference ordering will then be shown up in action when the agent is subject to those inputs. If eating apples has particular utility $u(A)$; and if causing the agent to believe that eating apples will reduce the rate of population growth, will cause $u(A)$ to change to $u'(A)$; and if $u'(A)$ will then be at the top of the ranking; then causing the agent to have that belief will allow us to confirm our ascription of the original value $u(A)$. The precise values of p- and d-functions will determine the effects of input; and these, in turn, will be determined by the structure of the preference ranking. Ascriptions of particular structures to the preference ranking will thus entail subjunctive conditionals of the form:

> C: If the agent had been subjected to input I, then S would have come to the top of the ranking.

And this, of course, will entail the functionalist thesis that this agent, subjected to that input, would try to bring it about that S; provided, that is, that doing S is a BASIC action.

Some writers on decision theory have treated preference as a matter of the subject's intuitions. Thus, von Neumann and Morgenstern say, of the hypothetical individual they are considering:

More precisely, we expect him, for any two alternative events that are put before him as possibilities, to be able to tell which of the two he prefers. (1947: 17)

But this is totally out of sympathy with a functionalist approach. What a functionalist will need is some output for the agent which will tell us what the agent's states are. It is perfectly true that we could read this passage as requiring that the relevant action be the speech-act of telling which of two options the agent prefers. But if that were the claim, which I do not think it was, then it would be absurd. Lots of things will affect whether agents will tell you their preferences, other than what their preferences actually are. Further there is no obvious reason why someone should know what their preferences are between *possibilia*: from the fact that Mary would always choose oranges rather than apples, it does not follow that she knows she would always do so. Freud taught us about the unconscious; we need not let von Neumann and Morgenstern deprive us of it.

The account I have been suggesting is not open to this objection. On our account, granted an initial state of the preference ordering and the probability and desirability functions which, given a metric, it entails, we have a good functionalist story of how the preference function shows up. It shows up when the new probabilities and desirabilities consequent upon some new input give rise to a new most preferred BASIC action.

We now have the answer to the suspicion I raised at the end of the last section. I pointed out there that, granted that a preference ordering is simply a matter of output, then the decision theoretic apparatus entails that we can characterise belief and desire purely in terms of output, contrary to my earlier claim that we should need input also. Now we see that the preference ordering is not simply a matter of output. In order to be able to discover the agent's preferences at all we must be able to make input claims.

In order to make good this story, we must be able to say what the constraints are: what the input claims are that will map a desirability function and p-function onto a new p-function and desirability function. This will allow us to say how the changes in the preference ordering come about when the agent acquires new beliefs in sensation and perception; and changes in degrees of belief will affect the agent's desirabilities – and thus utilities – in ways we shall be considering later.

On the account I intend to develop, the input claims are claims about how beliefs are changed by sensation and perception; claims about how evidence affects belief. For it is part of our *a priori* theory that what input must change is belief and not desire.

I am inclined simply to stipulate that what I mean by evidence is those states of affairs which our *a priori* theory treats as causes of changes of degree of belief. This is not to say that changes in the desirability function may not be brought about by way of input unmediated by changes in belief. It is a familiar observation that drugs can change a person's mood in ways that make them lose or gain desires; and this may be true of drugs which have no effect on their beliefs at all. But this fact is *a posteriori*; it is not part of our concept of desires that they do change in this way, it is simply that they may. Beliefs on the other hand *must* change in reaction to input; or, to put the matter another way, for a state to be a state of belief there must be inputs which would bring about changes in its degree, either directly or by way of changes in other beliefs.

I have claimed that it is part of our *a priori* theory that desires are insensitive to evidence; beliefs *must* respond to evidence, desires need not. But there might be objections to this claim from someone who held that moral attitudes were exceptional here: that someone with the concept of kindness as a virtue must come to assign a higher desirability to any act if they came to believe it *was* an act of kindness, and that this change must come about as a causal consequence of input that led to their having that belief. This would mean that some beliefs – evaluative ones – were like beliefs in that they responded to evidence, but like desires in the role they played in determining action. If this were right, I should lose part of my functional characterisation of the difference between belief and desire.

Such a view might be what is intended by some kinds of moral realist. And it is an interesting position, one that I do not think can easily be rejected; but to discuss it here would be to take us well out of the way. So I propose simply to avoid discussion of it by stipulating that my interest is in characterising an agent without concepts with this property. There is enough to be done in characterising agents anyway; and I worry less than I might about this stipulation because I doubt that this kind of moral 'realism' is true.

I intend, therefore, to begin by discussing those changes in agents which result from their acquisition of evidence. Later on I say how I think that these changes might be seen to result in changes in desirabilities.

3.6 CHANGING YOUR MIND

Once again I propose to help myself to Jeffrey's account. What Jeffrey has done is to define a method of deriving a new probability function consequent upon changes of degrees of belief which originate in a certain subset of the representations of an agent's system. We can describe a change of p-function as originating in a set of beliefs O, if

(a) the agent is caused by the experience to come to have new p-values for the members of O, and

(b) every other change in their p-function is caused by changes in the members of O.

It is quite clear, if we take, say, visual perception as our model, that the full description of the set O in English might be very extensive. As I look into an unfamiliar room I may acquire many new beliefs on the basis of what I see: but we may take, as Jeffrey does, a simple case, supposing that a complex one would not give rise to any new issues of principle.

Let me start with the standard Bayesian account, of which Jeffrey's approach is a generalisation. On that account of change in the p-function, p-functions change by simple conditionalisation. Every change of p-function is supposed to result from coming to believe some E with certainty, and adjusting $p(S)$ for every S, to

$$p'(S) = p(S/E)$$

(where p and p' are, respectively, the original and the new p-function). We do not need to consider why anyone might think this a reasonable procedure. For we can give two reasons why it will not do.

First of all, simple conditionalisation is irreversible. The reason for this is quite simple. $p(E)$ will have to be less than 1, or else $p'(S) = p(S)$, for all S. And $p'(E)$ has to be 1. But if $p'(E)$ is to be 1, there is no representation S, such that conditionalisation upon S will take $p'(E)$ to $p''(E) \neq 1$, where p'' is a p-function produced by conditionalisation upon p'. For if $p'(E) = 1$, then $p'(S/E)$ will be $p'(S)$ for all (S), unless it is undefined.

What this amounts to is that every change of belief is represented as the acquisition of a belief with certainty which can never be revised. This is objectionable because we are never caused by our experiences to come to believe something so strongly that no amount of logically possible further experience could change our minds. (Peter Unger (1975) tells many tales which reinforce this point.) The widely accepted thesis of the underdetermination of empirical beliefs by experience just is the claim that no amount of experience justifies the irreversible acceptance of any empirical proposition. If that is right, then a theory which made this not only possible but compulsory would be open to serious objection.

There are ways round this difficulty which make use of so-called Popper-functions; see, for example, Field (1977). For Popper-functions take conditional probability as basic, and not as introduced by a ratio of absolute probabilities; and define the absolute probability of A, for any A, as $p(A/T)$, where T is certain. Since this is so, the conditional probabilities on sentences of probability 0 can exist; they just are not equal to the normal ratio. In consequence, $p(S/E)$ can be defined where $p(E)$ is 0, so we could conditionalise on $p'(\neg E)$ to change $p(S)$, when $p'(E)$ is 0. But Popper-functions cannot be used in this way by someone who thinks, as I do, that probability functions should be regular. As I have said, I will discuss the issue of regularity later, in Chapter 4. For the moment, then, let me just accept that, for someone

60

who uses Popper-functions, this argument is not decisive reason for giving up simple conditionalisation.

The second reason why conditionalisation will not do *is* decisive, however, and is given by Jeffrey in the passage which follows. (Jeffrey's word 'proposition' can be used indifferently for 'representation' or 'belief'.)

The agent inspects a piece of cloth by candlelight, and gets the impression that it is green, although he concedes that it might be blue or even (but very improbably) violet. If G, B and V are the propositions that the cloth is green, blue and violet respectively, then the outcome of the observation might be that, whereas originally his degrees of belief in G, B and V were .30, .30 and .40, his degrees of belief in those same propositions after the observation are .70, .25 and .05. If there were a proposition E in his preference ranking which described the precise quality of his visual experience in looking at the cloth, one would say that what the agent learned from the observation was that E is true. If his original subjective probability assignment was prob, his new assignment should be prob_E,[9] and we would have

$$\text{prob}G \;=\; .30 \quad \text{prob}B \;=\; .30 \quad \text{prob}V \;=\; .40$$

representing his opinions about the color of the cloth before the observation, but would have

$$\text{prob}(G/E) \;=\; .70 \quad \text{prob}(B/E) \;=\; .25 \quad \text{prob}(V/E) \;=\; .05$$

representing his opinions about the colour of the cloth after the observation. But there need be no such proposition E in his preference ranking; nor need any such proposition be expressible in the English language. Thus, the description 'The cloth looked green or possibly blue or conceivably violet', would be too vague to convey the precise quality of the experience. Certainly it would be too vague to support such precise conditional probability ascriptions as those noted above. It seems that the best we can do is to describe, not the quality of the visual experience itself, but rather its effects on the observer, by saying, 'After the observation, the agent's degrees of belief in G, B and V were .70, .25, and .05'. (1965: 154)

How, then, are we to treat this case? First of all, to make it formally tractable, we must provide a logically more organised description of the set of beliefs in which the change originates. Thus we define, for any set of representations, S, with members $[S_1, S_2 \ldots S_n]$, an atom of the set as a conjunction of the form

$$(R_1 \;\&\; R_2 \;\&\; \ldots \;\&\; R_n)$$

where every R_i is either S_i or $(\neg S_i)$; and where the whole conjunction is logically possible. If the members of S are pairwise inconsistent, there will be n atoms; if they are not there may be as many as up to 2^n.

In this case of Jeffrey's, using Jeffrey's 'G' 'B' and 'V' to symbolise the

9. prob_E is the p-function obtained by simple conditionalisation on E.

agent's beliefs, the atoms are

$G \& \neg B \& \neg V$

$\neg G \& B \& \neg V$

$\neg G \& \neg B \& V$

$\neg G \& \neg B \& \neg V$

These are, of course, logically equivalent to G, B, V, and $\neg(G \lor B \lor V)$. Jeffrey assumes, for convenience, that $(G \lor B \lor V)$ is necessary, so the last of these is counted logically impossible and taken out of the set of atoms. Nothing hangs on this, so we can do likewise.

If we call the probability assignment – which results from the changes originating in the set $[B, G, V] - p'$, and the original assignment p, then Jeffrey requires that, for all S,

$$p'(S) = p(S/G) \cdot p'(G) + p(S/B) \cdot p'(B) + p(S/V) \cdot p'(V).$$

That is, he requires that the relative probabilities of representations on the atoms of the set in which the change originates should be preserved; and that the new probability $p'(S)$ for any S be equal to the sum of its probabilities conditional on the atoms, weighted by the new probabilities of the atoms.

Thus, suppose S is (It is my table-cloth). And suppose I believe my table cloth is green, so that

$p(S/G) = 0.90$

$p(S/B) = 0.05$

$p(S/V) = 0.05$

then, $p(S)$ will change to $p'(S)$, where

$$p(S) = (0.90)(0.03) + (0.05)(0.30) + (0.05)(0.40) = 0.305$$

$$p'(S) = (0.90)(0.70) + (0.05)(0.25) + (0.05)(0.05) = 0.505.$$

The general form of this rule for changing p-functions, which is called generalised conditionalisation, but which I shall usually refer to as conditionalisation hereafter, is this:

$$p'(R) = \sum_{i=1}^{i=n} p(R/S_i) \cdot p'(S_i)$$

for all R, where a change from p to p' originates in a set whose atoms are S_1 to S_n.

Given this method for changing p-functions we could, if we knew how to produce changes in some small subset of the agent's beliefs, predict what would come out at the top of the agent's preference ranking . . . provided we knew how to predict the consequent changes in the d-function as well. Finding the change in the d-function is not going to be easy however: for though we have the theorem

$$d(\neg S) \;=\; -\,(p(S)/p(\neg S))\cdot d(S)$$

(Jeffrey, 1965: 76, '5–6:'), this only gives us a new ratio for the desirabilities, not their numerical value.

How, then, are we to arrive at the new desirability function? I propose to give an account of change of p-function which justifies not only a rule for transition between d-functions but also the very rule for transition between p-functions that Jeffrey offers.[10]

Suppose someone's representations consist of an actual stock of n representations, $[R_1, R_2. . . R_n]$, and a potential stock of all the truth-functions of those representations. Thus, if they actually have some degree of belief that snow is white, one of the R_i will be (Snow is white) and, if they also have (Grass is green) amongst the actual stock, then (Snow is white and grass is green) is one of their potential representations whether they have any actual degree of belief about this or not. I argue in the next chapter for a functional account of the distinction between actual and potential states; but my basic position is just causal realism. Those states are actual which are available to play causal roles in the agent's mind. I shall call the set of representations $[R_1, R_2. . . R_n]$ the set of original representations.

We now define a set of basic atoms of the agent's system, of representations as follows. A basic conjunction of the agent's system of representations is a conjunction of the form $(S_1 \,\&\, S_2 \,\&\, . . . \,\&\, S_n)$, such that each of the set S_i is either R_i or $(\neg R_i)$, for every i between 1 and n. The set of atoms is the set of basic conjunctions which are truth-conditionally possible. Thus if R_i entails $(\neg R_k)$, then the basic conjunctions of the form $(S_1 \,\&\, S_2 \,\&\, . . . \,\&\, R_i \,\&\, R_k \,\&\, . . . \,\&\, S_n)$, are not atoms. If two atoms have the same truth conditions, or, more generally, if all the members of any subset of the atoms have the same truth conditions, we form the set of basic atoms by removing all but one of these truth-conditionally equivalent representations from the set of atoms. It does not matter which one we leave, but there will, of course, be a different set of basic atoms corresponding to each choice we might make. For what follows any such set will do.

A set of basic atoms is, of course, a set of representations which are

10. Paul Teller has offered arguments in defence of Jeffrey's style of conditionalisation before; but my argument here is different and starts, I think, with more plausible premises; see, however, Teller (1973). More sophisticated arguments is provided in Mellor (1980) by Skyrms. But the treatment there involves second order probabilities, which I shall not be considering.

truth-functions of the actual stock of the agent's original representations, R_1 to R_n. I shall now state eight important (but fairly obvious) results about basic atoms, which are proved in my 1981: Appendix 3.

1: Every basic atom entails the negation of every other; that is basic atoms are pairwise inconsistent.

2: The disjunction of all basic atoms is necessarily true.

If a representation is possible iff its truth conditions can hold, then

3: Every possible representation is equivalent to a disjunction of basic atoms.

It follows immediately from our definition of basic atoms that:

4: Every basic atom is possible.

for we have ruled out impossible basic conjunctions to get the set of atoms.

5: All basic atoms have distinct truth conditions.

Let us call the set of basic atoms whose disjunction is equivalent to a representation R, the basic atoms of R: call this set $A(R)$.

6: $p(R \lor S)$ is equal to the sum of the probabilities of the members of $[A(R) \cup A(S)]$, where '$\cup$' is set theoretic union

7: $p(R \& S)$ is equal to the sum of the probabilities of the members of $[A(R) \cap A(S)]$, where '$\cap$' is set-theoretic intersection.

8: $p(R)$ is equal to the sum of the probabilities of the members of $A(R)$.

The intuitive idea of the basic atom is simply that of a representation which specifies as completely as possible in an agent's system of representations a total state of the world. It is thus close to the notion of a possible world which plays so large a part in current discussions of semantics. I have said something in the introduction about why I do not use possible worlds as a device. For anyone who insists on doing so the translation is easy: a basic atom is a representation which specifies a class of worlds between which the agent is unable to distinguish. Given this equivalence I sometimes talk for expository convenience in terms of possible worlds; but this talk should always be seen as cashed out in terms of atoms. Once we had fixed someone's desirability for every atom, we should have fixed their preference ordering for total states of the world.

It is a fundamental part of our *a priori* theory of the mind that the desirability of a total state of the world is not something to which evidence is relevant. This is not perhaps immediately obvious. Mary's view of the desirability of states of the world in which there are clouds might seem to depend on what she believes about the connection between clouds and rain. But if Mary has in her system of representations some R, whose truth conditions are that it rains, and some S, whose truth conditions are that there are clouds: then amongst her basic atoms there will be some in which it rains and there are clouds, and some in which it rains and there are no clouds, and some in which it does not rain and there are clouds, and some in which there is neither rain nor clouds. And how she ranks these will not depend on whether she thinks clouds bring rain; for some of the atoms will entail that clouds bring rain and others that they do not. Nothing in the perceptual input of agents requires that they should have any particular ordering of these states.[11]

That is not to say that someone's ordering of basic atoms could not change. Mary might acquire a taste for cloudy days, even though she dislikes rain. But though the acquisition of a taste may be the causal result of an experience, it is consistent with our *a priori* theory that, for example, no amount of exposure to the taste of brandy should bring you to like the taste of it. And if that is so, then you will always prefer an atom R to an atom S if they differ only in that R entails you taste no brandy and S entails that you do.

We can express the point generally. Whether a certain state of affairs is desirable will, in the normal case, depend only on the intrinsic desirability to us of that state, but also on what else we think would happen if that state should come about. But a basic atom specifies not merely that something or other comes about, but also everything that comes about in consequence of this. Since the basic atom fixed how the world is in every respect in which we are capable of representing it to ourselves, its desirability cannot depend on what else happens if it comes about; for there is nothing further to come about that is left unspecified.[12]

The situation is fundamentally different with representations which are not basic atoms. Here, as Jeffrey's desirability axiom (DES, above) requires, where a representation R is equivalent to a disjunction of n basic atoms $[A_1, \ldots A_n]$,

$$d(R) = \frac{\sum_{i=1}^{i=n} p(A_i)d(A_i)}{\sum_{i=1}^{i=n} p(A_i)}$$

---

11. Notice that what I have claimed is not that there are no consequences in the desirability function which must result from input; only that there are no such changes which must occur which are either caused directly or mediated only by beliefs. It may help to bear in mind – what I shall argue later – that changes in beliefs cause changes in the desirability of a representation S only against the causal background of particular other desirabilities; while changes in belief may occur either directly as a result of input or mediated by other beliefs but causally independently of any desirabilities.

12. If this talk of basic atoms seems implausible because it is unlikely that anyone actually works out desirabilities from the desirabilities of basic atoms, then this problem will be cleared up in Chapter 4, where I give a more realistic view of decision-making. The talk of basic atoms is still useful: for the requirement that the basic atoms have desirabilities which are not necessarily changed by sensory input, is just a way of putting the requirement that the theory should not lead to our treating sensory input as evidence justifying our basic desires.

(This follows from DES by its multiple application to successive disjuncts; remembering that each disjunct is pairwise inconsistent with every other and that their negations never have probability 1; see my 1981: Appendix 3.)

Thus, where R is not a basic atom, its desirability depends not only on the desirability of its basic atoms; but also on their probabilities. And this is a simple consequence of our *a priori* theory. For the place of a representation in the agent's preference ordering depends, when it is not a basic atom, not only on what its basic atoms are, but also on which of them is most likely to be brought about. In reducing every representation to a disjunction of basic atoms we have shown that it is equivalent to a representation which can be true in a number of different and incompatible ways. Since some of the ways it can be true may be more desirable than others, how we value a representation may depend on which way we think it is most likely to be true; on which of the different and incompatible ways in which it might be true is most likely to be the way in which it *is* true.

More generally, our valuation of a representation may depend on the relative probabilities of its basic atoms. Since evidence is obviously relevant to our judgement of these relative probabilities, evidence may thus affect our valuation of a representation, even though it does not affect our evaluation of its basic atoms.

The first constraint on changes of probability and desirability function consequent on input, for a set of basic atoms, $[A_1, \ldots, A_m]$ is thus that $d(A_i) = d'(A_i)$, for i from 1 to m, where d is the original and d' the new d-function. It is, as I have said, possible that this condition should be violated; experience may cause us to change our desirabilities for basic atoms, by leading causally to the acquisition of tastes. But if this does happen, it will be an *a posteriori* feature of the experience that it causes this result, since, as I have said it is not *a priori* true that evidence will change the desirabilities of basic atoms. In what follows, then, I shall characterise the minimum change in the agent's probability and desirability functions that must come about on the acquisition of sensory evidence. If exposure to sensation, perception and input generally happens to produce other changes as well, then we can characterise these changes as independently caused modifications of the desirability of basic atoms.

The changes we are interested in, then, are those changes in the relative probabilities of representations that must come about on the acquisition of evidence. This process will occur in two stages. First, the experience will cause a change in some subset of their representations – in perception; and secondly these changes will produce adjustments in the probabilities of other representations in consequence – in the assessment of evidence. The first of these processes is characterised by what I have called input claims; which tell us how the sensory and perceptual interaction between agents and specified states of their environments will cause changes in the agents' degrees of belief. Let us begin, however, by leaving this question aside, and considering only the second process in which the initial changes act within the mind to produce new probability and desirability functions.

Consider, then, that subset of the agent's representations O, within which changes in probability are caused to occur initially. Call this the originating set. If the members of O are $[R_1, R_2, \ldots R_n]$, then, for i, from 1 to n, $p(R_i) \neq p'(R_i)$, where p is the original and p' the resultant p-function.

Given such an originating set, we can define a set of originating atoms: atoms which stand in the same relation to O as basic atoms stand to the total set R of an agent's representations. Thus, given the members R_1 to R_n of O, we can find the class of basic conjunctions of the form $(U_1 \ \& \ U_2 \ \&\ldots\& \ U_n)$, where every U_i is either R_i or $\neg R_i$, for the corresponding value of i. We then remove from the set of basic conjunctions any impossible members and all but one of any set of equivalent members. Then every member of the originating set will be equivalent to a disjunction of originating atoms: and the probability of every member of the originating set will be the sum of the probabilities of these atoms. Every member of O, the originating set, will be equivalent to a disjunction of some subset of originating atoms.

I propose to call the members of the set of originating atoms, O, $[O_1, \ldots, O_m]$; and the members of the set of basic atoms, A, $[A_1, \ldots, A_k]$. Because all the members of O are representations of the agent's, every O_i will be equivalent to a disjunction of members of A.

Now the set O of originating atoms will not be identical with the set of basic atoms. (That would have to be evidence which directly modified all one's beliefs at once!) So that if we adjust the probabilities of the originating atoms in such a way as to guarantee that $p'(R)$, the new probability of some R, is equal to the sum of the probabilities $p'(O_i)$ of its originating atoms, we shall still not have fixed the new probabilities $p(A_i)$ of the basic atoms. Thus, if we call the basic atoms of the originating atom O_x $[A_b, \ldots, A_c]$, then we shall have fixed that

$$p'(O_x) \ = \ \sum_{i=b}^{i=c} p'(A_i)$$

but we shall still not know how to redistribute the probabilities of the various A_i, for i between b and c, which are the basic atoms of O_x. Our final task, in relation to probabilities, is to decide how this must be done.

We know that the various A_i, for i between b and c, must change their p-values. For the p-value of the originating atom of which they are basic atoms, will have changed from $p(O_x)$ to $p'(O_x)$; and the sum of the values of the various $p'(A_i)$, i from b to c, must be equal to $p'(O_x)$. The obvious thing to do, granted that we cannot leave the p-values of the various A_i unchanged is to leave their relative probabilities unchanged. But we must be careful in giving our reason for thinking this.

Someone might argue that we should leave the relative probabilities alone because we have no reason to change them; but we have no reason not to change them either, or at least no immediately obvious reason. The evidence forces upon Mary certain changes in probability; why should she not change the others as she pleases? The answer, I think, is that we are engaged in characterising those changes which *must* be brought about by evidential input. We are concerned in other words, with that minimum derangement of the p-function that is required by the acquisition of input. Our theory is a causal theory and a realist theory about mental states. If there is any change in the p-function other than that caused by the evidence, then that change must be caused by something other than the evidence. For it is part of our conception of real causal states that changes in them do not occur uncaused. Since we are concerned with the changes which occur as the result of the acquisition of evidence, *qua* evidence – the changes which the acquisition of evidence must bring about – we can simply require that any changes not so caused should be ruled out.

It is still not enough to have a reason for leaving something or other alone; the question is why we should leave alone something highly specific, namely the relative probabilities, wherever we can. But this is just part of what it is to characterise a notion of evidence. If sensory or other evidential input causes Peter to change his assessment of the relative probabilities of two events then that is evidence relevant to those relative probabilities. The evidence we are considering produces changes in the relative probabilities of members of O, the originating set. We are obliged, in consequence, as I have shown, to change the probabilities of basic atoms. But though we are obliged to change their probabilities, we are able to leave their relative probabilities alone. And since we are interested in the minimum change, and since we cannot leave the probabilities alone, leaving the relative probabilities alone, where we can, is the best we can do.

In view of the sad history of indifference principles as attempts to ground inductive logics and to provide rationales for styles of statistical inference, I should insist that my task here is not normative. I am not recommending the preservation of relative probability where we cannot preserve absolute probability as a policy; I am saying that it is built into our *a priori* theory of mental states that, subject to important *caveats* I enter in the next chapter, we do so respond to evidence. Part of the support of this claim comes from its giving us what we should expect as a theory of the role of evidence; and part of the evidence for that I give later when I show that the resultant theory delivers a connection between conditionalisation and conditionals which conforms to our view of the latter; see 8.3.

I propose, then, that the model should leave the relative probabilities of basic atoms undisturbed wherever possible. This does not mean that the relative probabilities of all pairs of basic atoms are preserved; only that the relative probabilities of basic atoms of originating atoms do not change. Pairs of basic atoms which are atoms of different originating atoms will *always* change their relative probabilities.

Granted both that

(a) the desirabilities of basic atoms are undisturbed by the changes that produce the realignment of the probabilities of the originating set,

and

(b) the relative probabilities of basic atoms of originating atoms remain unchanged also,

we shall be able to map a pair of initial probability and desirability functions onto a final pair. And, we shall find, that mapping for probability functions is equivalent to Jeffrey's conditionalisation.

For, take any representation R in the agent's system, which is not in the originating set. It is equivalent to a disjunction of basic atoms, whose probabilities, when added equal its probability. Call these basic atoms of R, $[A_1, \ldots, A_n]$. Consider now any originating atom, O_r. This atom, O_r, is equivalent to a disjunction of basic atoms, also; call these $[A_k, \ldots, A_o]$. The intersection of these two sets will contain the atoms of the representations $(R \& O_r)$; see 7, above. Call the members of that intersection, if any, $[A_l, \ldots, A_m]$.

We have required that the relative probabilities of the basic atoms of originating atoms remain unchanged. So all members of the set of basic atoms of $(R \& O_r)$ should preserve their relative probabilities; since they are all members of the set of basic atoms of the originating atom O_r.

Thus we have, for any i, j, between l and m,

$$\frac{p(A_i)}{p(A_j)} = \frac{p'(A_i)}{p'(A_j)}$$

From this it follows that, for some constant b,

$$\frac{p'(A_i)}{p(A_i)} = \frac{p'(A_j)}{p(A_j)} = b$$

So that, for every i between l and m, $p'(A_i) = b \cdot p(A_i)$.

Now

$$\sum_{i=l}^{i=m} p'(A_i) \;=\; p'(R \,\&\, O_r)$$

and

$$\sum_{i=k}^{i=o} p'(A_i) \;=\; p'(O_r)$$

because the atoms of O_r are the A_i, i from k to o, and the atoms of $(R \,\&\, O_r)$ are the A_i, i for l to m. (The same result holds for the p-function p as for p'.) But

$$\sum_{i=k}^{i=o} p'(A_i) \;=\; \sum_{i=k}^{i=o} b \cdot p(A_i) \;=\; b \cdot \sum_{i=k}^{i=o} p(A_i) \;=\; b \cdot p(O_r)$$

and, similarly,

$$\sum_{i=l}^{i=m} p'(A_i) \;=\; \sum_{i=l}^{i=m} b \cdot p(A_i) \;=\; b \cdot \sum_{i=l}^{i=m} p(A_i) \;=\; b \cdot p(R \,\&\, O_r)$$

so that $p'(O_r) = b \cdot p(O_r)$ and also $p'(R \,\&\, O_r) = b \cdot p(R \,\&\, O_r)$. As a result,

$$\frac{p(R \,\&\, O_r)}{p(O_r)} \;=\; \frac{p'(R \,\&\, O_r)}{p'(O_r)}.$$

O_r is an atom of the originating set. In consequence it does not have either an initial or a final probability of zero; this follows from regularity, which I discuss in 4.5. And thus we can conclude, given the definition of conditional probability, that, for any originating atom, O_r, and any other representation R at all, $p(R/O_r) = p'(R/O_r)$. The conditional probability on any originating atom of any representation is thus preserved.

Jeffrey's conditionalisation rule follows swiftly. For given any partition of representations $[A_1, A_2, \ldots, A_n]$, such that, for all i, k, both $p(A_i \,\&\, A_k) = 0$, and

$$\sum_{i=1}^{i=n} p(A_i) \;=\; 1$$

there is a theorem of the probability calculus that, for all R,

$$p'(R) \;=\; \sum_{i=1}^{i=n} p'(R/A_i) \cdot p'(A_i)$$

and this, with the result of the last paragraph, entails

$$p'(R) = \sum_{i=1}^{i=n} p(R/A_i) \cdot p'(A_i).$$

where the (A_i) are originating atoms, which must form a partition.

Now we know how to get a new p-function, p', the derivation of the new d'-function is trivial. For we have as an axiom of decison theory that:

$$\text{DES } d(S \vee R) = \frac{d(S)p(S) + d(R)p(R)}{p(S) + p(R)}$$

where $p(S \,\&\, R) = 0$, $p(S \vee R) \neq 0$.

These last two conditions are satisfied for any pair of atoms: atoms are pairwise inconsistent and logically possible. So $p(S \vee R) = p(S) + p(R)$, and from DES it follows that $d(S \vee R) \cdot p(S \vee R) = p(S) \cdot d(S) + p(R) \cdot d(R)$, where S and R are atoms. From this it follows, by induction, that, for any K, which is a disjunction of basic atoms $[A_1, \ldots, A_n]$,

$$d(K) \cdot p(K) = \sum_{i=1}^{i=n} p(A_i)d(A_i)$$

Since we know how to find $p'(K)$ for every K in the agent's system of representations, and we know the desirability of a basic atom will be unchanged, we have all the materials we need to use this theorem to calculate the new desirability of any representation. Once desirabilities and probabilities, including probabilities of the subjunctive conditionals, are fixed, utilities are fixed also.

We are now in a position to say how the agent's preference ordering can be evoked. Suppose Peter has a p-function p and a desirability function d. It is an immediate consequence of this that there is at least one basic action which is at least as high in the utility ranking as any other; and that is what he will try to bring about. (As usual, if there are many at the same rank, we predict he will do one of them.) But we can now show how each other basic action in his desirability function which is not a basic atom can be brought to the top of his utility ranking. We introduce input which will change his degrees of belief in some subset of his representations. We can then say, given that the desirability function for basic atoms is unchanged, that this will determine which representation(s) will come to the top of the utility ranking. In giving agents evidence that actually produces this change we will be eliciting features of their previous preferences: for we need the total information about their original probabilities and desirabilities, and the changes of probability in the origination set, to fix the new desirability function. The ascription of a p- and a d-function thus entails subjunctive conditionals of the form: if

(a) a change in the p-function were to occur taking members in the originating set from $p(R)$ to $p'(R)$, and if

(b) no change were caused to occur in the agent's desirability ordering for basic atoms, and if

(c) there were no computational errors (this notion is explained in the next chapter),

then the agent would try to bring about some A; where this is a basic action, and $u(A)$ is a member of the (possibly unit) set of highest utilities for basic actions, which conditionalisation brings up the utility ranking.

We do not yet have an account of the *a priori* constraints on how experience causes changes originating in a certain subset of the agent's representations. That is the task in 4.4 of the next chapter. But once we have discovered this (and how to distinguish cases of computational error), then any case where there are no computational errors and conditionalisation fails to bring about the expected result, must be a case where the agent's ordering of basic atoms has changed; a case in which someone has 'acquired a taste'.

In this chapter I have stated the main outlines of a functionalist theory of belief, desire and action: but it is not yet in any way computational. In the next chapter I take up the modification of the theory to deal with computational structure.

4

Computation

1. The only psychological models of cognitive processes that seem even remotely plausible represent such processes as computational.
2. Computation presupposes a medium of computation: a representational system.
3. Remotely plausible theories are better than no theories at all.

(Fodor, 1976: 27)

4.1 OVERVIEW

Because our theory is computational it will treat beliefs as representations; and it says that some mental processes are computations with these and other representations.[1] Every representation which is a belief has also a property which reflects the degree of that belief; and every desire is a representation with a property that reflects its strength; i.e. in the technical sense introduced in Chapter 3, the subjective 'desirability' of what is thereby desired. Together these determine utilities, which determine action. What is required by a computational theory of decision is that our minds are so constituted that, given these materials, they compute the expected utilities that underlie our actions. This computation is a mental process, a process which is carried out in us by our central nervous systems, and which, like all processes, takes time. But it is a process which can also go wrong, a process in which computational errors can occur. If the computations are completed, then we come to be in a state of preferring some options to others and this causes us to do one of those most preferred basic actions; and if the computation is without error as well as complete, then that action will be a basic action with maximum expected utility. There are thus, on this view, two barriers to someone's action's displaying their preferences as computed by the pure decision theory. First, the necessary computations may not be carried out; secondly there may be some error in the computation.

This does not mean that we now have a theory which can treat anything at all as an agent, by regarding all deviations from predicted behaviour as computational errors. For computational errors have to be *deviations* from the *normal* functioning of the physical system that embodies the functional states.

[1]. Some mental processes are computational, please note. I do not make the extravagant claim that they all are; see Mellor (1984), who makes this very clear.

It follows that in calling something a computational error, we are committed to there being some explanation of it. A deviation from normal functioning is a deviation from what is prescribed by the functionalist theory. But this is not circular. What this means is that if someone's behaviour deviates from what the theory requires, this must be the result of an independently identifiable causal intervention with their mental functioning.

This is a general feature of functional specifications. So, for example, we can still treat a system as a thermostat when it is not *functioning* as one, provided there is some causal process interfering; a process which is both specifiable otherwise than as 'whatever is causing the interference' and one in whose absence the system would work as the functional laws governing thermostats require. (There might, for example, be an electrical storm interfering with the heat-sensor other than by heating it.) The analogous possibility exists for agents, for example in paralysis. Here there is a causal fact about the agent's musculature, which interferes with the route from belief and desire to action, and in whose absence the agent would do what the functionalist theory requires. It is important, on this view of what 'normal' means here, that there should not be a causal law which entails that there will *always* be some process interfering: otherwise there would be no true subjunctive conditional to the effect that the agent would perform as the functionalist theory requires if a certain factor was absent. And it is because of this that the fact that a system *never* behaves as the functionalist theory requires is evidence that it is not an agent: for that is evidence that there are no such true subjunctive conditionals.[2]

In this chapter, the functional role of computational structure is discussed. And when I say that if a representation R has computational structure C, it will, in virtue of this, change in such and such a way in reaction to certain stimuli, I must be understood as meaning that this is what will happen in the absence of computational error.

I begin in 4.2, by saying in a little more detail why it is that decision theory fails to distinguish truth–conditionally equivalent beliefs and desires. This is something we need to do, since computational structure is intended to solve the problems created for functionalism by this fact. In 4.3 I develop an idiom for describing computational structures (which is a notational variant of the

2. There is one slight problem for the claim that there must always be a causal explanation for deviations from normal functioning; since our world is apparently indeterministic, occasionally computational errors may occur as uncaused and improbable quantum events. Thus we should say, strictly: deviations from normal functioning are either caused by some independently specifiable process, or the results of rare uncaused events. This second disjunct means that, provided we identify the mental event which the functionalist theory predicts will not happen, with a physical event which can occur – according to general physical laws – uncaused, we may allow that there is, in this sort of case, an uncaused deviation from normal functioning. But it might be better to say that when these events occur we lack, for the moment, the relevant functional states.

standard syntax of the sentential calculus) and go on to say what computations are and how to specify some that agents can do.[3] In 4.4 I suggest how input and output claims will take account of computational structure and truth conditions. Section 4.5 delivers my earlier promise, in 3.2, to explain why probability functions should be regular; 4.6 completes the discussion, in 2.3, of the ways in which computational structure is and is not like sentential structure. Each of these sections settles questions we can answer most clearly in the light of a theory of computational structure. The next chapter shows more precisely how truth conditions figure in the theory. By the end of that chapter all the materials needed will have been assembled to put this functionalist, representational theory of mind to use in discussing the issues in the philosophy of language that takes up Parts II and III of this book.

4.2   TRUTH CONDITIONS AND DECISION THEORY

In the last chapter I said that decision theory is unable to distinguish between beliefs with the same truth conditions. I must say a bit more now about the notion of a truth condition involved here; particularly since I show later that, on this functionalist account, truth conditions do not have some of the properties standardly ascribed to them.

To begin with, then, let me stipulate that two representations R and S have the same truth conditions iff it is logically necessary that R is true iff S is true. This is certainly the standard assumption, in possible world semantics for example; see Lewis (1972b). For in possible world semantics the truth conditions of a sentence are given by saying in which of the logically possible worlds it is true; beliefs which are true in just the same logically possible worlds are thus beliefs with the same truth conditions. In our axiom system for probability we have required that if a representation has truth conditions which hold necessarily, then it has probability 1. That beliefs with the same truth conditions have the same probability follows swiftly from this, since if R and S have the same truth conditions ($R \equiv S$) (the material equivalence) has truth conditions which hold necessarily. Given this, $p(R \equiv S)$ will be 1; and then we can easily prove that: $p(R) = p(S)$.

This result can be derived – see, e.g. Field (1977) – from axiom systems which do not have it as an axiom that logically necessary truths have probability 1, so that it is not something that just happens to be built into Jeffrey's axioms. Our problem now is to explain why this is so. We can find

---

3. A more detailed treatment of some possible computational capacities is given in my 1981: Appendix 5.

the answer if we remind ourselves that decision theory takes no account of computation.

The process of working out the logical consequences of someone's beliefs is a *computational* process, on our theory. Since decision theory takes no account of computations, it assumes simply that all the computations necessary to calculate expected utility will be carried out. The reason decision theory is unable to distinguish beliefs with the same truth conditions is thus simply stated: if an agent has a belief that S, and this is logically equivalent to a belief that R, then decision theory assumes that the agent will carry out the computations necessary to discover this, and will then assign R the probability that S has. Let me state the point starkly: I claim that decision theory characterises the behaviour of computationally perfect agents, and that what this means is that it characterises the behaviour which actual agents (with the appropriate concepts)[4] would exhibit if they applied each one of the computations which they are physically capable of applying, instantaneously and without error. Call this class of computations the agent can perform the agent's set of feasible computations. Then, for example, amongst my set of feasible computations is one which takes me from the belief that John is coming to the belief that it is not the case that he is not coming. And I am capable of applying this computation to any belief, provided it is not too structurally complex. This fact is reflected in the decision theory by the theorem $p(S) = p(\neg(\neg S))$. It is the fact that I can apply that computation – even if errors of brain or mere structural complexity will sometimes produce the wrong answer – that makes this theorem a proper reflection of what I would do if computationally perfect.

Suppose, however, that there are no feasible computations which go from S to R: there is no reason then why the theory should treat the belief that S and the belief that R identically. For if someone were not capable of computations which would lead, if carried out perfectly, to their believing that R if they believed that S (and vice versa), then it does not follow from their believing one that they would believe the other, even if they computed perfectly. This fact is manifested in the formal structure of decision theory; for in order actually to prove that two representations have the same probability, it will be necessary to have axioms and rules of inference strong enough to prove that they are mutually entailing. Let us call the axioms and rules of inference which characterise the computational ability of some agent the proof theory for that agent. Then, a probability theory defined over a system of

---

4. By the possession of concepts here I mean only whatever capacities are involved in being able to have beliefs. Remember from Chapter 2 that there is no commitment at all to any capacity for linguistic expression; in this sense, dogs have concepts in virtue of the fact that their behaviour is explicable in terms of beliefs about such objects as cats and bones.

representations of the form of the sentential calculus will only allow us to prove that $p(S)$ must be equivalent to $p(R)$ if S and R are tautologically equivalent, if the proof theory includes an axiom system for sentential logic (and likewise for desirabilities in the desirability calculus). For the axioms and rules of inference in effect state what computations the agent can perform with the representations of the agent's system.[5]

We can now say what it is on our theory for a representation S to have a representation R as a logical consequence for someone. It is for them to be capable of computations which would lead them, if applied without error, to believe that R wherever they believe that S. More generally, using the theorem

If S entails R, $p(S) \leqslant p(R)$

we can say that R is a logical consequence of S in someone's proof theory iff they are capable of computations whose carrying out would guarantee that $p(S) \leqslant p(R)$ in every p-function that can represent their beliefs. But if, in the proof theory which characterises someone's computational capacities, there is no proof that R follows from S, nothing stops R from having a lower probability than S.

This fact, in itself, should afford us some relief. Field has pointed out that an account of belief that treats beliefs with the same truth conditions identically, will be obliged to allow that every one believes (say) Gödel's Theorem. But we can now see that this consequence only follows for people who are capable of computations leading from things they do actually believe to Gödel's Theorem; and that it still does not follow unless they have actually carried out those computations (Field, 1978).[6]

Admitting this much will still not quite do, however, to save decision theory from plain inconsistency with the facts. For Gödel's Theorem follows from things every number theorist knows, by familiar principles of inference, a grasp of which might reasonably be held to be constitutive of knowing what numbers are. Thus Mary, who knows what numbers are, and knows, as she must do if she is to understand number theory, what rules of inference are permitted, can still be proved to assign probability 1 to Gödel's Theorem. So if she has any belief about the matter at all, she has to be certain that Gödel's Theorem is true: even before she has ever seen a proof. Whereas, in fact,

---

5. In my 1981: Appendix 5 I showed how to generate an account of the computations which correspond to proving that S follows from R in some formal system. The general principle is this: unless an agent is in principle capable of deriving R from S and *vice versa*, there is no reason for treating S and R as necessarily having the same probability (or the same desirability).

6. Field actually discusses the Banach–Tarski theorem. But it helps to have an example whose content might be known to the reader.

someone who knows any number theory is likely to find a proof of it rather surprising; more surprising, in fact, than someone who knows no number theory at all.

We are now in a rather difficult situation. For if we do not assign Mary, *qua* number-theoretically informed agent, a p-function in which the theorem has probability 1, then we cannot guarantee that we can derive a preference ranking that is transitive, from her p- and d-values. If we do assign Gödel's Theorem probability 1, however, we shall have to explain how it is that a number theorist can appear not to believe it.

I propose to adopt the former course, allowing that agents may have beliefs that S and that R, where S and R are logically equivalent, such that $p(S) \neq p(R)$. But, I suggest, there is a way of doing this which does not make the decision-theoretic approach vacuous — the empty description of computationally perfect agents who never exist — or merely normative.

The first essential is to adopt a strong conception of the distinction between the agent's actual and the agent's potential beliefs and desirabilities. The actual representations are states of agents which play a part in the causal determination of their behaviour. Potential states are states which could be produced by computations feasible for an agent, which take his or her actual states as input. I propose to say that agents act so as to try to maximise actual expected utility: where this means that they try to perform the basic action of bringing about some state of affairs that S, where bringing it about that S has a utility at least as high as that of any other actual representation of a basic action. The actual states are all and only those which play a part in the causation of action.

The next two sections sketch the features of the processes by which someone can add new actual states, including new desirabilities. I allow that people's preference orderings for their actual representations may not satisfy the conditions necessary for defining p- and d-functions in the manner of the last section. If that is so, then, as I show later, what somebody does may depend on what computations they actually perform: on which potential states they actually add to their stock of representations. But we now face the problem of explaining why we suppose that agents have probabilities and desirabilities which sometimes perform in the way decision theory requires; for the only reason we had for adopting the formal constraints on the model at all was the assumption that the agent's preferences were transitive, complete and so on.

The answer to this question is that it is a part of our conception of the functional role of beliefs and desires that, if someone were computationally perfect, they would act in the way decision theory requires. So, for example, decision theory tells us what it is, in part, to believe to such and such a degree that snow is white, by saying what agents with a belief of that degree would do, given all their other beliefs and desires, if they carried out all the computations necessary to calculate expected utility. Actual people are not computationally perfect, but the states which determine their actual behaviour can still be characterised by how they would show up, given computational perfection. Analogously, the actual velocities of real gas molecules, which explain their less-than-ideal actual behaviour, may nevertheless be characterised as the velocities which would, if only gas molecules were perfectly inelastic point masses, produce the ideal gas laws predicted by the simplest version of kinetic theory.

In assuming computational perfection in characterising probability and desirability we are supposing that, given sufficient computational effort, a preference ranking of the right kind would result. As I observed in the last chapter, decision theorists have shown that, given a preference ordering of the right kind, probability and desirability functions exist; it is easy to see also that, given that someone's state can be characterised by a probability and desirability function, a preference ordering of the right kind exists. Thus, there is a reason to think agents will adjust their states in ways that tend to produce acceptable preference orderings, just in case we can show that where agents realise that their degrees of belief do not conform to the probability axioms, and their desirabilities fail to conform to the desirability logic, they must in fact so adjust them as to remove this defect.

But, of course, it is a condition of our making sense of someone that they remove inconsistencies of this kind when they arise. If a creature were to come, by computation – that is by thought – to believe that S, and to believe that not S, we could only continue to treat it as possessing those beliefs if it made some adjustment to remove the plain inconsistency. We can suppose that John has the belief that S and the n beliefs that R_i, (for i from 1 to n), where no p-function can assign $p(S)$ and $p(R_i)$ (for i from 1 to n) the values they actually have, provided he has not performed computations necessary to produce the belief that not S, where $p(\neg S)$ is greater than (or less than) $(1 - p(S))$. But if his beliefs *are* inconsistent, in this probabilistic sense, so that they cannot be represented by a p-function because no p-function can assign $p(S)$ and the $p(R_i)$ the values they have, then there will be computations he can perform which will produce a $p(\neg S)$ that differs from $(1 - p(S))$.

So computationally perfect agents, whose proof theory is strong enough to allow us to apply decision theory to explain their actions at all, will not assign the same representation two different p- (or d-) values; and that is why, where we are considering computationally perfect agents, it is reasonable to require that their states conform to the probability and desirability axioms.[7]

7. I do not here intend to rule out the possibility considered, *inter alia*, by Kyburg (1961), that we should allow that subjective p-functions could be 'fuzzy'; so that the probabilities of some

Let us say, now, that agents' actual representations are permissible iff there is at least one pair of p- and d-functions which assign to their representations the probabilities and desirabilities they actually have. Let us say also that a potential representation R – a type representation of which agents have no tokens amongst their actual states – has a p-value, $p(R)$, or d-value, $d(R)$, entailed by the p-values and d-values of the members of the actual representations in the class $[S]$, iff R has $p(R)$ or $d(R)$ in any pair of p- and d-functions which assign to the members of $[S]$ the probabilities and desirabilities they actually have. Whether the p- and d-values of the members of a particular agent's set $[S]$ do so entail that R has some $p(R)$ or $d(R)$ depends, of course, on the agent's proof theory.

Can we reasonably credit actual agents with proof theories strong enough to enable them to derive, say, Gödel's Theorem from beliefs about natural numbers? I want to insist that we can, for two reasons. First, the claim is weaker than it may initially appear. The route between a class of beliefs and its consequences may be indefinitely long and complex; and it might be that someone could not carry them out in sequence in their head because of limitations on memory, for example. Secondly, the notion of logical consequence in the theory is a descriptive notion, and it must somehow be possible to ground ascriptions of a logical structure to beliefs, in facts about mental structure. It is difficult to think of any requirement weaker than the one I have offered which will do this.

The model then is this: beliefs are representational states with degrees in the interval 0 to 1; and desires are representational states with desirabilities. Subsets of the class of beliefs and desires are brought to bear when an agent is deciding what to do on any occasion. The basic action whose utility consequent upon deliberation is highest, the agent then tries to perform. It is clear that there is some pattern to the way in which the classes of beliefs on which we are disposed to act at any one time are brought to bear – as suggested, for example, by Schank and Abelson (1977) – so that beliefs come in what we might call families i.e. sets of actual belief states such that only members of a single set need be invoked to explain any one piece of behaviour. Suppose

representations (or all) should be given an interval measure. If, for example, the agent's actual preference ordering contains too little information actually to find the materials we need to construct the metric, we shall certainly be in just such a position. What I *do* wish to rule out is any theory that allows that someone might both believe and not believe that S; or (if we allow interval measures) that not only permits someone to have probability values over an interval but actually allows that an agent may have two states of belief that S, for the same S, and that these might have as their measure distinct and determinate probability intervals. It is possible that we might even allow this, if we suppose that beliefs come in families, in the way I shall suggest in the moment. What we cannot allow is that an agent should have different degrees of belief (or non-overlapping intervals of degree of belief) that S in the same family of beliefs.

each family of beliefs is permissible; then we can see how it might be that agents can fail to rectify inconsistencies in their beliefs; namely by keeping their inconsistent beliefs in different families, so that the computation undertaken in deliberate action never brings the inconsistencies together. Actually I doubt even that the classes of beliefs we are disposed to act on at one time are always permissible: but I do think we ought to rule out the possibility that anyone has in one family at one time two states with the same computational structure and different probability values (or desirabilities, or utilities). We ought not to allow this possibility, because though it is just intelligible that someone might be so disposed that sometimes they act on the belief that S and sometimes on the belief that not-S, we can hardly allow the intelligibility of describing a single action as their trying to do both at once.

I have largely been discussing the p-functions of computationally perfect agents; my main focus throughout this book is on beliefs. But analogous points can be made about preference and desirability functions. Though there is no reason to suppose that actual agents have transitive preferences – the evidence, indeed (see Davidson and Suppes (1957)), is that they do not – *that* is no reason to deny that computationally perfect agents would have them. No one would be happy to find themselves preferring apples to oranges, oranges to pears, and pears to apples, in the same set-up. But anyone can be in a position where they would display intransitive preferences of this kind, without knowing that they are in it. It is because it is the theory of the computationally perfect agent that decision theory rightly assumes transitivity. So the overwhelming experimental evidence against transitivity for actual people does not, as I said in 3.1, worry me. It does not worry me for the same reason it does not worry anybody that there is plenty of experimental evidence that momentum is not conserved on billiard tables. We have an account of why that is, in terms of the elasticity of the materials involved; and we have an account of the deviations of agents from decision theory, in terms of computational structure.[8]

4.3 COMPUTATIONAL STRUCTURE

Computational structure, to repeat the central point, is that feature of propositional attitude states which affects their functional role and does not depend on truth conditions. To our account of beliefs as having truth conditions and

---

8. Donald Davidson suggested (in a 1980 talk) that we could only really come to grips with breaches of rationality if we allow that agents may have divided minds. The notion of a family of beliefs is one way of implementing this idea.
   A similar account of how an inconsistent corpus of beliefs can underlie behaviour, is mentioned by David Lewis in Lewis (1981*b*).

degrees, which conform, when all goes well, to the laws of probability, we must add something else: the computational structure of the representation. In building an account of computational structure, we can be guided by the analogy mentioned in Chapter 2: that between computational structure for representations and syntactic structure for sentences of natural languages. For the syntactic structure of a sentence S and that of a sentence R may differ, even where S and R have the same truth conditions. And the difference in the logical behaviour of two sentences with the same truth conditions may be accounted for in terms of their differing syntactic structures. In constructing a natural deduction system for a formal language, we write rules which take classes of formulae of a certain syntactic structure as input, and deliver a formula of related syntactic structure as output. We can thus take advantage of the familiar results about the syntax of formal languages in building up our picture of the computational structure of representations.[9]

As usual I shall be working with representations and truth-functions of representations and not with quantificational features. As before, I shall avoid the issue of how to handle the connective '⊓→'. When the truth-functions have been handled, the direction we would need to go to deal with the sub-sentential structure of representations, and with non-truth-functional compounds of them, is, I think, clear; and, indeed, I shall say a little about sub-sentential structure in Chapter 6, and a little more about the subjunctive conditional in Part III. This does not mean that I think that actually carrying out the programme would be easy either for quantificational representations or for subjunctives. But some of the major issues of principle can be worked out over the truth-functions.

We want to begin by specifying recursively the computational structure of truth-functionally compound beliefs and desires as functions of the computational structures of their components. This is easily done. Let us call the function from representations to their computational structures, C. So if the computational structure of R is $C(R)$, I write e.g.

1: $C(\neg R) = \langle C(R), o, \text{NEG} \rangle$

2: $C(R \;\&\; S) = \langle C(R), C(S), \text{CONJ} \rangle$

3: $C(R \lor S) = \langle C(R), C(S), \text{DISJ} \rangle$

Thus, we define a computational feature called 'NEG', such that, for any representation R, the computational structure of the belief that not-R is the

---

9. This does not, of course, mean that representations *are* sentences of a language, nor that computations are linguistic operations; see 2.3.

ordered triple consisting of the computational structure of R, a dummy feature o, and NEG.[10]

Similarly, we can define the features CONJ and DISJ in order to be able to set up the computational structures of disjunctive or conjunctive beliefs (and desires.) As is obvious these rules allow us to define recursively the C-value for any belief which has negated, conjoined or disjoined components, however deeply embedded, as a function of the C-values of the atomic representations of a person's system of representations.

From now on I propose to make explicit what has been an implicit *façon de parler* so far: I shall call any belief state — even where, since the p-value is small, it would normally amount to what we call disbelief — a 'belief'; and similarly I shall continue to call desires with negative desirabilities 'desires'. Treating belief, disbelief, not-knowing-whether-or-not, and so on as states of the same type is natural enough in the framework I outlined in the previous chapter. Given this notion of belief, we can now say that any belief can be specified by way of six features;

(1) a feature which marks it as a belief and not a desire —call it B
(2) its truth conditions — call these $T(S)$, for the belief that S
(3) its probability value (i.e. a real number between o and 1)
(4) its C-value, $C(S)$ for the belief that S,
(5) a feature marking it as being the state of some agent, A
(6) a feature indicating the time, t, at which the belief is held.

I shall show in Chapter 5 how the C-value of a belief is related to its truth conditions; and because the truth conditions of a belief have to do, not with its computational behaviour, but with its relations to the world, I shall not mention them in the discussions of this chapter. In fact, as we shall see in the next chapter, computational structure (along with features (5) and (6)) determines truth conditions.

Just as we can individuate a belief as a state with functional role determined by (at least) $\langle B, A, t, p(S), C(S) \rangle$, so we can fix desires by way of a quintuple consisting of a feature marking them as desires — D, a desirability, and four other features which are identical in the belief that S and the desire that S; thus: $\langle D, A, t, d(S), C(S) \rangle$. And, finally, where S is a basic action for A, we will have $\langle U, A, t, u(S), C(S) \rangle$ for utilities.[11]

It is obvious enough why we need the time to individuate a particular token belief of some agent's; for though the probability and computational structure

---

10. The dummy feature just allows me to talk about all these cases as triples; I have deliberately begun with this obvious arbitrariness in the notation to make it clear just how little the notation, *in se*, commits me to.

11. Since it is beliefs I am concerned about I shall say only the bare minimum about these affective states.

tell us about the functional roles of states of a belief-type, we need to know whose it is, and when, if we are to pick out just one token belief. And we need to know this for another important reason as well: if we did not know whose or when it was, we would not know in which body (and thus where) or when it would be causally active in the way the theory requires.

Given this specification of the features of beliefs that our theory seeks to account for, we can now define what I call a belief computation. A belief computation is any process in which causal interactions between the members of some class $[R]$ of the agent's beliefs produce a new belief (S), such that the pair $\langle p(S), C(S) \rangle$ is a function of the ordered n-tuple of pairs $\langle p(R_i), C(R_i) \rangle - i$ from 1 to n – where R_1 to R_n are the n members of $[R]$.

Thus a belief computation takes as input n beliefs and produces a new belief; a belief whose degree and computational structure are a function of the degrees and computational structures of the n input beliefs. The intuitive idea is simple. A belief computation is a mental process in which an agent with some beliefs comes to acquire another belief. Inferring will be a species of belief computation, for example, as well as someone's being reminded of one fact by another.

We can now specify a class of belief computations which, given a permissible set of someone's actual beliefs, would allow us to fix the set of the potential beliefs; beliefs which they would come to have if they thought through logically the consequences of what they believed already. There is an obvious way to characterise belief computations of this kind. For, on the decision-theoretic model, we have an account of what someone would do if they carried out perfectly all the computations necessary to calculate all desirabilities. The class of belief computations we are interested in is one which characterises the computations necessary to achieve this, in so far as they affect beliefs.

It is the class which, given any permissible set of beliefs as input, leaves someone in a state decision-theoretically equivalent to their original state. I shall call states of agents which are decision-theoretically equivalent to their actual states 'extensions' of their beliefs, just in case they differ from their actual states only in their having more actual beliefs.

Since computation is a causal process, two extensions of the same set of beliefs may differ in functional role; and the existence of extensions differing in functional role but decision-theoretically equivalent is another reminder of the fact that functional role is underdetermined by the truth conditions of beliefs. For truth-conditionally identical beliefs are, as I have said, decision-theoretically equivalent. Characterising the set of extensions of an agent's beliefs involves defining a class of operations on computational structures of those beliefs; it is in essence a syntactic characterisation of consequence for the logic of belief. The details are not relevant to my purposes here.[12] But I *do* want to give, by way of example, a couple of computations which, I suspect, agents regularly do perform. The first is a belief computation, corresponding to changing one's mind on the model of conditionalisation. The second is not a belief computation, but a computation which takes both beliefs and desires as inputs and produces desires as outputs. But it is a computation the capacity for which would make it possible for agents to calculate the desirability of a representation whose desirability was not initially amongst their actual states. This is something that agents need to be able to do in order to work out what to do: and producing an account of this computation adds to decision theory an account of the actual processes (as opposed merely to the ideal results) of evaluation. In order to define these computations I must introduce a further pair of computational features, of which the first will be particularly important in later sections of this book.

We have seen that in making transitions between p-functions, we make use of conditional probabilities, and in calculating utilities we make use of probabilities of subjunctive conditionals. I now define a new feature COND, such that if an agent's states include one which corresponds to the conditional probability $p(S/R)$, that agent has a representation with computational structure

$$\langle (C(S), C(R), COND \rangle.$$

Where $p(S/R) = k$, we can say that someone has a representation

$$\langle B, A, t, k, \langle C(S), C(R), COND \rangle \rangle$$

iff they have a state corresponding to a high conditional probability of S given R. I call such a state a conditional belief. I put the $C(S)$ first, so that we should read it as the conditional probability of S on R. For parity, I now define the feature corresponding to the subjunctive conditional, with the consequent first also, so that it should be read as 'S would happen if R were to.' So if someone has a belief that S would happen if R were to, they have a state

$$\langle B, A, t, k, \langle C(S), C(R), SUBJ \rangle \rangle$$

where k is $p(R \,\square\!\!\rightarrow S)$. I call this a subjunctive conditional belief.[13]

12. I characterise the extensions of a system of beliefs with the logical structure of the sentential calculus in my 1981: Appendix 5, and show how to use a simple notation to characterise a (very idealised) agent's proof theory.

13. It is inevitable, I am afraid, due to the fact that we write $p(S/R)$ for something that is, in effect, the probability that if R happens S will, that whichever way round you put the $C(S)$ and $C(R)$ here, there is scope for confusion. I have chosen this way round because my main interest is in the relations between conditional probabilities and conditionals; and $\langle C(S), C(R), COND \rangle$ goes with $p(S/R)$. To get it clear now which way round I have done it, using the mnemonic device in the text should make it possible to avoid confusion later.

It is important to be clear that the conditional belief state is not necessarily amongst someone's states just because $(S \ \& \ R)$ and R are amongst their actual beliefs, even though, by definition

$$p(S/R) \ = \ \frac{p(S \ \& \ R)}{p(R)} \quad \text{(where } p(R) \ \neq \ 0\text{)}.$$

Nor, conversely, does the presence of a state

$$\langle B, \ A, \ t, \ k, \ \langle C(S), \ C(R), \ \text{COND} \rangle \rangle$$

entail the presence of a corresponding pair of beliefs

$$\langle B, \ A, \ t, \ m, \ C(R) \rangle \langle B, \ A, \ t, \ n, \ \langle C(S), \ C(R), \ \text{CONJ} \rangle \rangle$$

(where $n/m \ = \ k$).

With these two new features we can take a computational look at conditionalisation and the calculation of expected desirability.

Let us take conditionalisation first. In order that someone should be able to change their probabilities in accordance with the rule of conditionalisation, they will need either to have the necessary conditional probabilities amongst their actual states, or to be able to compute them from their actual states. If they did not have these states then they could not carry out the computation corresponding to conditionalisation; for a computation is a process which takes actual states as input and produces a new state. It is not enough to say that someone's probabilities will just change in the right way when the evidence is presented: for there must be something about them, some state of theirs, which makes this happen, and the only candidate state is the conditional probability.

What would a computation corresponding to conditionalisation look like? Let us consider the simplest case, where conditionalisation originates in the partition $[S, \neg S]$. Then for every R, $p'(R) = p(R/S) \cdot p'(S) + p(R/\neg S) \cdot p'(\neg S)$. So what we want is a computation that, given the actual beliefs, $\langle B, \ A, \ T, \ k, \ \langle C(R), \ C(S), \ \text{COND} \rangle \rangle$ and $\langle B, \ A, \ t, \ l, \ \langle C(R), \ \langle C(S), \ 0, \ \text{NEG} \rangle, \ \text{COND} \rangle \rangle$, produces, in response to input that causes $\langle B, \ A, \ t, \ m, \ C(S) \rangle$ to change to $\langle B, \ A, \ t_2, \ n, \ C(S) \rangle$, the output $\langle B, \ A, \ t_3, \ n(k \ - \ l) \ + \ l, \ C(R) \rangle$ (where, of course, t is before t_2, which is before t_3).

Since I introduced conditional probabilities by a stipulation, saying that $p(C/A)$ is equal to the ratio of the probability of the conjunction, $(A \ \& \ C)$, to the probability of A, it might seem that this is all a good deal of fuss about nothing. We could just define conditionalisation using these ratios directly, and not worry about the conditional probabilities except as shorthand. But the reason why this will not do is simple: there is no guarantee that agents have the relevant $p(C \& A)$ and $p(A)$ amongst their actual states. I do not have a view about what the probability is that it will rain in the morning; but I do have a high conditional belief that it will rain in the morning, if the clouds are heavy. Given the whole range of my actual beliefs there are constraints set on what my degrees of belief in various possibilities would be if I were computationally perfect, and if I had any degree of belief at all. But I do not have to have any view at all.[14]

This *prima facie* case for conditional beliefs will be supported, as I have said, in Part III, where conditional beliefs, in this technical sense, will be argued to be conditional beliefs in a more familiar sense; beliefs that if R, S.

But we also have good reason to try to characterise some computations that will do the job of calculating expected utilities on a partition. And once we have done this we can make a parallel argument for the existence of subjunctive conditional beliefs. Take a case where the agent is computing the expected desirability on a partition $[(R), (\neg R)]$. For this case, we can define a computation:

EX.UT.: Where the agent's actual states include

$\langle B, A, t, k, \langle C(R), C(S), \text{SUBJ} \rangle \rangle$

$\langle B, A, t, l, \langle \langle C(R), \text{o}, \text{NEG} \rangle, C(S), \text{SUBJ} \rangle$

$\langle D, A, t, m, \langle C(S), C(R), \text{CONJ} \rangle \rangle$

$\langle D, A, t, n, \langle C(S), \langle C(R), \text{o}, \text{NEG} \rangle, \text{CONJ} \rangle \rangle$

---

14. Having introduced the feature COND, it is important to say as well that I have not offered any account of what the state

$\langle D, A, t, k, \langle C(S), C(R), \text{COND} \rangle \rangle$

would be, or indeed, whether there is any such a state at all. We have as yet had no use for a notion of the desirability of S conditional on T, which seems the most natural candidate. We should be able more easily to develop intuitions about this if we knew how we expressed the state

$\langle B, A, t, k, \langle C(S), C(R), \text{COND} \rangle \rangle$

in English; but that is the topic to which Part III of this book is devoted. For the moment I simply ignore the possibility that there are states of this form with 'B' replaced by 'D'. Such 'conditional desirabilities' at least play no part in the functional theory as far as I take it. In Part III I discuss conditional beliefs in some detail; but none of the plausible candidates for the status of conditional desires has the significance that conditional beliefs will there be shown to have. Note that $\langle D, A, t, k, \langle C(S), C(R), \text{SUBJ} \rangle \rangle$ seems pretty clearly to exist. 'I would rather the car did not collapse if I had an accident' means that I would like it to be true that: 'If I were to have an accident, the car would not collapse.'

there is a computation with these states as input that produces

$$\langle U,\ A,\ t2,\ ml\ +\ ln,\ C(S)\rangle.$$

This computation corresponds to the theorem of decision theory

$$u(S)\ =\ p(S\ \Box\!\!\rightarrow\ R)\cdot d(S\ \&\ R)\ +\ (S\ \Box\!\!\rightarrow\ \neg R)\cdot d(S\ \&\ \neg R).$$

Given the capacity for EX.UT., someone will be able to compute the desirability of, say, taking an umbrella, provided they have both a desirability for its raining and their taking an umbrella and for its not raining and their taking an umbrella; and they also have a probability for the conditionals which say it would and would not rain if they took an umbrella. And this fits well with other intuitions. For it is precisely these states we should expect to play a part in an agent's coming to judge that it is a good idea to take an umbrella.

I am often aware of having the representations necessary for EX.UT. Of course, the degrees of the desires and the beliefs do not manifest themselves to me as numbers; but the theory does not require that they should. All that it requires is that they should have features which determine, in the way the computation specifies, the place of S in my ranking of available actions, features of which I may or may not generally be aware.

I have given an example of a computation which agents might be capable of performing. I think human agents do sometimes perform EX.UT.; I think I do. In an empirical theory of actual agents we would look to characterise such computations as those which an agent carries out in inferring R directly from (If S, R) and S; or in inferring R from $(\neg(\neg R))$. But we need to be careful here that we are not misled by standard logical procedures. A belief is a state which has both a computational structure and a degree. Standard logics ignore the problem of specifying how the probabilities of the premisses of an argument affect the probability assigned to the conclusion; but see Adams and Levine (1975). In the cases I have considered the problem is relatively easy: for the probability of logical truths will be 1, and for any S, where S and R are mutually entailing, $p(S) = p(R)$. But if we have, for example, the belief that S and R as our input we cannot fix a unique value for the probability of S, unless $p(S\ \&\ R)$ is 1; for $p(S)$ is not a function of $p(S\ \&\ R)$ alone; though it is a function, e.g. of $p(S\ \&\ R)$ and $p(R/S)$.

The functionalist theory says that an agent must be able to perform computations which achieve certain effects. But it does not say directly which computations they must be. And in that respect talk of an agent's proof theory is like talk of sentential logic: there are lots of ways of actually doing it. What matters is what the theorems are. Of course, in sentential logic, some systems are more elegant, or notationally clearer, or more natural to use; so too, in us, the computations which we actually use may work more or less swiftly or reliably. But provided, if we made no errors and had all the time in the world, but no more input, we would come to have a belief with a certain computational structure, then our proof theory must have that belief as a theorem.

Let me put this another way: our theory says what it is for an agent to have a capacity for direct inferences of a certain form, but it does not say which inferences have to be direct. For an inference is direct if there is a computation which takes beliefs of the right computational structure as input and produces the right belief as output, and there are no intermediate steps involving the generation of beliefs. All the proof theory says is that we are capable of direct inferences which, taken in the right order, produce, with degree 1, belief in every theorem of your proof theory. That fixes our computational capacity, without fixing the specific computations through which the capacity is exercised.

It is likely, I think, to seem that ascriptions of computational structure to the states of actual agents, are heavily underdetermined by the outputs that they would produce in response to certain inputs. But there are two things which at least reduce the possibilities of underdetermination. And this is important because underdetermination threatens the individuation claim, that mental states can be distinguished by their functional roles.

First, the ascription of a capacity for a certain computation will have consequences for the relative speeds of different mental processes. In particular if Mary were to perform a sequence of n computations, that would take her less time than the same n computations and a further computation C which acts on the output of these n computations. For computations are processes; they take time. And if n computations take t seconds, then it will take further time to carry out a further computation.

This must be so, since we are realists about the mental states involved in the computations. As a result, since the output of computation C_1 is the input to C_2, C_2's input does not exist until C_1 has occurred. Nor can we allow that the sequence $\langle C_1, C_2 \rangle$ of computations takes less time than C_2, because the fact that it is followed by C_2 speeds up C_1. For whatever speeds up C_1 it cannot be C_2; it has not occurred yet and causation goes forward. And if what speeds it up is the fact that computation C_2 is going to happen, then, once more, as realists, we must suppose there is some state of the system which exists prior to C_1 and plays a part in its causal development.

This is not to say that every computation must take the same time on every occasion: indeed, we should expect that the computation's time depends on exactly what the detailed substructure of the representations on which it operates is. Thus, the same computation carried out with $(S \ \& \ R)$ as input may take more (or less) time with $((S \ \lor \ R) \ \& \ R)$ as input, even though each of these has the computational structure of a conjunction. Processing time will also be affected, presumably by such things as how tired agents are; on their general psychological state. The details of all this are a matter for experimental investigation.

The second factor that reduces the possibilities of underdetermination is that there are further functional features of computational structure, some of which I discuss in the section that follows. So far I have been discussing only the role of computational features in the interactions of the states inside our heads; I have been focussing on what, in Chapter 2, I called throughput. In the next section I discuss input and output claims about computational structure. In giving some of these we shall be able to see how an account of computational structure could 'go functional'; how, with sufficient output claims and input claims, we could begin to distinguish decision-theoretically equivalent, but functionally distinct, representational states.

4.4 OUTPUT AND INPUT

On our theory beliefs and desires are representations with degrees and computational structure. In order for them actually to produce the mental events which immediately precede action, we must suppose some actual computational processes go on. Even the simplest change of degree of belief is a computation, provided it is *caused* by changes in the properties of other representational states. For a computation, by stipulation, is just a process whose input is a state of a certain computational structure and whose output is a state whose computational structure is a function of that of the input states. Sometimes, in perception, our degrees of belief are changed directly as a result of the action of events on our eyes; so changes of belief can occur without computation. But once this process has occurred the consequent changes of belief and desire are normally computational. Prior to any action, a utility for doing it has to be available, has to be computed. Even where someone acts on a settled intention, the belief that the time for its execution is *now*, must occur, and must lead to the production of a utility for that action, which exceeds that of all other options the agent considers. The conclusion is plain: action presupposes computation.

If the relevant computations are carried out correctly and completely, then a series of processes occurs, each of which is isomorphic with a calculation we could carry out on paper in a decision-theoretic model; and examples of such computations were given in the preceding section. Our theory so far tells us what someone does if they carry out all these computations; but what might happen if they did not?

Consider two cases in which the fact that an agent is not computationally perfect allows us to explain something that decision theory could not explain on its own. Each corresponds to a different kind of extension of the explanatory power of decision theory, once computation is taken into account. The first case is the sort of case in which, for example, someone who, as we say, knows perfectly well that there is a quicker route from their college to the library, nevertheless goes by a slower route. Here the explanation seems to be simply that they have not brought to bear one of their beliefs, and have thus wrongly concluded that the longer route is the most desirable.

In the second case we can see how what people do will depend on which of their beliefs they actually bring to bear; so that whether or not they will do something depends not simply on their states of belief and desire but on whatever other factors determine which of the many computations open to an agent at any time they actually perform. This too is a familiar phenomenon: 'If only I had thought about it that way', we say, 'I should have done something different.'

I propose to show in a simple way, using the computation EX.UT. how each of these possibilities can show up in the theory.

Suppose, then, in the first case that Peter's p- and d-functions are defined over a set of actual representations sufficiently rich to determine the p- and d-values for all truth-functions of those representations. A set of actual representations is permissible, we recall, iff there is a pair of p- and d-functions which entail that those representations have the p- and d-values they actually have. Suppose, also, then, Peter's beliefs and desires form a permissible set. (This is not very likely, but we can consider in a moment what happens without this constraint.)

Consider now the class of basic actions available to Peter. If he is to conform to decision theory, a utility must be computed for each of them, and the action with the highest utility will be the one he tries to perform.

Thus, for each such basic action, A_i, a computation should occur, taking the set of states of the form

$$\langle D, \text{PETER}, t, k_i, \langle C(A_i), C(R), \text{CONJ} \rangle \rangle$$

$$\langle D, \text{PETER}, t, l_i, \langle C(A_i), \langle C(R), \text{o}, \text{NEG} \rangle, \text{CONJ} \rangle \rangle$$

$$\langle B, \text{PETER}, t, m_i, \langle C(R), C(A_i), \text{SUBJ} \rangle \rangle$$

$$\langle B, \text{PETER}, t, n_i, \langle \langle C(R), \text{o}, \text{NEG} \rangle, C(A_i), \text{SUBJ} \rangle \rangle$$

as input, and produces

$$\langle U, \text{PETER}, t + dt, (k_i m_i + l_i n_i), C(A_i) \rangle$$

as output. Suppose that if each of these computations occurred, A_j would have highest utility. But if Peter does not carry out this computation, then some A_q will have highest utility and Peter will do, not A_j, as the decision theory predicts, but A_q.

Consider, now, the second case, one in which Mary's states are not, as in

91

general we should not expect them to be, a permissible set. Suppose, in particular, by way of example, that she has amongst her states the following:

$\langle D, \text{MARY}, t, k_R, \langle C(A), C(R), \text{CONJ}\rangle\rangle$

$\langle D, \text{MARY}, t, l_R, \langle C(A), \langle C(R), \text{o}, \text{NEG}\rangle, \text{CONJ}\rangle\rangle$

$\langle B, \text{MARY}, t, m_R, \langle C(R), C(A), \text{SUBJ}\rangle\rangle$

$\langle B, \text{MARY}, t, n_R, \langle\langle C(R), \text{o}, \text{NEG}\rangle, C(A), \text{SUBJ}\rangle\rangle$

necessary to produce the utility of action, A, on the partition $(R, \neg R)$

$\langle U, \text{MARY}, t + dt, (k_R m_R + l_R n_R), C(A)\rangle;$

and the corresponding states

$\langle D, \text{MARY}, t, k_S, \langle C(A), C(S), \text{CONJ}\rangle\rangle$

$\langle D, \text{MARY}, t, l_S, \langle C(A), \langle C(S), \text{o}, \text{NEG}\rangle, \text{CONJ}\rangle\rangle$

$\langle B, \text{MARY}, t, m_S, \langle C(S), C(A), \text{SUBJ}\rangle\rangle$

$\langle B, \text{MARY}, t, n_S, \langle\langle C(S), \text{o}, \text{NEG}\rangle, C(A), \text{SUBJ}\rangle\rangle$

which are needed to produce the utility on the partition, $(S, \neg S)$,

$\langle U, \text{MARY}, t + dt, (k_S m_S + l_S n_S), C(A)\rangle.$

If Mary's states were permissible, $(k_R m_R + l_R n_R)$ would be equal to $(k_S m_S + l_S n_S)$; but suppose Mary's beliefs and desires do not form a permissible set. Then there is no reason why these should be equal. Suppose, then, that Mary has computed the utilities of a set of basic actions, and suppose that one of them has the highest actual utility computed so far, and

$\langle U, \text{MARY}, t + dt, x, C(A')\rangle$

is such that x is greater than $(k_R m_R + l_R n_R)$ but less than $(k_S m_S + l_S n_S)$. Then whether Mary will do A or A' will depend upon whether she applies EX.UT. to give

$\langle U, \text{MARY}, t + dt, (k_R m_R + l_R n_R), C(A)\rangle$

or

$\langle U, \text{MARY}, t + dt, (k_S m_S + l_S n_S), C(A)\rangle.$

For agents who are not computationally perfect, and for those who have sets of actual states which are not permissible, what they do may depend simply on what computation they perform.

These, then, are two kinds of consequence of the fact that agents maximise the utility of their *actual* states by *actual* computations; they try to perform not that basic action whose utility would be highest if they did all possible computations, but rather the (or one of the) basic actions such that $\langle U, A, t, k, C(S) \rangle$ is a member of the set A of their actual states, and no other basic action has a higher actual utility than k. This follows from the functional significance of the distinction between actual and potential states; only actual states play a part in the causation of action.

Computational structure is important in determining the output of an agent because what computations someone will perform depends on the states they actually have, and the computational structure of those states.

The computational structure of the actual states thus determines how much computation is necessary to add new actual desires, and thus determines how long it will take to add them, as well as which ones are likely to be added. It is facts such as these that allow us to use output claims in our specification of the way computational structure helps fix functional role. Let us now turn to the role of computational structure in determining the content of input claims.

In talking about input to the agent we are talking, at least in so far as beliefs are concerned, about perception and sensation. To make our account of computational structure operational we need also to show how input to agents, which leads to beliefs with truth conditions T^*, determines what actual belief with truth conditions T^* is produced. We know there are many beliefs with any particular set of truth conditions; we need to know which ones will be produced when.

Let us begin with a simple case. The belief that a rose is red is truth-conditionally equivalent to the belief that it is not the case that that rose is not red. Now whatever the details of our account of perception the following will have to be a consequence of it: the belief that a rose is red will be caused, *ceteris paribus*, by sensory interaction with a rose before one that is red. This may not seem to offer us much help. For if Rabbie Burns sees that a rose is red, then the state of affairs visual interaction with which produces his belief, is also the state of affairs of its not being the case that a rose before him is not red. But the fact is that the computational structure of the belief that is caused will normally be not

$$\langle \langle \langle C(\text{This rose is red}), \text{o}, \text{NEG} \rangle, \text{o}, \text{NEG} \rangle$$

but simply

$C(\text{This rose is red})$.

Now it would not take long for most agents with the concept of negation to carry out the computations necessary to move from:

R: This rose is red

to

> S: It's not the case that this rose is not red.

But the belief that R is going to precede the belief that S, according to our *a priori* theory; and it is the belief that R whose acquisition will causally explain the acquisition of the belief that S (if it occurs), and not vice versa.

From the particular case we may move to the general point: a functionalist theory will sometimes assign different causal roles to a belief and a computationally more complex belief with the same truth conditions, because it will entail that the second is derived (in certain circumstances) from the first.

This is not to say that someone could not move the other way. If I am told that it is not the case that a rose is not red, I may come to believe that this is so, and only then carry out the computations necessary to come to believe that it is red. Indeed, in this case, the theory may *require* that in interpreting the sentence 'This rose is not red', we come first to have the belief that S and then infer that R later.

Once again the theory tells us something about computational structure without telling us everything. Thus, though it follows from our theory that the belief that S is derived from the belief that R by computation, where the belief that R derives from sensation, it does not follow that it should, for example, take a particular amount of time. My interest in this book, as I have said, is in a particular kind of output, namely assertion; I do not intend to develop, therefore, a fuller account of the causal role of input. I have wanted only to suggest how input determines aspects of the computational structure of beliefs along with some of their other properties. I shall assume that a theory of this kind can be constructed which allows us to say under what circumstances people will (normally) be caused to change their beliefs in a way that originates (in the sense of 3.6) in changes of the degrees of a subset of their actual beliefs. This theory will classify causal environments of agents in such a way that it allows us to tell what beliefs those environments will (normally) produce by way of the senses. The details will depend on issues in the philosophy of perception, into which I do not want to enter.

So far I have been trying to set out an account of computational structure and to show how it might 'go functional'. I have shown that the computational features of the theory allow for minds that breach the laws of logic – and this is achieved by building onto the decision theory which demands perfect logical acumen.

4.5 REGULARITY

It is the assumption in decision theory of perfect logical acumen which explains why, as assumed since Chapter 3, the p-functions have to be regular.

Remember, a p-function, p, is regular iff

REG: if a sentence S has $p(S) = 1$ then it is an *a priori* truth.

Now the *a priori* is what is knowable by *reason* alone; and a computationally perfect agent is someone who gets all reasoning right. The *a priori*, then, is what every computationally perfect agent would know. But if computationally perfect agents get all reasoning right, then they know that unless a sentence is *a priori* true, there could be evidence that ought to count against it; and that unless it is *a priori* true, there are, in consequence, some odds that are unacceptable on a bet on it. The latter, given familiar betting interpretations of personal probability (see Mellor (1971: Chapter 2)), gives us that only the probability of *a priori* truths should be 1; and the former suggests the same result, as I can now show, if we suppose that beliefs change by conditionalisation.

There are two forms of conditionalisation, which are offered as models of those changes in a computationally perfect agent's p-function that come about when they acquire evidence; and they are simple and generalised conditionalisation. I shall consider the implications for regularity of both of them. For regularity was part of my reason for rejecting simple conditionalisation, and I do not want to argue in too tight a circle. For whether we use simple conditionalisation or generalised conditionalisation, we are likely to want to have regular p-functions.

Suppose that a p-function is not regular. Then there is some *a posteriori* S, such that $P(S) = 1$. If, for all i, $P(R_i) \neq 0$, then generalised conditionalisation (and, therefore, simple conditionalisation), will not make it possible to get to a $P'(S)$ that is not 1. For $P(S/R_i)$ will be 1, for every R_i; but then, by the definition of generalised conditionalisation, and given that the sum of the probabilities of a partition must be 1, it follows that $P'(S)$ will be 1 also. Suppose, however, that, for some k ($k \leqslant n$), $P(R_k) = 0$. Then $P(S/R_k)$ can take any value in the interval 0 to 1. This will only help us get $P(S)$ down from 1, if $P'(R_k)$ is not 0.[15] So $P'(S)$ can be less than 1, if $P(S)$ is 1, only if there is some $P(R_k)$ such that $P(R_k) = 0$, and $P(S/R_k) \neq 0$; and such that $P'(R_k) \neq 0$. In sum: you can get $P(S) = 1$ down to $P'(S)$ less than 1 iff you have direct evidence which leads you to revise some $P(R_k)$ from 0 up to some $P'(R_k)$ greater than 0.

But what evidence could lead a computationally perfect agent to bet on a proposition on which he or she had been previously unwilling to bet *at any odds*? A computationally perfect agent must be supposed to have no difficulty with logic: for the evidence of *proofs* should not change their degrees of belief

---

15. Otherwise we are just back where we were with all the $P(R_i) \neq 0$; the $P'(R_i)$ sum to 1 as do the $P'(S/R_i) = P(S/R_i)$, so that $P'(S)$ would be 1.

at all. So it is only empirical evidence that is relevant; and, though I cannot prove this is so, until an argument is offered, it seems to me unlikely that any empirical evidence should so change the beliefs of a computationally perfect agent.

It may seem that the introduction of conditionalisation here has added little: the only way to change from believing something – call it S – to degree 1, to believing it with degree less than 1, is to come to believe something – call it R – with degree more than 0 that we used to believe to degree 0. This is hardly surprising: R might, for example just be $(\neg S)$. But the point is that if conditionalisation is how a computationally perfect agent acquires beliefs, then, for a computationally perfect agent, changing the subjective probability of S from 1 to less than 1 involves having *direct* empirical evidence that leads us to change from accepting no bets at all on some proposition (the attitude we have to a contradiction) to accepting some bets if the odds are sufficiently favourable (the attitude we have to, say, the proposition that the current deliverances of our eyes are all illusory). In my view, *empirical* evidence of this sort is simply very hard to imagine; and if there is no such empirical evidence computationally perfect agents will have regular p-functions.

If p-functions are regular, only *a priori* truths have probability 1. I have argued that, assuming generalised conditionalisation is the right account of change of degrees of belief, the only way someone could cease to believe a sentence which had an initial probability of 1, would be to have *direct* evidence that some sentence on which he or she had been unwilling to bet at any odds at all, was now reasonably to be betted on. I think that direct evidence of this kind is inconceivable for a computationally perfect agent; and the p-functions should, therefore, be regular.

There is a possible exception to this general rule, and it has to do with beliefs about infinitesimal magnitudes. We might conceivably want a value for a conditional probability when the probability of the sentence conditionalised upon was 0 in the kind of case considered by Field (1977). He looks at a case where $p(R/S)$ is defined, though $p(S) = 0$, because R is a sentence which describes the occurrence of one of an infinite set of possible occurrences which is a proper subset of the set of occurrences to which the event described by S belongs:

Suppose a point were picked at random from a cube. The probability of the point being on a particular vertical plane b through the cube would be zero (since the plane would be 'infinitesimally thin'); the probability of the point being in the top half of b (more accurately, the top half of the square common to b and the cube) is also zero. But the probability of the point being in the top half of b, given that it is on b, is surely 1/2. (1977: 381)

But this is a very special case which involves infinitesimals and limits; and a theory of beliefs and degrees of belief of this kind with philosophical underpinnings is lacking. It is not obvious, for example, even if the probabilities are as Field says they are, how we can make sense of subjective probabilities corresponding to them. At any rate, until we have a theory of this sort of case, it seems to me unwise to assume that allowing the subjective conditional probability to be defined in this case is the most perspicuous solution to the many technical problems raised. And, at all events, this kind of case does not help to show that there is use to be made of values of conditional probabilities where $p(S) = 0$, and S and R do not involve infinitesimals. I do not think that it is wise to identify an infinitesimal probability with a 0 one, in any circumstances. But if anyone disagrees, I am prepared simply to say my account does not cover the restricted class of cases of beliefs about infinitesimals.

4.6 BELIEFS AND SENTENCES

I want to end by returning to an issue discussed in 2.3, when I first introduced the idea of computational structure. I said there that I did not think that beliefs were isomorphic with sentences, but the treatment of this chapter might seem to be going back on that claim. I have, after all, only suggested computational features, NEG, CONJ, DISJ, COND, SUBJ, which appear to correspond to features of sentences: 'not', 'and', 'or' 'if . . . , then . . .' and 'if it were that . . . , it would be that . . .'. Have I not just assumed that beliefs *do* have the structure of sentences?

I can begin my defence against this charge by observing that computational features correspond to very abstract features of syntactic structure. The presence of a 'not' in the right place to turn a sub-sentential expression into its negation is not a simple unitary feature. It is only at some level of analysis that

John and not Mary came to lunch

is equivalent to

John came to lunch and NOT (Mary came to lunch).

So the first thing to say is that calling beliefs 'sentence-like' makes the task look easier than it is. But more than this, picking on the features of representations which make it true that they have NEG or CONJ in their structure in a certain way, simply does not rule out that the relevant beliefs have a richer structure than sentences. Nothing I have said rules out that (John comes to lunch) is stored as a three-dimensional image or a two-dimensional map; and even though, when I come in the next chapter to make some suggestions about how 'John' corresponds to a computational feature, I shall suppose that (John comes to lunch) is of the form $\langle C(\text{John}), C(- \text{ comes to lunch}) \rangle$, that

97

too is consistent with its being encoded as an image. An image of John at a dining table could have the right structure if it functioned in the right way. And to see that this is so, it will help, I think, to give a summary of the way computational structure determines functional role.

Computational structure plays two related roles. On the one hand, given the proof theory which fixes how the presence of states with one computational structure leads to states with other computational structures, we can say how states of mind interact with each other to produce new states of mind. On the other, given input and output claims, it fixes how states of mind produce and are produced by, external states. To produce a basic action, A, of John's, there has to be a sequence of computations which gives rise to $\langle U$, John, now, k, $C(A)\rangle$; and k has to be bigger than other actual utilities. To produce John's belief that a rose is red, there has to be an experience which gives rise to $\langle B$, John, now, k, $C(A$ rose to red$)\rangle$. What computational structure allows us to do is to fix an abstract pattern of possible causes and effects, in input, output and throughput, which depend on the presence of computational features. When we refer to John's belief that something is red, or his desiring to do A, we rely on these abstract patterns to give the ascription of belief an explanatory function. Because we refer to the belief in English, we use the structural features of English sentences to latch onto those abstract features.

But in doing so we will suppose that the causal relations are in fact mediated by causal connections of which we know nothing. Those complex routes may well depend on features of beliefs – such as their being stored as images – which are not part of their *a priori* causal powers, and thus not part of their functional role. And that is the crux.

Though computational structure, which relies on the sentences of the natural languages we use, determines functional role in terms of sentence-like features, nothing excludes the *a posteriori* possibility that beliefs and desires have other features which determine their causal behaviour in ways which depend on features which are not at all sentence-like. The causal roles of beliefs and desires, which are both *a priori* and *a posteriori*, can depend on un-sentence-like features, even though their functional roles do not.

Remember the analogy I drew with antigenicity in 2.4. There I said that the causal definition of antigenicity entailed that antigens caused antibody production, but that antigenicity was causally connected with many other features – for example the possession of certain chemical functional groups. To insist that beliefs have only sentence-like structural features is a bit like insisting that antigens only act through antibody production. The pressure to treat beliefs as sentence-like depends upon the fact that the way we individuate them, in natural languages, relies on sentence-like features; but the states can have non-sentence-like features as well; it is just that it will be *a posteriori* what they are.

I have been discussing those beliefs which we express in natural languages. But another reason beliefs have non-sentence-like features, is that there are beliefs we do not express in English, but which we believe to be encoded in images. These states are not expressed directly in natural language: from the image, which we cannot express directly, we compute sentence-like beliefs, which we can. In sum, computational structure is part of functional role. What a belief's computational structure is, is, therefore, *a priori* and, for the beliefs we express in natural languages, the computational structure is sentence-like. But there are other beliefs which we do not express in natural language: these we individuate by other structural features, those of images, for example. That is one reason not all structural features are sentence-like. But a second is that states of mind have features other than their functional roles. And these features, which psychology, whether formal or informal, studies, are, as it turns out, not generally sentence-like at all. (See Block (1981: Section 2).)

5

Truth conditions

even though in a sense truth-conditions don't need to be mentioned in specifying the functional roles of . . . beliefs, those functional roles *determine* the belief's truth conditions.

(Loar, 1980: 67–8)

5.1 OVERVIEW

In this chapter I wish to draw together conclusions about the way the conventional notion of a truth condition fits into the framework of a functionalist theory as I have set it out. I want to consider whether, as Loar puts it, the truth conditions of beliefs are *determined* by a functionalist theory; and to draw some consequences of the fact that the resources available to a functionalist theory are more limited than those which classical accounts of truth conditions take for granted.

A functionalist theory of the mind looks to individuate mental events by their functional roles: by their causal antecedents and consequences within and without the mind. Mental states are characterised by the way in which they determine the functional roles of mental events. When we approach an account of the sentential attitudes – those psychological states, like belief, desire, hope, and so on, the English verbs for which take sentential complements in 'that'-clauses – we are left with a problem. For the sentential attitudes seem to have the general form of a relation between an agent and what philosophers have called a proposition. John's belief that snow is white and his desire that snow should be white are, on a traditional view, just different relations between John and the proposition that snow is white. Similarly, John's belief that snow is white and his belief that grass is green are identical relations, so that story runs, between John and these two different propositions. The problem is to say how a functionalist theory accommodates these facts.

I have already provided an idiom which allows us to state the issue without talk of propositions. What John's belief that snow is white and his desire that it should be white have in common is that they are both tokens of the type-representation (Snow is white). And this means they are tokens with the same truth conditions. The core of the problem, then, is to explain the relations between representations and their truth conditions.

The truth conditions of a belief (so much by way of definition) are the logically possible conditions under which it would be (or is) true. For representation type S, then, we can say that S's truth conditions are the logically possible circumstances under which the belief that S would be true. I have already argued that we cannot individuate beliefs by their truth conditions alone: but I have also carried on the discussion on the assumption that beliefs generally do have truth conditions. It is hard to see how anyone could quarrel with this. Perhaps there are states which should be called 'beliefs' which have no truth conditions: the aesthetic belief that Prokoviev was a better composer than Borodin, perhaps, or the moral belief that lying is wrong. What does not seem possible is that no beliefs at all should have conditions under which they are true. My belief that there is a building less than 80 yards from the window at which I write, is, probably, true. And even if it is not, it would have been if there had been such a building. Antirealists, in the style of Dummett (1973), may think this fact uninteresting; in particular because it may be insufficient to ground a theory of meaning. But I should find it very hard to see what anyone meant by denying it; see Appiah (forthcoming).

Disagreement of a legitimate kind will arise, however, the moment we try to say what it is for a condition to be the truth condition of a belief, at least if we stray from the definition offered above. I hold that a correct account can be given consistent with functionalism. In this chapter I try to say how. I begin in 5.2 with decision theory once more, saying how the role of truth conditions shows up in the computationally perfect agent. I suggest how we can make sense of a basic intuition about truth conditions, in a functionalist framework: namely, the intuition that a truth condition for S is a condition sufficient for the success of actions explained by the belief that S. Section 5.3 observes and defends an anti-Cartesian consequence of this theory: that what someone's state of mind is, in respect of their beliefs, is not determined by their phenomenology. In 5.4, I show that the notion of a truth condition as a certain kind of condition connecting action, belief and success, is not identical with the classical notion, because it allows for conditions which are necessary and sufficient for truth but not *logically* necessary and sufficient – I call these causal truth conditions. I show how to build in to a functionalist theory this distinction between causal truth conditions and truth conditions *simpliciter*.

5.2 DECISION AND TRUTH

As we saw in Chapter 3, decision theory makes no distinction between beliefs with identical truth conditions. That is, if it is logically necessary that S is true iff U is true, then $p(S) = p(U)$ and $d(S) = d(U)$. An account was offered of why decision theory has this feature. I said it was because decision theory assumes computational perfection: it predicts what will happen on the assumption that the agent carries out all the computations necessary to calculate which basic action has highest utility and then tries to perform that action. The necessity for an account of computational structure arises because agents are not computationally perfect. If they were we should need to say nothing about computation in our *a priori* theory.

Now since decision theory is indifferent between representations with identical truth conditions, it seems that it will be decision theory that allows us to assign truth conditions to the representations. For representations have the same behaviour from the perspective of decision theory iff they have the same truth conditions. Identity of decision-theoretic properties for beliefs should thus suffice to fix truth conditions.

In fact, as we have seen, this is not quite true. What is true is that those representations that are assigned the same p- and d-values in every probability and desirability function fall into equivalence classes of representations with the same truth conditions. So there will be at least a pair of such classes for each truth condition, one for beliefs, one for desires. But what these truth conditions are is not fixed in a functionalist theory until they are related to the effects of perception and the effects on action; that is, decision theory fixes the truth conditions of beliefs and desires when supplemented by what I have been calling 'input' and 'output' claims.

The theoretical significance of this fact is simply put: assigning a state which is a member of one of these equivalence classes to a computationally perfect agent results in exactly the same predictions for action as assigning any other. But the decision theory needs supplementation by input and output claims before it can be functionalist at all. Until we have these there is nothing to connect these equivalence classes with things outside the agent, truth conditions or anything else. But if the basic thought of the last paragraph is right, we should be able to assign truth conditions to each of these equivalence classes, once we have the input and output claims.

Once we know both how events outside people give rise to changes in their p- and d-functions; *and* how the state of the world outside them affects which of their tryings-to-act will produce successful actions, then we have a functionalist account of the behaviour of the computationally perfect agent. Given these input and output claims, we should know how events outside the agent would lead to changes in the agents p- and d-values: given a knowledge of these changes we could tell what actions they would try to perform: and given knowledge of which tryings would be successful, we should know what the agent would do; since, granted computational perfection, they would try to do what the decision theory predicts.

From now on, then, let us suppose our functionalist decision theory to be supplemented by the input and output claims necessary to say how changes in the probability function originate (in the sense of Chapter 3) and how tryings-to-act relate to action. Then this supplemented decision theory should be sufficient to fix the truth conditions of representations.

Can we say, then, in a general way, what makes a condition a truth condition? If we start by asking ourselves a simpler question, I think we shall find that we can. Let us begin then by asking why we want our beliefs to be true. The obvious suggestion is that if all our beliefs were true then the actions we undertook on those beliefs would satisfy our desires; and the obvious extension of this, when we act, as decision theory requires, on degrees of belief, is that the truth of the beliefs we act on will make the action more likely to satisfy our desires. But what, in this extended case, is it to act on a belief: when my $p(S) = p(\neg S) = 0.5$, for instance, do I act on the belief that S or the belief that not S?

We might be tempted to say that someone acts in the belief that S iff they both

(a) act having calculated the expected utility of the action on the partition $\langle (S)(\neg S) \rangle$; and

(b) have a high degree of belief that S.

But because we are dealing with computationally perfect agents, we cannot use (a). For a computationally perfect agent will get the same expected utility for an action on every partition, so that this suggestion would have agents acting on *every* belief that satisfies (b). (The reason for this is that computationally perfect agents do not *calculate* at all: they already know all the answers.) And (b) is wrong on other grounds also. For consider the case below, where the action contemplated is A and the expected utility is calculated on the partition $\langle (S), (\neg S) \rangle$

p	S	$\neg S$		d	S	$\neg S$
A	0.9	0.1		A	-1	20

Now suppose that $u(A)$ here is Mary's highest utility. Then she will do A, and she has a high degree of belief that S. But she would clearly prefer the outcome in which it is not the case that S. For $d(A \ \& \ \neg S) \geqslant d(A \ \& \ S)$. So, on this definition of what it is to act on a belief, it would not be true to say that her action is more likely to satisfy her desires if the belief she acts on is true.[1]

What is required, I think, for the notion of acting on S is that believing S to whatever degree you do, you do A; *and* that you would desire to do A more if you believed S more. That, I think, also captures the intuition that it is S's being probable that makes the act more desirable than it would otherwise be.

But another condition is required for acting on a belief: namely that you think that S is fixed, independently of your action. Otherwise S is not part of the background of belief for the decision, but part of what the action is directed at achieving. So I suggest the following definition:

ACT: a computationally perfect agent, X, performs act A on the belief that S iff,

(a) X does A, and

(b) X believes that whether or not S is causally independent of whether or not X does A; and

(c) if X believed that S more strongly X would also desire more strongly that A.[2]

ACT looks as though it has the right properties. For in the case just considered, if the agent's degree of belief that S had been greater, $u(A)$ would have been less, not more. So, in this case, we should say that the agent is acting, not on the belief that S, but on the belief that not S. But it is very odd to say that Mary is acting on the belief that S, when in fact she believes that not S more strongly than she believes that S. What we can say, however, is this. Provided that we mean by 'coming to believe that S more strongly', an agent conditionalising on the partition $(S, \neg S)$, where $p'(S)$ is greater than $p(S)$, then

E: An agent would desire that A more strongly if they came to believe that S more strongly iff $d(A \;\&\; S) > d(A \;\&\; \neg S)$.

If an agent does A, where $d(A \;\&\; S)$ exceeds $d(A \;\&\; \neg S)$, we would

---

1. An obvious simplification of this suggestion would be more direct: You do A on S iff you do A and if you believed S more strongly you'd still do A. But that is wrong. Suppose I decide to jump into the safety net held out by some firemen because I believe that there's a chance I would survive, if I were to jump, and much less chance if I did not. If I were more certain of the safety net, I would want to jump more. But I would also believe that I could wait a while, since, if jumping is really safe, I can leave it until the last minute. So I would decide to throw out my suitcase first. Because it is in fact risky, I think I should act fast: it will get more risky the longer I delay. So, believing it was safer would actually lead me to do something different: delay, throw the suitcase, and jump later. This sort of thing can be worked out in the decision theory; but the principle is clear without the formal theory.

2. This definition has the nice consequence that you never act on the belief that you are going to act; for whether or not you act is *never* causally independent of whether you act.

naturally call this *acting on the belief that S*, as ACT requires, only if they also had a high degree of belief that S; if they had a low degree of belief that S we should more naturally call it *acting in the hope that S*. But these two cases form a coherent kind just because in them $d(A \& S)$ exceeds $d(A \& \neg S)$; which is why, in ACT, I called them both acting on the belief that S.

We can now state one way in which truth and success in action are connected, for representations of states of the world outside the agent:

TRUTH: the truth condition of the representation S of an agent is that condition whose holding is sufficient to guarantee that, for every action A, if they were computationally perfect and performed A on the belief that S, then the outcome would be the one they preferred.[3]

So now we can see one way in which it is true that if Mary acts on the belief that S, and S is true, then the outcome of her action will be one she prefers; and that this is a fact we can take advantage of in setting out to discover the truth conditions of a representation.

TRUTH is a truism. If you act on the belief that S, so that evidence for S would increase the utility of your action, then, if S is true, the outcome will be: S and you did A. And you'll prefer that outcome, of course, because, as I have said, $d(A \& S)$ is greater than $d(A \& \neg S)$, which latter is what would have been true if S had been false. TRUTH is a truism because, if you would want to do A more if you believed that S more, it must be that you would prefer a world in which S and you do A, to a world in which $\neg S$ and you do A. But TRUTH still gives us a connection, however trivial it may seem, between representation and reality; and that is all we need.

Or rather, it is almost all we need. For though TRUTH is true, it still does not give us a functionalist account of truth. For the functional significance of the fact that an outcome is preferred by an agent depends not simply on its being preferable but on the agent's recognising that a preferred outcome obtains. If I lift the switch, acting on the belief that my doing so will make the light go on, then my future reactions will depend not simply on whether the light goes on, but on whether I come to believe that it is on. To make TRUTH into a functional account of truth we should have to say how the fact that an outcome is one an agent prefers to another will affect the agent's future dispositions to action. And to do this we should need to say how the fact that a preferred outcome obtains will affect the agent's beliefs about what is the case. We should need, in other words, once more to rely on input claims: claims about how the holding of a certain condition would change agents' mental states, in particular their beliefs.

3. This definition will not work for token-reflexive states; for the condition sufficient will be a disjunction of all the truth conditions of the different tokens.

Our theory is functionalist. In consequence the input claims relate states of the world and states of the agent; just as the output claims relates states of the agent and states of the world. In giving an account of truth of the kind I am suggesting, we have to say how the agent's actions give rise to states of the world. We must also say how those states of the world change the agent's beliefs and thus produce the satisfaction of desire. It is essential to see, however, that this feedback loop could not be specified just by saying directly what the effects of the agent's attempts at action will be on his states of beliefs: the reference to the world is not an optional extra. It is a crucial element in the specification of the mental states that the route from attempts to act to the satisfaction of desire should go through the world.[4]

It is true that sometimes, as when we turn our heads to look at a clock, part of the object of our action is to produce a change in our beliefs: we wish to come to believe that the time is whatever the clock says it is. But in general the objects of our actions are external states, and it is part of what it is for a state to be a state of desire that it leads in certain contexts to the agent's changing the world in certain ways. The consequences for someone's actions of the fact that their desires are satisfied will depend on whether they recognise them to be so; and it is for this reason that we need input claims. (Even in the case where what someone is trying to change is their own beliefs, they must come to believe that their beliefs have changed before they recognise they have achieved their desires. So this case is an instance of, not an exception to, the general rule that action aims first at changing the world — in this case a state of the agent's mind — rather than at changing the agent's beliefs about it.)

Though I cannot say in detail how this would actually be done, I can say something about how an account of computationally perfect agents should assign truth conditions to beliefs. For this would be done, in part, as we have seen, by way of input claims relating beliefs and their truth conditions. Thus, for example, we might have an input claim which entailed for each agent something of the following form:

1: If Peter has representations R_1 to R_n over which p- and d-functions are defined; and if conditions C obtain; and if an object with visually detectable properties in the class V, with members V_1 to V_m, were to come before him; then, given computational perfection, his p-values for representations R_1 to R_m, whose truth conditions, for each i, are that there is something before the agent with property V_i, would change from $p(R_i)$ to $p'(R_i)$, where $p'(R_i)$ is nearer to 1 than $p(R_i)$.

The details of this formulation should not be taken too seriously. All I want this suggestion for is to make plausible the view that there will be truths which

4. This fact is of importance when we come to consider the problems raised in 5.3.

are, at a higher level of abstraction yet, of the form:

2: If it were the case that S; and Mary became appropriately causally related with the state-of-affairs in virtue of which it is true that S; then, given computational perfection, she would increase her degree of belief that R to near 1,

where R is any representation whose truth conditions are that S. Truths of this form will help fix the truth conditions of R: for at least part of what it is to be a belief with R's truth conditions, is that it is to be a belief which would, in certain circumstances, be caused by events occurring when it is the case that S.

Though the general idea is straightforward, there are going to be problems in the application of 2 to the cases of general beliefs, *a priori* beliefs and existential beliefs, problems which, however, I hope I may be forgiven for not answering in this book. For though they are not trivial, I see no reason to think them insoluble, given solutions to the simpler problems I am tackling. Thus general beliefs look to be a counterexample to the claim that there are instances of 2 for every proposition (because causal relations hold between agents and token states-of-affairs, and a general truth, not being a token state of affairs, is not something to which one can have a causal relation).But we can here say that, in a sense, what we call general beliefs are what Ramsey called 'habits of singular belief'. That is, the functional role of general beliefs can be specified by saying, for the belief that all men are mortal, for example, that people who have it are so disposed as to come to believe x is a mortal whenever they come to believe x is a man.

It is true that we should need as well as this, some account of how general beliefs are acquired; and this would amount to giving an account of the inductive logic that is built into our system of beliefs. Once more I must excuse myself from saying how this is to be done. I develop a logic of singular conditionals in Part III, and thus have no need to say anything explicit about quantified beliefs. I believe that the extension from singular to quantified conditionals[5] will be achieved by applying to conditionals a general account of quantified beliefs, of the kind found in Field (1977), where the matter is

5. I mean to include conditionals of the form

> If a is P, then it is Q

for example, where there is what linguists would call an anaphoric connection between antecedent and consequent; it is at least not obvious that these can be handled by normal quantificational devices.

It should be noted that many apparently singular conditionals are in fact quantified. Conditionals where the main verb is in a continuous tense, for example, – as in

> If John comes, Mary does –

are, in effect of the form,

> (t) (If John comes at t, Mary comes at t).

dealt with by saying what constraints the possession of quantified beliefs lays on the extension of agents' probability functions as they add further singular terms of their system of representation.[6]

The problem with *a priori* truths is just that there need be nothing at all that we can call a state-of-affairs to which they correspond. Here, as I have said, a belief is *a priori* iff any computationally perfect agent who has the capacity to form the belief, will form it with probability 1. Since no external evidence is needed for *a priori* beliefs there are no input claims about what will elicit them in agents who are not computationally perfect. People do, of course, come to have new *a priori* beliefs, as a result of thinking about a subject, for example, or as a result of someone's telling them. But granted that an agent has representational items sufficient to form a particular *a priori* belief, the only external stimulus necessary to produce it will be something that starts off the computations which lead to it.

As for existential beliefs, their functional role seems to be given by their relation to singular beliefs (through the computation corresponding to existential generalisation, in particular) Once more I should expect a full treatment to follow from a proper general account of quantification.

So, in the hope that these problems *can* be solved, let us return to 1: it is obviously directed to the visible properties of middle-sized objects. And so the conditions *C* will say something about the light, about the absence of barriers between the agent's eyes and the objects with properties V_i, and, of course, about the agent's eyes being sufficiently sensitive to differences between visible properties. (The blind and the colour-blind will not satisfy *C*.) But sentences of the general form of 2 are not restricted to dealing with beliefs for which the truth conditions are that something should have a certain 'observational' property. For we conceive of agents as causally located in the world with all its properties. Thus, if it is true, for example, that there is an electron hitting the screen of the oscilloscope, and if that will cause a certain scintillation, and if Mary is before the screen and conscious and the light from the scintillation is sufficient to cause sensation in her visual system; and if Mary has certain beliefs about scintillations, electrons and oscilloscopes, she will come to believe that an electron has hit the screen. This complex conditional is also of the form of 2. And there are many more, known to all of us with the necessary

6. I should remark in passing that this way of proceeding has a certain advantage in the case of the conditional over older approaches. For, as will become clear in Part III, I doubt that conditionals have truth conditions. Any reading of the quantifiers which required the notion of an object's satisfying an open sentence of the form

If *x* is *P*, then *x* is *Q*

would be open to the objection that, since an object satisfies an open sentence iff substitution of the object's name into that sentence produces a truth, the notion of satisfaction is here inapplicable.

concepts, which help fix the relations between its being the case that S (for some S) and an agent's believing it to be the case that S. These are the truths which will allow us to fix S's truth conditions.

In TRUTH I speak of an agent's doing A. In order to connect doing A with the mental states of the agent we shall need to know under what circumstances agents trying to perform basic actions will actually succeed. We know that whenever computationally perfect agents have $u(A)$ greater than the utilities of other basic actions, they try to do A. But we can only make functional sense of trying to do A if we know under what sorts of circumstances trying to do A produces A-ing. So, if input claims help fix the truth conditions of representations by fixing the truth conditions of beliefs, output claims will help us in fixing the truth conditions for representations by telling us about the truth conditions of desires. Thus, we might have

> 3: If someone is in state M, where u(I bring it about that S) is the highest utility amongst their basic actions, then, provided they are computationally perfect, they will try to bring it about that S.

Since, if u(I bring it about that S) is highest, the computationally perfect agent will try to bring it about that S, it follows that there exists some class of possible conditions C, such that

> 4: If a computationally perfect agent is in state M, and conditions C obtain, then, they will bring it about that S.

Here too, in specifying the content of C, we rely on our general beliefs about the way agents are causally located in the world. If doing S is a bodily movement of the agent, then all C has to say, perhaps, is that the agent is not paralysed, and that he knows how to bring it about that S. And we can say at least this about what it is to know how to bring it about that S: it is to be so constituted that normally trying to bring it about that S brings it about that S. And 'normally' here means, as I said in 4.1, not 'usually', but 'unless prevented by independently specifiable causes'.

5.3 PHENOMENOLOGICAL PROBLEMS

The line of thought we are pursuing, in which truths like 1, 2, 3 and 4 play a role in determining what the truth conditions of beliefs and desires are, has, however, a *prima facie* implausible consequence. Investigating it will bring out more clearly the relations between beliefs and their truth conditions. The problem is best seen if we begin with an analogy with the simple case of the thermostat with which the notion of a functional theory was introduced in Chapter 2.

Suppose we take a thermostat whose heat-sensor is a bi-metallic strip, and whose heater is an electrical element. From the electric lead to the heater we take off a lead to a new device. That device contains a clock. Whenever there is an electric current in the lead, the device waits two minutes and then mechanically bends the bi-metallic strip in the thermostat in such a way as to break the circuit and cut off the electric supply to the heater. Then, after a few minutes, the machine bends the bi-metallic strip the other way, and once more the heater is on. The thermostat now behaves exactly as it would have done if the external temperature had been changing in a certain regular way. But it is no longer functioning as a thermostat.

What has now changed, of course, is that the thermostat no longer satisfies the condition that its behaviour should be appropriately sensitive to the temperature of the external world; and that it should do its bit in regulating that temperature.

Now the analogy I want to pursue also relies on taking a system which satisfies a certain functional description – in this case an agent – and changing the way it is connected to the world, so that it becomes differently sensitive to the states of the world around it. We shall see that it is true of agents, as of thermostats, that changing the way they are 'wired into' the world may substantially affect their functional descriptions. In fact the case I want to consider suggests that two people could have beliefs with identical phenomenology while the truth conditions of every pair of phenomenologic-ally identical beliefs were different. This conclusion runs clearly against many people's intuitions, and I must now try to establish that it is both a consequence of the line of thought I have suggested, and true.

Suppose that

P: if sensory input and motor output are mediated by nerve impulses, then the phenomenology of an agent is independent of which events outside the agent cause incoming nerve-impulses; and of what results causally from outgoing impulses.

The antecedent of this conditional seems to be pretty likely to be true, and the conditional as a whole is a consequence of the fact that mental events are supervenient upon physical ones. By 'phenomenology' I mean what might otherwise be put simply as 'what it feels like' to have experiences; thus, pains, visual images, and what have been called by some philosophers 'qualia', and by others 'raw feels' – all the sensations and other contents of consciousness count as part of an agent's phenomenology.

Consider, now, the following possibility. A human brain – yours, say – is removed from its body by skilful surgeons while its owner – you – is asleep. Each nerve-ending is carefully labelled as it is removed and is connected up to a giant computer. The computer contains a program which guarantees that the following subjunctive conditional holds; whenever there is a sequence of motor output which would have led, if the brain had still been in your body, to a certain sequence of sensory input, the sensory nerves are stimulated in exactly the manner they would have been. If the brain produces a pattern of motor output of the kind that would have occurred if you had tried to lift your arm, then the computer produces the input that would have occurred if your arm had gone up.

Now the significance of the principle, P, I assumed earlier is obvious. For it enjoins us to accept that, as far as you are concerned, this transfer of your brain from your body into the bath of saline that is its new home, should make no difference. Phenomenologically, your position will be the same. Whenever it seems to you that you have decided to set about making a cup of tea, it will seem to you that the kettle boils and you pour hot water over the tea-bags. Indeed, granted the principle, P, the hypothesis is simply a familiar sceptic's tale: Peter Unger (1975) might even ask you how you knew that it was not true.

Now consider again 1, 2, 3 and 4 above. There ought to be truths corresponding to each of them for you. But, after the transfer of your brain to its new home none of these corresponding truths is true. You have visual experience, but no eyes; you try to do things but all that ever happens is that the machine mimics what would have happened if you had tried to do those things while still the inhabitant of your body. So that if 1, 2, 3 and 4 were really the sorts of truths which have to be true of someone if their beliefs are to have truth conditions, you would now be in the strange position either of having beliefs without truth conditions; or in the equally strange position of being in the state you were always in when you smelled a rose before, but having a belief whose truth condition was not that there was a rose before you, but reflected some state of the computer that now invents your experience; or, some might say, in the position of seeming to yourself to have beliefs while, in fact, having none. None of these options seems attractive.

The temptation to say that the states of this brain have the same truth conditions as before is hard to resist. But we should resist it. For one thing we could produce a machine which had going into it an array of electrical impulses patterned exactly as the input in to the brain in the saline; and from which came an array of output patterned exactly as the brain's output. If we were to call one of these an agent, why not the other? Yet surely, all this new machine is is a complex device for producing patterns of electrical output in response to patterns of electrical input.

That we could make a machine which would produce the same electrical output for any input as your brain in the saline does not, of course, mean that your brain in the saline differs in no way from a machine with those complex electrical dispositions. For one thing, such a machine lacks many of the physical properties that your brain has, and these might be crucial in the causal determination of whether the machine had a phenomenology. For another, your brain has a history within a body, so that even if it is not now true that the states of your brain are standardly caused in the usual ways, it was once true of it. And we might want to say that its states were beliefs, not because they would now be caused in the usual way but because they *were* caused in the usual way. This line of thought would be encouraged by thinking that, after all, what is going on in your brain when you have the experience that used to be caused by looking at a red rose, is just the same experience, caused differently. But, granted that this is true, this would oblige us to treat a brain with no history within a body, manufactured by simply making a physical copy of your brain, as having the belief that a rose was before it, whenever it has this experience. And this would be because this pseudo-brain was in a certain physical state, not because that state was caused in any particular way.

I think, then, that we should just accept that a brain might exist with the same experiences as an actual agent, while having beliefs with different truth conditions. After all, if TRUTH is right, then the truth condition of a belief is a condition sufficient to make action in that belief satisfy one's desires: and for the brain that condition will be a different one in most cases from the one that is sufficient to make a person's wishes come true.

There is, as I have said, an analogous problem for the thermostat. For just as a brain, and the mind that it embodies, can be reconnected to the world in novel ways; so, as we saw above, a thermostat could be reconnected to the world in novel ways. And, just as the brain would then cease to satisfy that part of its functional description that reflects general connections between its internal states and states of the world; so too would a thermostat. So much so, indeed, that we should not call it a thermostat at all; nor, I suggest, by analogy, should we call our rewired and actually ineffective brain an agent, or credit it with beliefs and desires. As stated in 5.2, the reference to the external world in the functional characterisation of mental states is not really an optional extra.

Just as the full functional description of the thermostat depends for its truth on how that system is causally located in the world; on what it is hooked up to; so, I maintain, does the full functional description of agents and their mental states.

5.4 TRUTH CONDITIONS AND CAUSALITY

Whether we consider input or output claims of the form of 1 to 4, their general form is of a claim that a relation obtains between four things: an agent, a set of conditions, the state of affairs that S, and a state of the agent with the truth conditions of S. And that relation is causal. It holds because of causal relations between mental states and other states which are not mental. That the relation holds *a priori* does not show that the underlying facts are not causal: what is *a priori* is that the existence of things which satisfy that causal relation makes it true that there is a certain functional state; what is *a posteriori* is that there are any things which satisfy the causal relation.

Causal relations between events, like all relations, are extensional.[7] If event C causes event E, then, if C' is the same event as C, C' causes E. If the misting on the glass is caused by the water's boiling, and the water's boiling is the vaporisation of H_2O molecules; then the misting on the glass is caused by the vaporisation of H_2O molecules. From this sample fact it follows that it is not only the case that if

(a) A-type events cause B-type events

and

(b) all A-type events are C-type events; and *vice versa*,

then

(c) C-type events cause B-type events;

but also that if

(d) A-type events in circumstances of type C cause B-type events

and

(e) circumstances of type C occur iff circumstances of type C' occur

then

(f) A-type events in circumstances of type C' cause B-type events.

These facts have important consequences for our account of truth conditions. Recall again 2:

2: If it were the case that S; and Mary became appropriately causally related with the state-of-affairs in virtue of which it is true that S; then, given computational perfection, she would increase her degree of belief that R to near 1. (Where S is a truth condition of the belief that R.)

7. That causal relations are thus extensional does not mean that causal explanations are extensional also: the fact that the ball passed through a point 20 metres to the left of the pine tree does not explain why it broke the window, even if its passing through that point *was* its passing through the window; see Anscombe (1969).

Let 'R' be

R: Something before Mary is red.

and suppose that red things emit light in the range of wavelengths w; then

2': If it were the case that something before Mary emitted in the range w; and she became appropriately causally related with the state of affairs which makes this true; then, given computational perfection, she would increase her degree of belief that something before her is red.[8]

And indeed, all the truths about the causal role of the belief that something in which reference is made to red things will correspond to truths in which reference is made to w-emitters. If it is a necessary and sufficient condition for a state of affairs to be the truth condition of a belief, that tokens of that state of affairs stand in just those causal relations to tokens of that belief, then, surely, we must conclude that S's truth conditions are that something before the agent emits in the range of wavelengths w? This is just a reflection of the facts about causation I noted above. In so far as our theory of truth conditions is causal, it will apparently assign to beliefs (and desires), as 'truth conditions', states of affairs which are true whenever the beliefs are − not out of logical necessity, but simply as a matter of fact.

In fact, however, this does not follow at all. For our functionalist theory individuates mental states by their functional roles: that is by *a priori* features of their causal role. And though it is true that, if 2 is true and red things are w-emitters, 2' is true: it is not the case that if 2 is *a priori* true and red things emit in those wavelengths, 2' is *a priori* true. The truth conditions of the representation are fixed by the *a priori* truths of the form of 2 and 3 which form part of the theory, not by *every* truth of one of these forms.

The significance of this fact is most easily seen if we consider what it would be like to have a functionalist theory of the mind of an agent with concepts different from one's own.

Consider, then the case of a dog. Let us call him Charles. Suppose that Charles has special vision; his eyes are sensitive to emission of electro-magnetic radiation in a certain range of the ultra-violet. Let us call things that emit (or reflect) light in just that range of frequencies 'ultra-violet'; and likewise let us call the light they emit (or reflect) 'ultra-violet' also. Sometimes a thing is before Charles' eyes and we switch on a source of ultra-violet light. Suppose the room is otherwise unilluminated. Then we see nothing. But, as we can confirm by looking at the room with an ultra-violet sensitive camera, Charles goes about roughly as he does when the room is normally illuminated. Of course, he bumps into things that are transparent to ultra-violet, just as we should expect.

8. I abbreviate 'emits in the range of wavelengths w' from now on to 'is a w-emitter'.

There is no doubt that Charles is having experiences, and, on the account of belief I have proposed, there is no doubt, either, that he is forming beliefs; including beliefs that things are the colour that ultra-violet objects look to him. For there is a system to his preferences and the behaviour consequent upon them, that can be captured by p- and d-functions, subject to computational error. In the end, then, after watching Charles for some time, we shall be able to give a functionalist account of the beliefs he forms when presented with ultra-violet objects.

UV: Charles believes something is R if an object before him is ultra-violet, *ceteris paribus*. Further his belief that something is R is true iff that thing is ultra-violet.

We do not ourselves know what it is for something to be R: for there is no sensory organ of ours that leads to our having beliefs that something is R, and there is, in consequence, no functional state of ours with these properties of the belief that something is R. But there is no doubt that the states of this dog's that we pick out are states of belief, even if they are states which we cannot ourselves have; compare Nagel (1974).

Amongst the things we cannot believe, and Charles may, is that the belief that something is R is true iff that thing is R. We do not believe it because we do not have any beliefs about things being R, and cannot, therefore, have beliefs of the form

S is true iff — is R.

Since a truth condition is a condition logically and not just causally necessary and sufficient for the truth of a representation, and since we do not know such a condition, it follows that we do not know a truth condition for the belief that something is R at all.

Granted that we do not know what Charles' belief that something is R is, there is still a question as to what we do believe about him. And the answer must be that we believe he is in a state which is

(a) caused in certain circumstances by certain standard routes, and

(b) true — a notion for which, as we have seen, we can give some causal rationale — when certain conditions hold.

If this is right, then it looks, as I have said, as though we have a functionalist conception of his state. But this conception differs from his: and though it in fact picks out those states of his which are beliefs that something is R, it does not pick out those states by way of the properties they have *a priori qua* beliefs that something is R for him. Indeed, it is precisely because what is *a priori* for him differs from what is *a priori* for us that we have different concepts.

Remember what this means: R is *a priori* true just in case any computationally perfect agent who had the concepts necessary to have the belief that R, would believe that R to degree one. The *a priori* truths about the belief that snow is white, are truths which would be known to any computationally perfect agent who had the concept of the belief that snow is white.

The reason why we do not know the truth conditions of the belief that something is R is simple: we do not have the concept of the belief that something is R at all. We have seen that we can have the conception of a state, which I called the belief that something is R. But this might more properly be written as 'the-belief-that-something-is-R'. For it is, for us, an unanalysable primitive notion: it is not one we can decompose into a relation between an agent and something-that-is-R. For the only conceivable candidate for 'R' is 'ultra-violet': and we know that this is not an acceptable candidate, because we can distinguish the belief that something is R and the belief that something is ultra-violet, functionally.

For someone who has the concept of the belief that something is R, on the other hand, it is *a priori* that that belief is true iff that thing is R. And it is only possible to have the concepts necessary for coming to think this as a result of computation, if you have the concept of R-ness. Consequently, only someone with the concept of R-ness can have the concept of the belief that something is R.

Our relation to Charles is, obviously, like the relation between someone who is blind and someone who is sighted. Suppose again that red things emit in the wave-lengths w, so that red things are all, as we can say, w-emitters. Then a blind man could know that I have beliefs-that-something-is-S which I form on the basis of visual exposure to things that w-emit, and which are true iff those things do w-emit. But he cannot, not having the capacity to form any beliefs that something is red at all, believe that I sometimes believe that things are red.

In giving my theory so far I have been talking about what is known (or knowable) about our functional states for anyone with our concepts. Here is one way that the distinction between knowing conditions causally necessary and sufficient for the truth of a representation – call these causal truth conditions – and knowing conditions logically necessary and sufficient for its truth – i.e. truth conditions *simpliciter* – can be explained in the context of my theory. To know the truth conditions of a representation it is not enough to know the causal truth conditions; it is necessary further to specify them by way of the very same concepts that the representation contains. And that, I claim, is what we cannot do for Charles' belief; and the blind man cannot do for ours.

There is something rather curious about this situation. Our notion of a truth condition – that which is shared by every computationally equivalent belief – turns out to be compounded of two elements, at least from the perspective of a functionalist theory which is fundamentally causal. On the one hand,

116

there is the causal truth condition, a notion which makes good sense in the context of a functional theory; on the other is a constraint on the way in which agents must represent that causal truth condition to themselves if their knowledge of that causal truth condition is to be knowledge of the truth condition *simpliciter*. Indeed, we might feel, looked at from a functionalist perspective, the notion of a truth condition which is not just a causal truth condition is just a tremendous muddle. Why not stick with the notion of a causal truth condition, while making sure to put into the functionalist theory, the very interesting, but surely separable fact, that anyone with the concept of the belief that *S* must be able to specify that causal truth condition by way of the very concepts which make up the belief that *S*?

But there is another way of seeing the matter that makes clear what the real significance of the truth condition is. I mentioned at the beginning of the chapter that beliefs could be separated out into equivalence classes consisting of members with the same truth condition. In computationally perfect agents any member of this class has the same causal role as any other. Not only are they all always true together – that condition is satisfied by the members of classes of beliefs with the same causal truth condition – but, in a computationally perfect agent, they will be caused in the same circumstances. This condition is not satisfied by beliefs with the same causal truth conditions in general. And the identity of causal role, with respect to decision theory, of beliefs with the same truth condition is one that may be seen to justify the importance which that notion has played in the philosophy of language and of mind.

5.5 SUMMARY

I have tried in this chapter to fit truth conditions into the framework of the general theory. I began by arguing that it was in the computationally perfect agent that we would find the key to truth conditions: for the computationally perfect agent has equivalence-classes of beliefs and desires with the same truth condition. I suggested that what made a condition a truth condition was the fact that it was a condition whose holding was sufficient to guarantee that an action on the relevant belief was successful; and I then suggested what, in terms of the computationally perfect agent, that might mean.

In 5.3 I observed and defended a consequence of my account: the consequence that identity of phenomenology does not entail identity of truth conditions for mental states. The thesis that it does entail identity of truth conditions is what Putnam has called 'methodological solipsism'; and it is an advantage of my view that it entails that methodological solipsism is, as Putnam (1975a) has argued, false.

Then I went on to point out that the conditions we call truth conditions are distinct from what I called 'causal truth conditions'; and to argue that we could still have room for logical truth conditions in our theory. Talk about truth conditions can be restated in terms of talk about equivalence classes of decision-theoretically equivalent beliefs with the same causal truth condition.

Chapter 2 ended with 11 constraints on a functionalist theory of the mind. I repeat them here, and show what progress we have made towards satisfying them for a functionalist theory of beliefs and desires. I claimed that there must be a functionalist theory of the mental which

(a) characterised the causal role of mental states, by

(b) stating *a priori* truths about the mind which were

(c) sufficient to identify each mental state as the state with such and such causal powers.

I then called these *a priori* features of causal role functional role. Then I said that the theory must be

(d) computational, individuating sentential attitudes partly by their computational structure,

which I defined as that feature of sentential attitude states which was not determined merely by their truth conditions, I claimed that

(e) mental states are not conceptually tied, unlike many dispositions, to a unique display, but that a functionalist theory *will* entail a unique output for any input to a total state.

I added that the theory must require

(f) that it is changes of mental state that cause action, and called truths about how mental states cause action 'output claims'.

I then required that the theory

(g) ascribe token-referential beliefs, and

(h) that it have input claims – *a priori* truths about the non-mental causes of changes of mental state,

as well as

(i) laying constraints on the way changes of belief lead to changes of other beliefs, by way of what I called throughput claims.

Finally I also required that we should allow for

(k) throughput claims with a richer structure than entailments.

I fear I have said nothing, apart from what I said towards the end of 2.6, to meet (k). But all that I have said in this chapter and the last three has been an attempt to state facts about the causal role of mental states of belief – and, to a lesser extent, desire – thus satisfying (a). I have claimed that it is *a priori* also, satisfying (b). The claim that what I have said would be sufficient to individuate beliefs by their functional roles remains to be established; but I have offered support for it, in showing how to characterise such features of beliefs as their computational structures and their truth conditions, in terms of functional roles. So much, then, for (c). I have satisfied (d) by saying a great deal more about the causal features of computational structures; and gone some way towards meeting (e) by showing how a decision theory, computationally expressed, and supplemented by a mechanism for changing states of belief in response to evidence, allows us to predict what someone will do, subject to error in their computations, if they are subjected to input which causes changes in the degrees of an originating set of beliefs. Point (f) is satisfied in two ways. First, by our treatment of utilities: for it is when a state $u(S)$ comes to the top of the preference function at some time that it leads to action; and it is the event of its coming to the top that causes the action. Secondly (in a little more detail in one case), by the account of the way computations produce new states — as for example when EX.UT. (see 4.3) produces new states of desire. For the end product of those computations may produce a utility value which is at the top of the preference ordering; and the event of its production causes action.

I have claimed that (h) could be satisfied by a full account of perception and must be satisfied if we are to have a functionalist theory of truth conditions; and (i) is satisfied because the theory allows for belief-computations.

As for (g), I consider token–referentiality in the next chapter for sentences; and in Chapter 7 I extend the treatment in an obvious way to apply to beliefs.

We now have an account of beliefs as states which can be characterised by a quintuple, $\langle B, A, t, p(S), C(S) \rangle$, with the truth conditions of the belief fixed as a function of all its members, save $p(S)$ (and B).

With this in hand, we can turn from mind to language.

Part II *Meaning*

6

Realism and truth-theory

To know the meaning of *s* is to know under what conditions *s* would count as true.

(Wiggins, 1971)

6.1 OVERVIEW

I turn now from an account of certain general features of the mind to an account of declarative meaning. In doing so I begin by examining the main stream of thought about meaning; what I believe to be the central theory in philosophical semantics. I mean what Michael Dummett, amongst others, has called 'realism'.

Realism, in semantics, as I characterise it, is the claim that the meaning of a central class of declarative sentences can be given by stating their truth conditions.[1] This way of putting the matter leaves much open. Which class of sentences is central? Do we give meanings to token sentences or to types? And, above all, what, for sentences, are truth conditions? Without answers to these questions realism is just a scheme for a theory of meaning; a scheme we might acquiesce in without being clear what it entailed. The service Donald Davidson has done us is to offer a way of filling out the scheme; a way that allows us to ask and to answer these and many other questions. But it is just one way. And if we end by rejecting it, that is not the end of realism. Some other way of filling out the scheme might do the job.

We have already offered some account of truth conditions for beliefs; and it might seem that this settles the question what truth conditions are. But there is no guarantee that the truth conditions of sentences bear any particular relation to the truth conditions of beliefs, at least until we have developed an account of the relation of beliefs and sentences. It will turn out that though truth conditions will not do *as* meanings, they do play an important part in semantic theory. So, throughout my discussion of Davidson, bear in mind that

---

1. This is a deliberate expository simplification. Most current realists think that truth conditions are only part of meaning, and I shall be explaining why that is at the end of the chapter. For a typical realist view of which does not *identify* meaning with truth conditions, see Lewis, (1972*b*).

what is under consideration is not the thought that sentences have truth conditions which speakers know, but Davidson's way of specifying them.

I propose therefore, in this chapter, to examine Davidson's form of realism and the claims he makes about truth conditions. Once we have seen that Davidson's theory fails as an account of meaning, we return to the question whether we can give an alternative account of truth conditions for sentences which does any better. At that point I shall draw on our account of the truth conditions of beliefs to throw doubt upon the possibility of giving a theory of meaning in terms of truth conditions: and to do this I need to develop a theory of the relations between beliefs and sentences.

None of this would be necessary if Davidson's theory worked; and so I have made it my first task to show that it does not. This project is not, however, simply negative. For, in the course of it I shall be both explaining features of Davidson's theory that can be of use in the development of a theory of truth conditions, *and* discussing many of the central questions of the theory of meaning.

6.2 MEANING AND TRUTH CONDITIONS

What does a theory of meaning tell us? Obviously, what sentences and other expressions mean. And what is that? Obviously, that is what people who know the language must know about the word and sentences and such. For someone who knows the language knows what all these expressions mean. One kind of theory of meaning will be an account of what people who know the language know. And Davidson's theory is just such an account.

On Davidson's view, a theory of meaning is a statement of the implicit knowledge of speakers: a statement of a theory, knowledge of which allows speakers to use the language in acts of speech and writing and to understand such uses by others. This claim is not obvious. For consider a parallel account of a theory of bicycling.

'What is a theory of bicycling? Obviously, a theory that tells us what people who know how to bicycle know. So one kind of theory of bicycling is a theory which states the implicit knowledge of bicyclists: a statement of a theory, knowledge of which will allow people to use bicycles in acts of bicycling.'

It is clear from this example what is odd about the assumption that a theory of meaning must state the implicit knowledge of speakers: it is that it is not obvious that what speakers know about the language is propositional knowledge, knowledge *that* sentences have certain properties, rather than knowledge *how* to use them. Just as, though bicyclists know how to ride, it is not at all clear that there is anything they know which constitutes a theory of how bicycles are to be ridden. And even if there is, why could there not be an adequate theory of how bicycles are ridden which was different from the theory, propositional knowledge of which underlay the capacity of bicyclists to bicycle?

In the development of Davidson's view we should keep in mind the possibility that what speakers know is simply how to use the language; and that this knowledge is not constituted by way of a theory. I do believe that speakers know that the sentences they utter have certain properties and that this knowledge explains their competence. In 7.2 I return to this question in the context of my own positive theory. The question I want to address in this chapter is whether the knowledge that Davidson ascribes to speakers would be sufficient to underlie their competence. But I want to insist from the very beginning that I do not assume that any theory would do, just because it stated propositions, knowledge of which would allow speakers to use the language properly.

Davidson insists that the knowledge of speakers is implicit and not explicit. This could be taken in various ways. The most plausible interpretation, I think, in the framework I have been developing, is that implicit knowledge is the body of beliefs which agents are capable of deriving, by way of computation, from the body of actual beliefs which constitute what they explicitly know. This is plausible because Davidson would presumably agree that I have implicit knowledge that, say, factorial 10 is

$$10 \times 9 \times 8 \times 7 \times 6 \times 5 \times 4 \times 3 \times 2 \times 1 \ = \ 3,628,800$$

because that this is so follows from what I know already, even if I have not actually worked it out.

If I am right in this, then the test we need to apply is not whether speakers would, for example, agree to the claims of the theory that Davidson develops; it is rather whether the claims of the theory follow from things that speakers believe, by computations of which they are capable; even if, since they have often not carried out the requisite computations, they may sometimes act as if they do not believe those claims.

Let us now consider what it is that Davidson says every speaker knows. His initial idea was both simple and appealing. If truth and meaning are connected in the way that realism requires, then a theory which said for every sentence of the language what it was for it to be true, would apparently do as a theory of meaning. Now Tarski had already shown how to characterise truth for formal languages. All we had to do, Davidson claimed, was to look at Tarski's theory in a new way. Tarski had said:

Let us consider an arbitrary sentence; we shall replace it by the letter '*p*'. We form the name of this sentence and we replace it by another letter, say, '*X*'. We ask now what is the logical relation between the two sentences 'X is true' and 'p'. It is clear from the point of view of our basic conception of truth these sentences are equivalent. In other words, the following equivalence holds:

T: X is true if, and only if, p.

We shall call any such equivalence (with 'p' replaced by any sentence of the language to which the word 'true' refers, and 'X' replaced by a name of this sentence) an 'equivalence of the form of (T)'.

Now, at last, we are able to put into a precise form the conditions under which we will consider the usage and the definition of the term 'true' as adequate from the material point of view: we wish to use the term 'true' in such a way that all equivalences of the form (T) can be asserted, and *we shall call a definition of truth 'adequate' if all these equivalences follow from it.* (1943/44: 344)

And he had constructed for a series of languages a definition of truth-in-the-language which was, in his sense, adequate. Davidson suggested that instead of using the theory to define truth, we could take the notion of truth as one of our primitive theoretical ideas and treat each of the sentences of the form (T) as giving the conditions under which the sentence it mentioned was true. Looked at not as a definition of 'true' but, taking the notion of truth as primitive, as a specification of the truth conditions of all the sentences of the language, a Tarskian truth-theory could be seen as a theory of meaning.

If we are to put Tarski's theory to this new use, a number of modifications are in order. To begin with, Tarski was concerned only with languages in which, if one token of a certain sentence-type is true, all are. But a theory of meaning will have to cope with token-reflexive sentences; sentences the truth of tokens of which depends on who says them, where and to whom, and may depend on yet other features.

I: I want you to fetch that pig

for example, is true iff it is uttered by someone at a time when they want a person whom they are addressing to fetch some contextually indicated pig.

T(I): A token of *I* is true iff I want you to fetch that pig

(which satisfies nicely the adequacy condition that Tarski lays down in the passage above) is not even true: we should go wrong if we required of a theory of meaning that it should have T(I) as a consequence. And, as is obvious, we should do no better with the sentence type.

Still, this problem is easily avoided. What we need to do is to give sentences like (T) which assign truth conditions not to types, but to tokens, and allow the sentence which gives the truth conditions − 'p' − to be something other than the very sentence which 'X' picks out. One way we can achieve this is to assign truth conditions to ordered *n*-tuples, consisting of a sentence-type, followed by a speaker, followed by a time, followed by a place, followed by an audience, followed by . . . ; followed, in fact, by whatever we find we need to do the job. Thus, to give an example which deals with just a speaker and a time:

T(TR): For all speakers, A, and all time intervals t, the triple $\langle$'I am happy', A, $t \rangle$ is true iff its first member is produced by its second member during its third member and there is some interval t_2 which includes the third member, during which the second member is happy.

I shall simplify this proposal in what follows to:

T(TR'):$(A)(t)$('I am happy' uttered by A at t is true iff A is happy at t)

and analogously for other sentences. But the full formulation helps to keep us aware that, though the principle underlying the treatment of token-reflexives is clear, the details are far from unmessy. Except where it matters in what follows I shall stick with the Tarskian format, ignoring token-reflexivity. But we can begin, at least, by admitting that this obvious extension of Tarski's work makes precise some of the ways in which the truth of what we say may depend on what we sometimes loosely call 'context'.

Next we need to look more closely at the way we name sentences. Given what Tarski says,

T(N): 1 is true iff snow is white

will do as a sentence of the form of (T), provided '1' is the name of the English sentence 'Snow is white'. There are lots of ways of naming sentences of English: one is to assign a natural number to all the words in the lexicon – in alphabetical order as in a dictionary, say – and then assign to each sentence a name which is the ordered n-tuple of the numbers assigned to the words it contains. For all Tarski says we could use such a name. But we standardly use tokens with the same shape as the written sentences, placed between inverted commas. It is natural to think, therefore, that what Tarski wants is really a sentence of the form

T(SN): 'Snow is white' is true iff snow is white.

Indeed, this is his most often quoted exemplar. It is important, therefore, to see that, so far, T(N) will do just as well; and that it lacks a feature which T(SN) has; the feature, namely, that the name used in T(SN), unlike that in T(N), not only picks out the sentence, but does so in such a way that we can recognise, once we understand the convention of quotation that is being used, whether *any* token is of the type whose truth conditions are being given. The fact is that the expression i.e. ' "Snow is white" ' is not, a name at all: it is a disguised description of a type of sentence – the type whose tokens consist of a token of the letter 'S', followed by a token of the letter 'n', followed by a token of 'o', followed by a token of 'w', followed by a space . . . and so on. I shall restrict myself here, as in what follows, to discussions of written tokens; but, given the conventions of pronunciation, i.e. ' "Snow is white" ' also tells us how to recognise spoken tokens of the type.

If we are to turn a theory of truth into a theory of meaning, our sentences of the form of (T) must use a name of the sentence whose truth conditions they give, which picks out the sentence in this perspicuous way; they must use what we oxymoronically call a 'structural-descriptive' name. The reason for this is important, for it brings out the nature of the claim that a theory of truth will do as a theory of meaning.

Because, for Davidson, a theory of meaning is a statement of the implicit knowledge of speakers, meaning is given by way of sentences of the form of (T) only if these sentences pick out the sentences whose meaning they give under descriptions which will allow speakers who know all these (T)-like sentences, to use the language in virtue of that knowledge. For speaking and writing are, standardly, intentional actions, which occur, like all actions, under a description which is the agent's description. If the knowledge in sentences like (T) is to help with such linguistic actions, then it must connect truth conditions with sentences under the descriptions under which they are standardly produced.

It is this condition which T(SN) satisfies and T(N) does not. And it is for this reason that Davidson has to require that the name the theory uses for each sentence must be a structural-descriptive name. In this, it seems to me, Davidson is clearly right: any theory that states implicit knowledge of speakers by pairing sentences with their meanings – whether by way of truth conditions or not – would do well to follow him in this.

We have suggested two consequences of the change from a theory of truth to a theory of meaning. We must cope with token-reflexivity and we must insist on structural-descriptive names. So far so good.

But if Davidson's adaptation of the theory was to work, Tarski's adequacy condition would need to be further restated. To begin with, Tarski's account, in the version I cited above, is explicitly committed to stating sentences of the form of (T) in such a way that 'X' is a name of the sentence that takes the 'p' position. What is required for this is that the metalanguage – the language in which the T-theory is stated – should contain every sentence of the object-language – for which 'truth' is being defined. But a theory of meaning for, say, German, ought to be statable in English (or at least in an extended version of English to account for the things Germans do talk about that

English speakers do not) and

T(1): 'Schnee ist weiss' is true iff schnee ist weiss

which satisfies the adequacy criterion stated above is not a sentence of English (or any other language!). Tarski, well aware of this, offered an alternative to his 'homophonic' adequacy criterion:

[I]t suffices to assume that the object-language can be translated into the metalanguage; this necessitates a certain change in the interpretation of the symbol 'p' in (T).

(1943/44: 350)

The obvious change, as Tarski realised, would be simply to require that the sentence of the metalanguage in the 'p' position should be a translation of the sentence in the object-language of which 'X' is a name.

Now it is all very well for a theory of truth to take the notion of translation for granted: but it will hardly do in a theory of meaning. For a sentence S of L is a translation of a sentence R of L_1, just in case S and R mean the same. To presuppose the notion of translation in a theory of meaning would be to presuppose the notion of sameness of meaning.

It might be objected that the fact that it presupposes the notion of sameness of meaning is not in itself an objection to the use of the idea of translation in our account of meaning. After all, there is a perfectly standard account of what the natural numbers are, due to Frege and Russell, which takes for granted the notion of two sets being equinumerous; which amounts to explaining 'number' in terms of sameness-of-number. If this is permissible, what is wrong with a theory of meaning which presupposes a notion of sameness of meaning? So, at least, it might reasonably be asked.

There are important differences, however, between these two cases. For there is a good operational sense of what it is for the members of two sets to be in one-to-one correspondence, a sense which is plausibly conceptually prior to our conception of number. We *can* grasp the pairing of objects without the concept of natural number. On the other hand we do not seem to have a good grasp of the notion of sameness-of-meaning for sentences which is prior to our conception of the meanings of sentences. Such candidates as 'used by native speakers of the two languages in the same circumstances' are either too restrictive – circumstances are never the same in different linguistic groups – or too vague; and it is no use suggesting 'accepted by all bilinguals as equivalent' for that fails to tell us the content of the judgement the bilinguals are supposed to be making. At the very least, then, some account of what translation is, independent of the notion of meaning, is required.

But there is a second problem for the proposal to start with the notion of translation in an explanation of meaning: namely that to do so is simply to take ourselves one step back into a regress. We cannot explain the meanings of an object-language's sentences by saying what their translation is in some metalanguage: for what, then, is the meaning of the metalanguage sentence, which is what *we* know in understanding it? We do not want to answer that its meaning is given by translating it into some meta-metalanguage; this will leave us with a regress we cannot accept because we are trying to give an account of what speakers know. We must not lumber ourselves, as semanticists, with an infinitely ascending hierarchy of metalanguages.

Suppose we stop the regress, then, by saying that understanding sentences in the metalanguage is not knowing a translation, but is, in some way, given; does not need explaining. Then, of course, our knowledge of the meaning of the sentences of the metalanguage must consist in *something*; and if there is such a thing then it follows that we can explain meaning without appeal to the notion of translation.

The problem for Davidson, then, is what to substitute for Tarski's proposal that '*p*' should translate X.

Davidson's solution to the problem takes him a step away from Tarski. What he adds is not a further or different constraint on the sentences of the form of (T), but rather a constraint on the form of the whole theory of meaning, a constraint on how the sentences of the form of (T) are derived. In adding this holistic constraint, however, Davidson relies once more on Tarski: for what he too requires is that the theory of meaning should have some of the features of the theory of truth, which Tarski had proposed as satisfying his adequacy condition. To understand how this constraint works, we must say more about Tarski's theory of truth.

6.3 TARSKI'S TRUTH-THEORY

For this purpose, let us consider a very simple quantificational language, L, which has names

$$'a_1', 'a_2', \ldots .$$

and one-place predicates

$$'P_1', 'P_2', \ldots .$$

of each of which there is, of course, a finite number. We also have the symbols '&', '$\neg$' and '$\forall$' (for the universal quantifier), along with '(' and ')' to keep the syntax in order. Finally we allow ourselves a denumerable infinity of variables

$$'x_1', 'x_2', \ldots$$

We can define the syntax in the standard way for predicate calculi of the first order. Names and variables are singular terms. A predicate followed by a singular term is a formula. Negations and conjunctions of formulae are formulae; as are the universal quantifications of a formula. Finally we say what it is for the quantifier to bind a variable, and we can then define a sentence as a formula in which no variable occurs which is not bound.

With the simple language, L, we can display the essential features of a Tarskian truth-definition. For this purpose we need the notions of reference, of satisfaction, and of a sequence. Of these three none needs much introduction. For reference is just the ordinary notion: the reference of a name is whatever it names. And the root idea of the notion of satisfaction is easily grasped also. For simple subject–predicate sentences, satisfaction is the relation which holds between an object and the predicate iff the introduction of a name for the object in the subject position would make a true sentence. Satisfaction is just one of the relations which holds between my red pencil and 'is red': the relation, in fact, that makes the sentence 'My pen is red' true. What Tarski did was to generalise this notion so that we could specify the satisfiers for all sentential functions recursively: in a way that showed that the satisfiers of a sentential function could be picked out by functions from

(a) the satisfiers of the predicates it contained and the referents of the names, and

(b) the properties of its logical operators.

Sequences, finally, are just functions from the natural numbers to objects; they correspond to ordered sets of objects whose members are denumerably infinite in number.

Given this notion of a sequence, which we can regard as a purely formal device, going along with the co-ordinate notion of satisfaction, we can define the true sentences of the language L as those that are satisfied by all sequences.

I shall use a predicate variable, 'P_i', a name variable, 'a_i', a pair of sentence variables, 'U' and 'R', 'S' and 'S''' as variables for sequences, and the convention that

'n' + 'm'

(where 'n' and 'm' are names of any symbols in the language) is the structural descriptive name of the symbol which consists of what 'n' denotes followed by what 'm' denotes. Thus,

'(' + '&'

is a way of referring to the symbol which follows: (&

Then we can proceed, thus;

(1) *Names*

For each name we have an axiom of the form:

N: 'a_i' refers to a_i.

(2) *Predicates*

For each predicate we have an axiom of the form:

P: an object, O, satisfies the predicate 'P_i' iff $P_i O$.

And we can now specify satisfaction . . . and then truth.

(3) Any sequence S satisfies a predicate P_i concatenated with a name a_i iff the object to which the name refers satisfies P_i.

(4) Any sequence S satisfies a predicate P_i concatenated with the kth variable iff the kth member of the sequence satisfies P_i.

(5) Any sequence satisfies the sentence '(' + '$\neg$' + 'P_i' + ')' iff it does not satisfy P_i.

(6) Any sequence satisfies the sentence '(' + 'U' + '&' + 'R' + ')' iff it satisfies R and it satisfies U.

(7) Any sequence S satisfies the universal quantification of a formula R with respect to the kth variable, iff R is satisfied by all sequences S', which are like S, except in at most their kth term.

(8) A sentence is true iff it is satisfied by all sequences.

It is a little laborious to show that this truth-definition satisfies Tarski's adequacy definition, but, as he showed, it does. (This version comes from Platts (1979), where this is demonstrated.) It is easy to see, however, simply by glancing at (3) of the truth-definition, that, for any sentence formed by placing a name after a predicate, we can easily derive a sentence of the form of (T).

Take '$P_1 a_1$'. Rule (3), in conjunction with the axioms

a: 'a_1' refers to a_1

and

P: An object O satisfies 'P_1' iff $P_1 O$

allows us to conclude that a sequence satisfies '$P_1 a_1$' iff $P_1 a_1$. Since *which* sequence it is plays no part in the argument, we can conclude that '$P_1 a_1$' is satisfied by all sequences iff $P_1 a_1$. And this, with (8), gives us that

'$P_1 a_1$' is true iff $P_1 a_1$.

Tarski's theory uses satisfaction as one of its primitive concepts, and, in effect, defines truth in terms of it. All the other concepts involved seem pretty unproblematic. It has sometimes been objected against Tarski's account that it achieves little, since our grasp of the notion of satisfaction – which is, after all, a technical term of Tarski's – is parasitic upon our grasp of the concept of truth. Though I think this objection is misguided, it is anyway not necessary for Davidson to answer it. For he can put the definition the other way round.

Since he is using the theory to illuminate not truth but meaning, he can, as he does, take the notion of truth explicitly for granted. Granted the notion of truth, we can introduce satisfaction in terms of it, in rather the way I did intuitively earlier: an object O satisfies a predicate P_i, just in case concatenating a name of O with P_i would produce a true sentence. To get the full notion employed above we should need to change rule (4), for example, to read:

(4'): A sequence S satisfies a predicate P_i concatenated with the kth variable, iff concatenating a name of the kth member of the sequence with that predicate would produce a true sentence.

Provided we think, reasonably enough, that we could find a name for any object, this view of satisfaction would seem to do the job just as well as Tarski's.

It was the notion of satisfaction, along with the correlative notion of reference for names, which provided Davidson with his second constraint on theories of meaning. For he required not only that the theory should satisfy Tarski's adequacy condition – generating all the true sentences of the form of (T) – but also that it should derive them from true reference axioms for names and satisfaction conditions for predicates (and relations). Let us call this second constraint the requirement that the theory should be 'componential in Tarski's sense'; 'componential' for short.

We might ask why Davidson requires any second constraint at all. Why not require simply that a theory of meaning should allow us to derive all the sentences of the form of (T)? Davidson originally stressed as a motivation for the requirement (that the theory of meaning be componential) the fact that this would guarantee that the meanings of all sentences could be derived by recursions on finite axioms. This was important because, as I have said, he thought that a theory of meaning ought to be a theory which stated the implicit knowledge of speakers about their language. It would be absurd to suppose that speakers' knowledge was embodied in an infinite set of actual beliefs of the form of (T): first, because such an infinite set of actual beliefs could not be acquired in a finite time – which would make the meanings of the sentences unlearnable; and secondly, because on reasonable physicalist assumptions, only a finite number of actual mental states can be ascribed to anyone. People might, of course, be said to have an infinite number of beliefs in the sense of potential beliefs: beliefs they could have if they went through the necessary computation. But the class of potential beliefs is generated recursively from the finite set of actual beliefs. And if speakers' knowledge consisted of an infinity of beliefs about linguistic items, that infinity of beliefs would have to be potential; and it would have to be an infinity of beliefs, each of which could be generated recursively from the base of finite actual states.

But the finite axiomatisability of the truth-theory in Tarski's form is a feature it shares with many possible theories of meaning; possible worlds theories, for example. Davidson's main reason for insisting on componential theories comes out if we ask how he interprets the Tarskian adequacy condition.

In the passage from Tarski I quoted above, he uses in sentence (T) the expression 'if and only if' and he might be supposed to mean what he says. In the truth theories Tarski actually developed, however, the derived sentences are of the form

(T'): 'X' is true $\equiv p$.

So that Davidson has some warrant for the reading he gives of the 'if and only if' in (T) as being material equivalence. I shall, for this reason, state Davidson's interpretation of the Tarskian adequacy condition (familiarly known as 'Convention T') as follows:

> DAVIDSON: For a theory of truth to be a theory of meaning it must be possible to derive in it, for every sentence S, a true theorem of the form
>
> T: S is true $\equiv p$.

I shall call sentences of this form 'T-sentences', following Davidson; up until now I have been speaking of sentences of the form of (T), where (T) is Tarski's original formulation with 'if and only if' and not '$\equiv$'. Now it will be clear why I shall say that Davidson's first constraint was that the truth-theory should be extensionally adequate; for

S is true $\equiv p$

is true just in case 'S is true' and 'p' have the same truth-value.

Once we know what extensional adequacy is, we can see why Davidson had to have a second constraint. Take

G: 'Snow is white' is true $\equiv$ grass is green.

Given only Davidson's condition that a theory of meaning should allow us to derive for every sentence some true T-sentence, and given – what we can admit at least by way of hypothesis – that all tokens of

' "Snow is white" is true'

and

'Grass is green'

have the same truth-value, G is true. A truth-theory that allowed us to derive G but not

G': 'Snow is white' is true ≡ snow is white

would thus satisfy the adequacy condition, DAVIDSON. It is, at least *prima facie*, totally implausible that such a theory could give the meaning of 'Snow is white'.

Still, extensional adequacy has a great appeal, even if it will not do the job on its own. Truth conditions are defined as conditions logically necessary and sufficient for the truth of a sentence: if we could fix when a sentence would and would not be true in terms of when it actually is true, this would make the task of constructing a theory of truth conditions significantly easier than we might have expected. For one thing, there is much disagreement about the proper analysis of 'if' and 'only if' sentences, and none about the behaviour of material implication (and thus equivalence). If 'if and only if' in the T-sentence is just material equivalence, we can avoid this problem. For another: alternative accounts of truth conditions, which treat T-sentences as being governed by some modal operator, will involve us in more – and more doubtful – theoretical apparatus. Extensional adequacy is methodologically more parsimonious and relies on no controversial assumptions about conditional logic.

What is achieved, then, by the Davidsonian condition of componentiality? Davidson's intuition, I think, was that though it is easy enough to produce a trivial T-sentence like G if we lay down no constraints on how it is derived, it is much harder to see how we could derive it, if we had to derive it from an axiom for 'snow' and an axiom for the predicate 'is white'. The axiom

g: 'Snow' refers to grass

allows us to derive the true G', in conjunction with

w: an object O satisfies 'is white' ≡ O is green.

But add

h: 'Grass' refers to grass

and we get the false

S'': 'Grass is white' is true ≡ grass is green.

And anyway, g and w are not even true.

If Davidson's intuition had been correct, and we had been able to produce a theory that entailed the plausible

G': 'Snow is white' is true ≡ snow is white

just by producing a componential, extensionally adequate truth-theory, then he would have achieved the 'reduction' of the concept of meaning in terms of an austere list of other concepts – *object, sequence, expression, reference, satisfaction* – plus a little logical apparatus. Given the reducibility of satisfaction to truth which I suggested above, this list contains only notions we seem to have uses for anyway. If we had a theory which elucidated 'reference' causally, we should have a theory of meaning that used only one semantic concept essentially: that of truth. Seen this way, the Davidsonian programme seems to offer at least as much excitement as illumination.

As is now well known, however, Davidson's original claim that a theory of truth could provide a theory of meaning – a statement of the implicit knowledge of the competent speaker – just in case it was extensionally adequate and componential, has turned out to be ill founded. For reasons which are well stated by Foster and Loar in Evans and McDowell (1976) – reasons, of which it should be said in fairness, Davidson has been aware for some time (1976: 33-4) – these conditions are not enough. For it is possible to provide trivial variants of any truth-theory that are extensionally adequate and componential without being at all plausible as accounts of truth conditions, just because what replaces the '*p*' in many T-sentences does not look like an adequate truth condition at all. Thus to take an example of Foster's, suppose we had a truth-theory of the right form that had as consequences sentences like

    F: *S* is true $\equiv$ *a* is a part of *b*

then we can construct a similarly adequate truth-theory which has

    F': *S* is true $\equiv$ the earth moves and *a* is a part of *b*

as a consequence, just because the earth does move (Evans and McDowell, 1976: 12-14). All we need to achieve this result is to notice the English predicate:

    M: 'The earth moves and – is a part of – '.

Any ordered pair satisfies *M* iff it satisfies

    M': '– is a part of –'.

Consequently, since *M* and *M'* are coextensive, the axiom

    F (*A*): An ordered pair $\langle O_1, O_2 \rangle$ satisfies *M'* $\equiv$ the earth moves and O_1 is a part of O_2

will allow us to derive a T-sentence whenever

    F (*A*)': An ordered pair $\langle O_1, O_2 \rangle$ satisfies *M* $\equiv$ O_1 is a part of O_2

will; where a T-sentence is just a true sentence of the form

    T: *S* is true $\equiv$ *p*.

We could try to avoid this unhappy consequence by requiring that the T-theory which is simplest is the one that explains grasp of meaning. But this notion of simplicity is hard to make precise. Why, for example, does this satisfaction axiom seem intuitively adequate, even though not simple:

S(ACE): An event O satisfies the predicate '– is a tennis ace' iff O is a tennis service and O is 'in' and the designated receiver of O fails to return O.?

There seems to be a fatal difference between $F(A)$ and S(ACE) which has nothing to do with simplicity: $F(A)$ looks contingently true, while S(ACE) seems necessary. And we are inclined to think, as we saw in Chapter 5, that truth conditions are conditions which are logically – and not merely actually – necessary and sufficient for truth.

Davidson's reaction to these problems is, in essence, to give up the goal of an extensional theory: to return to interpreting the 'iff' of the T-sentence as a genuine (subjunctive) conditional.

Let me now trace the trail of that retreat. In his comments on Foster's paper, Davidson says this:

Foster's point is . . . that although my interpreter [who knows the T-theory] has a theory that satisfies Convention T, nothing in the theory itself tells him this.

We get a precise parallel if we ask what someone must know to be a physicist. A quick answer might be: the laws of physics. But Foster would say, and I agree, that this is not enough. The physicist must also know, (and here I speak for myself) that those laws *are* laws – i.e. that they are confirmed by their instances and support counterfactual and subjunctive claims. (1976: 36)

What consequences can we draw from these remarks? Davidson's proposal apparently amounts simply to this:[2] we must give up the old analysis – T – in favour of

T_s: S would be true iff it were the case that p

where – stipulatively – the conditionals are read however law-supported subjunctive conditionals should be read.

I call a theory which delivers sentences with this force a T_s-theory ('s' for 'subjunctive'); T_s exhibits the form of a T_s-sentence. Convention T_s says:

DAVIDSON': For a theory of truth to be a theory of meaning it must be possible to derive in it, for every sentence S, a true theorem of the form
T_s: S would be true iff it were the case that p.

The trouble with this is that there are objections to T_s-theory analogous to those that Davidson accepted against the original extensional T-theory. Consider for example any sentence which expresses an *a priori* proposition:

2. If this seems brisk, I charted the various options for Davidson more thoroughly in my 1981: Chapter 5.

e.g.

N: There are not any married bachelors.

Then, for any S which would be true iff it were the case that p, it is also true
that

1: (A) (t) (An utterance of S by A at t would be true iff it were the case
that p and there were not any married bachelors.)

We should be in even worse case if we could find some sentence R, clearly
different in meaning from S, such that it would be the case that p if and only
if it were the case that R; for then we could leave 'p' out of our T_s-sentence
altogether. We would still have the true

2: S uttered by a speaker at t would be true iff it were the case that R
at t

but this would not have much claim as an account of meaning.

There is now a dilemma for anyone who prefers T_s – to T-theory, a
dilemma to which Davidson could appeal by way of defence. On the one
horn, we can rule out apparently irrelevant T_s-sentences like 2 as accounts of
truth conditions on grounds other than straight falsehood – after all, they are
all *ex hypothesi* true – but then why could the original T-theory not be saved
by a similar strategy? On the other horn, we can accept sentences like 2,
leaving ourselves with implausible accounts of truth conditions as determining
meaning.

A priori truths like N raise problems for a truth-conditional theory of
meaning which we shall have to face anyway. So far, for example, since they
are all necessarily always true, we seem to have to give them all the same
meaning. But if there are cases where R is not equivalent to the conjunction
of 'p' and some *a priori* truth, a general solution to the problem raised by *a
priori* truths will not obviously address the problem created by 2.

Are there, then, any cases where we can find something to play the role of
R? The thought that there are is prompted by the fact that subjunctive
conditionals in the relevant interpretation are supported by natural laws. Now
amongst such consequences of laws are biconditionals of the form:

E: P happens iff Q does

where, if the standard account is correct, E has subjunctive force. Thus, for
example, not only is it a consequence of the law that all water is H_2O, that
(for some time t)

E': Water boils at t iff H_2O boils at t,

it is also a consequence of that law that

E'': Some water would have boiled at t iff some H_2O would have boiled at t.

And this fact will allow us to produce true T_s-sentences like

T(Water): 'Water is wet' would be true at t iff it were the case that H_2O were wet at t.

And the trouble with this is that it does not seem to be something every speaker must know implicitly. We might escape this sort of consequence of these subjunctive bi-conditionals for the T_s-theory, by insisting, as Davidson reasonably did for T-theory, on componentiality; by insisting that T_s-sentences be derivable from the satisfaction conditions for predicates and the references axioms for names. But the laws of nature also give us reason to think that there are predicates which are (or would be) satisfied just when other predicates are (or would be) and these would avoid this device as successfully and less artificially than Foster's counterexample (cited above as F) avoided it for T-theory.

Some philosophers, I fear, would embrace this result. Putnam, in one mood, has suggested that we state the truth conditions in our preferred language of science (1975b): what will allow him to distinguish between different forms of the T_s-theory, all of them true, is that only some of them have satisfaction conditions (and thus truth conditions) given in terms of fundamental particles. Thus, an extra, theoretical, constraint will reduce the available number of T_s-theories for him; and he might just agree that all these syntactically distinct theories were merely equivalent formulations of the same facts.

Davidson's thoughts about modifying the T-theory, with which we started, are not, however, meant to be so radical. And there is, from the point of view of an interest in the T_s-theory as a theory of meaning which characterises the speaker's implicit knowledge of their language, a fundamental flaw in adopting Putnam's proposal: no one can plausibly be held to govern their use of a language by way of rules stated in terms of particles about which most of us seem to have no beliefs at all. If Putnam thinks that 'every Hottentot and every Eskimo' has, appearances notwithstanding, beliefs about muons and leptons and such, an argument is needed to show that this is so. If it is not so, there is an argument against the proposal precisely on the same grounds as the argument against using anything but structural-descriptive names of sentences in stating truth-conditions. And those arguments are both to the effect that a theory of meaning must characterise sentences and their meanings under descriptions which are available to speakers, descriptions which determine which action they intend to perform in producing those sentences. It is no use knowing that a sentence S is true iff a class of particles is in a certain state, if we do not know anything about those particles or that state: any more than it is any use knowing that 1 is true iff snow is white. if we do not know how to produce a token of the type '1' picks out.

The only way left, then, seems to be to return to the strategy of dealing with deviant truth conditions by way of constraints on the T_s-sentences other than truth. What these would be is still, I think, mysterious.

6.4 TRUTH CONDITIONS ARE NOT ENOUGH

At this point we should do well to go back to our first intuitions. The view that the meaning of 'Snow is white' is known by anyone who knows both

(a) that 'Snow is white' is true if snow is white

and

(b) that snow is white if 'Snow is white' is true

(where the conditionals 'have subjunctive force') was what gave Davidson's original proposal all its plausibility. Surely this, at least, is true?

Unfortunately the answer to this question, whatever the details of the correct theory of the conditional, must be: No. These may be necessary conditions for a knowledge of the meaning of the sentence 'Snow is white'; but they are certainly not sufficient. For, if they were, to know of any sentence S that

(c) S is true if snow is white

and

(d) If snow is white S is true

ought to be enough to know that S means that snow is white. But consider the sentence

'Frozen H_2O crystals reflect the light throughout the visible spectrum'

(and suppose it to be true; this is bad physics, but the point is good). I shall abbreviate this sentence as L. I know, of 'Snow is white' that

(A) 'Snow is white' is true if L

and

(B) If L, then 'Snow is white' is true.

But it does not follow from this fact that 'Snow is white' means that L.

Even the requirement of componentiality will not help us here. For that is just the requirement that one's knowledge that A and that B should be derived from satisfaction conditions for predicates and reference axioms for names;

and (treating 'snow' for convenience as a name) we can derive the T_s-sentence

T(L): 'Snow is white' would be true iff it were the case that L,

from axioms of this kind. For

a('snow'): 'Snow' refers to frozen crystals of H_2O

and

P('white'): An object O does or would satisfy the predicate 'is white' iff O reflected or reflects the light throughout the visible spectrum.

The problem is simply stated: it is *a posteriori* that 'snow' denotes frozen crystals of H_2O. What is *a posteriori* is an epistemic question. And it is *epistemic* considerations that matter here, for we are trying to capture speakers' knowledge. If it is not known to speakers that 'snow' denotes this frozen H_2O, then an axiom for 'snow' like a('snow') cannot form part of the implicit knowledge of a speaker; and we cannot ascribe that knowledge to speakers by allowing it in the T_s-theory.

This objection to T_s-theory relies on intuitions about meaning. But provided we can avail ourselves of a simple theory of the relations between beliefs and sentences (used in assertion), we can draw on the account of the truth conditions of beliefs in Chapter 5, to make this objection depend not on intuition but on theory. The assumption we need is

EXP: that the truth conditions of a sentence, in a certain context, are the truth conditions of the belief it would express in that context.

I defend a view with this consequence in the chapter that follows, but it is a plausible enough assumption, so let us make it provisionally.

I argued in Chapter 5 that the truth conditions of a belief were conditions such that, *a priori*, the belief would be true iff those conditions held. What this meant was that anyone who had the concept of the belief and who was computationally perfect would know that the belief was true if and only if those conditions held. Now T_s-sentences can be sentences like T(L). And though this is, *ex hypothesi*, true it is not true that any computationally perfect agent with the concept of the belief that snow is white must know that that belief is true iff frozen H_2O reflects throughout the visible spectrum. Far from knowing it, a computationally perfect agent might even not have the concept of H_2O at all.

The reason we have been misled is, of course, that though T(L) will not do the job, there are sentences of the form of T_s-sentences that do have on their right-hand side a sentence that states the truth conditions of the sentence named on the left-hand side. Thus

'Snow is white' is true iff snow is white.

Anyone who was computationally perfect and had the concept of the belief that snow is white, would know that that belief is true iff snow is white; so that the condition on the right-hand side of this biconditional is, in fact, the truth condition of the belief the sentence expresses, and, assuming EXP, is thus the truth condition of that sentence. The problem is that we do not have in Davidson's work any account of how we are to develop a theory which entails only T_s-sentences of this acceptable kind.[3]

But even if we did have such a theory, there is an irresistible objection to regarding it as a theory of meaning, at least on the assumption that sentences express beliefs. For I pointed out in Part I that we cannot individuate beliefs by their truth conditions. That Mary has at some time a belief whose truth conditions are that S does not entail, for any particular S, that she believes that S. Even if we had a theory that assigned to every sentence the truth conditions of the belief it expressed, we would still not know what belief each sentence expressed. If knowledge of the meaning of a sentence is knowledge of what belief it expresses, a theory of truth conditions could not, therefore, be a theory of meaning. As I say, this consequence depends on assuming that sentences express particular beliefs, and that I have not yet argued.

It is important to see that what I have argued is that a theory of truth conditions will not do as theory of meaning, not that there is no place for assigning to sentences truth conditions at all. Indeed, quite the contrary: for the assumption of EXP entails that sentences have truth conditions. And it follows from the theory I shall give that speakers know implicitly the truth conditions of beliefs. So if it is *a priori* true that a belief has a certain truth condition, then any agent who knows a mapping from the sentence to the belief it expresses is capable of making computations which will show that the sentence expresses a belief with those truth conditions. If a theory is 'realist' iff it ascribes truth conditions to sentences, and requires that speakers have an implicit knowledge of them, then none of this chapter challenges realism at all.

I have spent most of this chapter arguing that Davidson's T-theory, even modified in a way hinted at in his reply to Foster, will not do: it will not do as an account of truth conditions and it will not do as an account of meaning. Still, the problems I have raised for Davidson have to be solved by any adequate theory, and it will turn out that we can put some of the materials of his theory to good use in solving them. Thus we have seen any theory of meaning must map structural-descriptive names of sentences into meanings, and deal with token-reference; and any theory of truth conditions can use the *form* of Tarski's theory. Each of these facts is relied on in the next chapter.

It is time now to turn to this positive account.

3. Though his work on radical translation (Davidson, 1974) is excellent, I do not believe it solves this problem.

7

Assertion

The truthful speaker wants not to assert falsehoods, wherefore he is willing only to assert what he takes to very probably true.

(Lewis, 1976: 297)

7.1 OVERVIEW

In Part I of this book I was concerned almost exclusively with minds. The last chapter was concerned very largely with language and relatively little with mind. In this chapter I want to give my own view of assertion, a view which connects language and mind. I want to show how, given our theory of the nature of beliefs, it is relatively easy to give an account of declarative meaning. This task will seem to some of our contemporary anti-psychologists – such components of 'psychologism' in semantics as Dummett (1973: *passim*) – absurd. It is not possible, they have held, to carry out this project because, in Davidson's (1975) words, 'without speech . . . we cannot make . . . fine distinctions between thoughts'. My project, from this point of view, is circular. For I assume that we can ascribe beliefs and then go on to say what terms in the agent's language mean; whereas they hold that I need meanings to ascribe the beliefs.

Let me mention three reasons why I have ignored their position here. First, and importantly, I can simply admit some of what Davidson is claiming. There is no doubt that many of the fine distinctions between thoughts we often rely on only exist, as a matter of causal fact, in language speakers. So we cannot make these fine distinctions in prelinguistic animals because there are no such distinctions to make. It may even be that there are kinds of belief which you could not have without possessing a language: indeed, if knowing a language is, as I argue in this chapter, a matter of having beliefs about linguistic items, this is indeed so. My project would only be threatened if there was reason to think that we should need to know the meanings of the words speakers used in order to ascribe to them the beliefs which constitute knowledge of meaning. And this I deny.

Secondly, as I said in Chapter 1, there is much recent philosophical writing, for example by Jonathan Bennett (1976) and Jerry Fodor (1976), which devotes much time and energy to arguing that the fine distinctions in thought we can make in speakers, we could in principle make independently of ascribing meanings to utterances. My position is thus, at least, one that has been seriously defended recently.

Finally, as promised in Chapter 1, I have tried deliberately in the first five chapters to discuss minds in ways that presuppose nothing about whether the agents have a language or about the meanings of their utterances if they have. Part of the support for my view that we can develop the rich psychological account of agents I presuppose, without knowledge of the meanings of terms in the agents' language, is just that I have done so.

7.2 UTTERANCE

I have already said roughly what I take the role of assertion to be: speakers use sentences in assertion to express their beliefs. Someone knows what a declarative sentence means, I think, if they know what belief that sentence expresses, whether uttered by them or by others. My task in this chapter is to make this claim more precise. I seek to show what kind of mapping from sentences to beliefs competent speakers have a grasp of; and in doing this I am able to make use of the T-theory I introduced in the last chapter. At the end of this chapter we shall have a theory we can put to use in addressing the semantics of indicative conditionals.

Because I am interested in assertion I shall be talking about declarative sentences: sentences whose grammatical form shows that they are primarily used in assertion. I do not want to try to characterise the class of declarative sentences any more precisely than this. In the end, in my view, we should characterise the declarative sentences of a language as those sentences which are (standardly) used, in the ways I shall now be specifying, to express beliefs. At this stage I wish only to rely on our intuitive grasp of the distinction between those sentences which we call, colloquially, statements or assertions, on the one hand, and, on the other, such classes of sentences as questions or imperatives or what used to be called 'optatives' – sentences of the form 'Would that . . . ' It is the sentences we call statements or assertions that I mean by the term 'declaratives': and part of my task is to give a systematic account of the features of such sentences.

I have spoken so far simply of sentences, leaving it open whether I am speaking of types or tokens. But we cannot suppose that those rules which give the grammar of a sentence are attached to tokens: for competent speakers have a capacity which they can exercise with any token of the type. In fact, there is also a problem about trying to specify which type sentences are declarative. The difficulty is quite simple: two utterances of the type sentence 'John is coming', of which one has a 'flat' intonation profile and the other a

144

rising intonation, will count in English as a statement and a question respectively. And even if we were to include the intonation profile as part of the specification of a type sentence (which we should probably want to do anyway), we should still be left with problems. For a sentence such as 'You will be coming' may count in certain dialects of English as sometimes a statement, sometimes an order. And though it is possible to think of ways in which the utterance of a sentence in someone's presence expressing the belief that they will come, might sometimes constitute an order, it is not clear *prima facie* that these reasons sufficiently explain why, say, an utterance by a sergeant-major of the sentence 'You will come at 10.00 a.m., sir', to a young officer training at Sandhurst or West Point, feels very unlike a standard assertion.

For these reasons I shall prefer to speak of declarative uses of type sentences, rather than of declarative type sentences. And I wish to give an account of the declarative meaning of type sentences: where that is what a competent speaker has to know about sentences in order to understand declarative uses of them. Because some sentences in English have both declarative and non-declarative uses, this will involve, amongst other things, a knowledge of how to bring information to bear about the context in which a sentence is uttered, in order to decide whether it is being used declaratively. Thus, if I utter the one-word sentence 'Snow', in answer to the question 'What shall I bring you from the Antarctic?', then that sentence is not the expression of a belief, but of a desire. But if I were to utter it in response to the question 'What is all that white stuff?', then it would express a belief; the belief, namely, that that white stuff is snow. Competent speakers of English know how each of these two questions provides a context for the sentence 'Snow'; and that it is only in response to the second question that it constitutes an assertion.

I have already assumed that an account of the meaning of a sentence is an account of what competent speakers have to know about that sentence in order to know what it means. Dummett has put the matter thus:

what a theory of meaning has to give an account of is what it is that someone knows when he knows a language; that is, when he knows the meaning of the expressions and sentences of the language. (1975: 99)

It may seem truistic that the meaning of a sentence is what someone who knows the meanings of that sentence knows. But Dummett's way of putting the matter is not, in fact, a truism. First, because, as he has expressed it, we are required to have a theory which says what competent speakers know; and thus, it may be assumed, we are required to have a theory which talks about speakers' knowledge. Dummett himself allows that a theory of meaning might consist of sentences of the form 'The sentence/expression X means that

. . . ', where there is no explicit mention of speakers or their knowledge. But even if we were to have a theory of this form, we should still need to know how knowledge of the meaning, so conceived, results in the capacity to use the language. This task is especially urgent for me, as I am committed to functionalism. Knowledge of meaning is presumably a psychological state: and I should like to be able to give an account of that state in terms of the notions of belief, desire, intention and the rest, for which I think that functionalism will do. Such an account will show how being in the state of knowing the meaning of a sentence will lead to action – including linguistic action – in response to events – including linguistic events – in the world.

This brings me to the second respect in which Dummett's claim is not a truism. *Prima facie*, what competent speakers know is *how* to use their language. It is not at all obvious that their knowledge is the kind of theoretical 'knowledge-that' which we should capture in a sentence saying that an expression has a certain meaning, or expresses a certain belief. Perhaps, when competent speakers wish to express the belief that snow is white, they are simply caused to utter the sentence 'Snow is white'; not because they know that the sentence expresses in that context the belief that snow is white; not in virtue of knowledge of the truth of any theoretical proposition saying what that sentence means at all.

Why, then, should we treat knowledge of meaning as theoretical knowledge, knowledge-that, rather than knowledge-how?

We need to begin by saying, what should be sufficiently obvious, namely that utterances are actions. The utterance of a sentence is a performance in whose causation the beliefs and desires of a speaker play a part. I say 'There is a car we can use' partly because I think that if I say this you will come to believe that there is a car we can use; I think you will come to believe this partly because I think that my saying it will cause you, provided you believe I am honest, to believe that I believe there is a car we can use. Since I believe you also think that I am likely to know whether there is such a car, I expect you to come to believe that what I believe is true; and thus to come to believe it also. This background of my beliefs about your beliefs, together with my desire that you should believe that there is a car available, means that if I calculate the utility of the basic action of uttering the sentence, it comes out higher in my preference ranking than any other basic action. So I utter the sentence.

Notice first that nothing in this explanation involves ascribing to me beliefs about what the sentence 'There is a car we can use' means. I have referred to beliefs about relations between the sentence and my own and other people's beliefs; and the explanation is only correct if I do have such beliefs. It is beliefs of this kind that I shall ascribe in my account of what it is to know the meaning of a sentence; and my claim is that no part of my account involves ascribing to speakers beliefs which we do not in fact normally rely on their having in our everyday explanations of what they say and their reactions to the utterances of others. At the end of 7.4, I shall have a theory of meaning that works in such a way that the explanation I have just offered of the psychological background to my utterance, establishes it as a display of my knowledge of its meaning. My answer to the question why we should ascribe to speakers knowledge-that, about sentences, and not merely knowledge-how, then, is simply that speakers do seem to have such 'theoretical' knowledge. And the evidence for this, I claim, is that we advert to this knowledge regularly and successfully, in explaining the utterances of competent speakers. Indeed, as I think, we could not explain some of the linguistic acts which speakers perform in virtue of their knowledge of meaning unless they had these beliefs.

7.3 SENTENCES AND BELIEFS

We must look now for a specification of the declarative meaning of a type sentence S, in terms of a function from contexts of utterance to the belief that tokens of the sentence would express in that context. This function must be specified for sentences under structural descriptions, for the reasons we considered in the last chapter. And having said what that function is, we must say what a speaker has to know about the relations between the sentence and the belief to know that the sentence expresses the belief.

In English it is a relatively trivial task to say what belief a sentence expresses. Where the sentence S contains no token-referential expressions, we can usually pick out the belief that it expresses simply by calling it the belief that S. 'Snow is white' expresses the belief that snow is white.

For sentences containing token-referential expressions, the problem is a little more difficult. Thus an utterance by John of the sentence 'I am happy' expresses John's belief that he is happy. And, in general, an utterance by a speaker A of a sentence of the form 'I am . . . ' expresses the speaker's belief that A is . . . For 'now' and 'here', however, an account which is less natural, but equally adequate, is available. 'John is now happy' uttered at t expresses the speaker's belief at t that John is then happy. It certainly does not express the belief that John is happy at t: for the speaker may not know that it is time t. Nor would it be right to say that every utterance of this sentence does or did or will express the belief that John is *now* happy; for that belief is only true if John is *now* happy, at the moment I write, and not at the time that the utterance was or will be made.

It would, at any rate, be an interesting task to settle for English how we go from a sentence S to the belief that it expresses. And, indeed, I have just assumed until now, that we can do this, because I have called the belief that a sentence S expresses the belief that S; relying on the fact that, in English, simply placing 'the belief that' before a sentence will often produce a term that picks out the right belief. I shall continue to use my 'belief that S' convention for the moment, supposing that, where the sentence is token-referential the proper adjustments have been made to account for the fact that it is so.

But even when this is done, we shall not have characterised the mapping from sentences in contexts to beliefs that we need for our theory of meaning. For though we write our theory of meaning *in* English, we do not wish to be restricted to writing theories of meaning *for* English. And we cannot pick out the belief that, for example, 'Schnee ist weiss' expresses in German, by way of an English expression, such as 'The belief that schnee ist weiss'. For there is no such expression in English.

How, then, are we to proceed? In the first part of this book I characterised beliefs in a functionalist theory. That theory individuated beliefs as states of the form $\langle B, A, t, p(S), C(S) \rangle$.

Consider now the last member of this quintuple. It seems that if we are to find a belief for a sentence to express we must be able at least to find a mapping from sentences in contexts to the computational structures of the beliefs they express. We saw in Chapter 5 that computational structure determines truth conditions of beliefs, but not vice versa; for beliefs with the same truth conditions may differ in computational structure. It will not be enough, then, to state the truth conditions of a belief expressed by a sentence: for that will not individuate a single belief as the belief that sentence expresses. Rather, we must state a mapping from sentences to their computational structures. In 7.5 I give an account of a theory that allows us then to assign truth conditions to sentences, as a function of the computational structure of the belief each sentence expresses.

For the moment let us suppose that we have a theory which allows us, given any sentence of language, to map that sentence, S, onto the computational structure of the belief that it expresses in a given context. We can turn, then, to an account of what the competent speaker has to believe about the relations between utterances of sentences and the beliefs they express: to an account, in other words, of expression.

7.4 CONVENTIONS OF EXPRESSION

David Lewis has provided us with a theory which says that it is for conformity to any regularity of behaviour to be conventional. I simply cite that account now in order to apply it to the case in hand: for I shall claim that all that is necessary to know the declarative meaning of a sentence is to be a member of a population every member of which conventionally uses tokens of that sentence to express a belief, and to know, for each context and each sentence, what belief that is.

Let us begin then with Lewis' account of convention. A regularity in the behaviour of an agent X exists iff there is some A which the agent does when or only when a certain condition, C, obtains. If there is a regularity in the behaviour of some person, X, I say, following Lewis, that they conform to the regularity of doing A when (or only when) some condition obtains. In general, where the regularity R consists in X's doing A when (or only when) C obtains, I say that X conforms to the regularity R. Now we can give Lewis' account of what it is for conformity to a regularity to be conventional.

A regularity R is a convention for a population P iff

(1) Every member of P conforms to R;
(2) Everyone in P believes the others conform to R;
(3) This belief (2) gives every one a good and decisive reason to conform to R themselves.
(4) There is general preference for general conformity to R, rather than slightly less than general conformity;
(5) R is not the only possible regularity satisfying the last two conditions;
(6) (1) to (5) are matters of common knowledge: they are known to all members of P, it is known to everyone that they are known to every one, and so on.

Someone conforms to the convention R iff they are a member of P; see Lewis (1975a).

Given such an account of what it is for a regularity to be conventional all that is needed for our purposes is an account of what the regularity is, conformity to which constitutes a person as knowing the language of a certain linguistic community.

I am developing the view that assertion is the expression of belief. The obvious place to begin, then, is by stating the regularity as one of uttering a sentence only when we want to express the belief it expresses. We have already assumed that we know how, given a sentence and its context, we can specify what belief it expresses. And I shall show how that specification is to proceed in the next section. We shall have for every sentence, S, and for every context specified in the appropriate way, C, a function that gives a certain belief as its value for the pair $\langle S, C \rangle$. Let us call the belief that S expresses in the context C the belief in C that S, for short. Then the relevant regularity will presumably be:[1]

---

1. This is not a terribly good way of putting it for token-reflexive beliefs. But we must just remember that 'S' itself in 'that S' may be of the form 'he is . . .' or '. . . then . . .' or '. . . there . . .' etc.

R1: For all $\langle S, C \rangle$, using S in a context C only if you intend to express the belief in C that S.[2]

There are objections, however, to stating the regularity this simply. First of all, and less seriously, there are in English conventions about the intonation profile of a sentence which allow us, in irony and sarcasm, facetiousness and so on, to use a token of a sentence to express beliefs other than those we are 'literally' expressing (where, I take it, what we are literally expressing is just what we would be expressing if we used the sentence with the normal intonation profile). This problem arises because we specify sentence tokens usually without saying anything about their intonation. From now on, then, let us assume that the intonation profile of a sentence is part of its structural description; and that, in all examples, the intonation is the standard 'literal' one.

There is a second and slightly more difficult problem, in that we use sentences when acting or in fictions in ways that do not amount to expressing any beliefs at all. In the absence of any contrary indication – such as the fact of our being on a stage, or, in the case of written fiction, the fact of introducing utterances as fiction – we shall be taken to be expressing beliefs. So that we can take account of this by modifying R1 so that it requires not that speakers utter sentences only when they intend to express the relevant belief, but that they utter sentences only when this condition holds, *and* no other convention is prevailing. I shall call all these other conventions non-assertion conventions. Then we can modify R1 to get

R2: For all $\langle S, C \rangle$, using S in context C, only if either
   (a) you intend to express the belief in C that S, or
   (b) a non-assertion convention is operating.

We could deal with this problem in another way, marking contexts for the presence or absence of those features which mark the fact that such a non-assertion convention is or is not operative. Either way, we shall need to take care that what we say in specifying non-assertion conventions is not directly parasitic on our account of assertion. Otherwise the account would be circular. But there is no reason why this should not be done. We could, for example, mark the context of an utterance with a 'PLAY' marker, and explain what the convention is for such utterances in plays; and we need only say that the presence of the features of the context that make the marker apt,

---

2. I say 'only if' and not 'if and only if' because many sentences in the same language may express the same belief.

I have not offered a functionalist analysis of the concept of intention. I am inclined to think that one could be given in terms of the concepts of belief, desire and causation. But I do not want to offer any suggestion, since the analysis does not look to me to be easy; and all that I require is simply that it should be possible.

mean that the convention R1 does not apply. From now on, however, I ignore this problem. We might call this 'speech-act' ambiguity; and I also ignore problems raised by lexical and syntactic ambiguity in the sentence uttered.[3]

We need now to say what it is to express a belief: the required answer is quite simple. It is to do something which gives others evidence that you have that belief. I realise that this is a somewhat extended notion of expression. We would not normally be held to have expressed a belief which was displayed in the course of an attempt to conceal it. Thus, if someone, lying, says 'No' to a question and rattles their tea-cup, thus revealing their dishonesty, then we would not normally speak of the rattling of the cup as their expressing the belief they were trying to conceal. But I think that the reason that it is incorrect to say that Mary expressed her belief by rattling the cup, is that the rattling of the cup was not intended to express the belief; and we normally speak of people doing one thing, E, *by* doing another, M, when they intend that doing M should bring it about that E. If E is the unintended consequence of doing M, it is at least misleading to say that someone did E, *simpliciter*. So I do not say that this will do as a general account of expression; only that it will do here; see Schiffer (1972). So now we have as the upshot,

K: knowledge of the (declarative) use of the sentences of a language, L, in assertion is conformity to the convention
R: For all S in L, and for all C, use S in C only when you intend to give other members of P who come to believe you have uttered S in C, a reason to believe that you believe in C that S.[4]

I shall now fill in one final detail of an account of mastery of declarative usage. On my account of belief, it admits of degrees. We can write the degree of the belief expressed by a sentence S in a context C as $p(C[S])$. Now it seems reasonable to suppose that we do not only utter sentences of whose truth we wish to make others believe we are certain. If we did, we should have to say a great deal less than we do. For, on our theory only *a priori* truths will have probability 1 in computationally perfect agents; and, since most people know enough about us to realise that we are not going to be absolutely certain

3. This could be dealt with in an obvious way by recognising that there is no function from sentences in contexts to beliefs but rather a function from sentences in contexts to sets (sometimes one-membered) of beliefs; we can call the members of these sets, for any sentence S and context C, the beliefs that S may express in C and then have the rule
   R3: For all ⟨S, C⟩, using S in context C, only if you want to express one of the beliefs that S may express in S.
4. Remember we are leaving aside considerations of 'speech-act', lexical and syntactic ambiguity. (We need the extra requirement – that the utterance should be addressed to a member of P – because speakers must know there is no point in addressing remarks in their own languages to non-members of P.)

of most of what we believe, we are hardly likely to succeed in persuading them that we are certain. The modification of R that this suggests is

R$_{prob}$: For all S in L, and for all C, uttering S in C only when you intend to give other members of P who hear a reason to believe that your $p(C[S])$ is fairly high.[5]

So, if people know a mapping for every S and C to the belief in C that S, we know now what they would do with it: they would conform to a complex convention R, in the specification of which that function would play a part. We can now say what a theory of that mapping must be like.

7.5 SENTENCES AND COMPUTATIONAL STRUCTURE

Agents with all our concepts, can be said to know what our sentences mean iff they both

(a) have beliefs about linguistic items sufficient to generate by computations of which they are capable, the mapping from sentences to the computational structures of beliefs; and

(b) know how to use that knowledge in conformity with the convention R$_{prob}$.

I have already argued that our functionalist theory is *a priori*. It would be known, in consequence, to any computationally perfect agent with our concepts. Since that theory entails a mapping from the computational structure of beliefs to their truth conditions, it will follow that a mapping from sentences to the computational structures of beliefs, will entail, along with the general theory, an account of the truth conditions of the beliefs expressed by all sentences.

And, if the truth conditions of a sentence are the truth conditions of the belief that it expresses, then a computationally perfect agent will know what the truth conditions of every sentence are.

Following this route from sentences to their truth conditions, by way of the beliefs they express, will allow us to put to use results in T-theory to construct the mapping from computational structures to truth conditions, as I shall show. But it will also guarantee that the knowledge we ascribe to

---

5. In fact, there are cases where what is required is not that the probability of S be high; but rather that the probability of some related representation should have a probability in some range. For an example, see 7.5 and 11.4, where I consider the case of epistemic modal sentences like 'Mary may be coming'.

How high e is, will, of course, depend on C: idle gossip may make more (or less!) demands than conference discussion or the courts.

speakers – in supposing them to know the function from sentences to beliefs – is sufficiently rich to account for their mastery of their language, because it tells us more about the beliefs expressed than just their truth conditions.

Following this route also suggests that there are two sets of problems about the mapping from sentences to their truth conditions: first, problems about the mapping from sentences to beliefs; secondly, problems about the mapping from beliefs to truth conditions.

How, then, first, are we to get from sentences to the beliefs they express? We must begin by making full use of the specification of a belief I urged in Part I. I argued there that a token belief is really specified by a quintuple $\langle B, A, t, p(R), C(R) \rangle$; that is by saying that it is a belief, whose it is, when, that it has a certain probability, and a certain computational structure. Strictly what we need is a function which takes as input ordered pairs consisting of contexts of utterances and sentence tokens, specified under structural descriptions as for the T-theory of the previous chapter, and produces as output, appropriate quintuples of the form: $\langle B, A, t, p(R), C(R) \rangle$. The $p(R$ value will most usually simply be specified as being near to 1. But we cannot ignore it in general, since some elements of sentences reflect not the computational structure of the belief, nor whose it is, nor when; but facts about the probability value. But the general idea is simple (see 11.5): 'Mary may be coming' uttered by John at t, reflects the belief $\langle B,$ John, $t, (k > e), C$(Mary is coming)$\rangle$, (for some small e.) That is, it expresses a belief state of John's which is not of very low probability. In saying it, John gets us to see that he does not have a low degree of belief that Mary is coming.

I have already said that I intend to say very little about the computational structure of beliefs below the 'sentential' level. But – at the level of truth-functions of representations – the mapping from sentences to the computational structures of beliefs will, for example, take every sentence of the form 'S and R' into a belief of computational structure $\langle C(S), C(R), \text{CONJ} \rangle$; and similarly for 'or' (using DISJ) and 'not' (using NEG) in the way suggested by the model of computational structure of Chapter 4.

Clearly a full theory would have to say how words mapped into representational elements at below the 'sentential' level; so that, for every name, for example, such as 'John', there will be an element in the representational system onto which it maps, C(John). And similarly, for predicates, such as '– is red', there will be analogous elements of the system of representations such as C(Red). Suppose then we are considering a system of representations which is just of the form of the language we considered in Chapter 6: it has just a list of those representational items corresponding to singular terms (which I shall call singular elements)

'a_1', 'a_2', . . . , 'a_n',

and to predicates (which I shall call predicate elements)

'P_1', 'P_2', . . . , 'P_m'.

Then there will be a system of axioms in our theory which go from every name to its $C(a_i)$; and from every predicate to its $C(P_i)$. And finally there will then be rules which, given the structural description of a sentence and the computational structures of the representational elements corresponding to each of the words, produce a computational structure for the belief expressed. We may identify this with the ordered n-tuple of the computational structures corresponding to each word of the sentence. So that for a simple sentence, such as 'John is coming', we could identify the computational structure of the belief with the ordered pair $\langle C(\text{John}), C(- \text{ is coming})\rangle$.

Even saying only this little about the computational structure of representations, we can now see that there is an obvious way to put to use the T-theory of the last chapter, in giving an account of the truth conditions of representations.

For we can now give the outlines of a function from computational structures to truth conditions. In general, then, we suppose that at the sub-sentential level, every $C(R)$ for representation R, is a function of the ordered n-tuple of minimal representational elements. So we might as well identify $C(R)$, where R has the elements

$\langle (a), (b), . . . , (n)\rangle$,

with the ordered n-tuple

$\langle C(a), C(b), . . . , C(n)\rangle$.

For each minimal representational element, (a), we shall need an axiom which gives its $C(a)$.

Suppose the system of representations has the very simple structure I suggested above, consisting only of singular elements and one-place predicate elements. Then we can set up a function *den*, which, given as argument, $C(a)$, for any singular term (a), the time, t, and the agent A, gives as its value an object, for that agent at that time, which is the object which (a) denotes. *Which* object *den* $(A, t, C(a))$ is, for any $C(a)$, is a problem in the theory of reference.

There will also be a function *ext*, which, given $C(P)$ for any predicate (P), the time t, and the agent A, gives as its value the extension of that predicate.

Thus, if the class of things that satisfy *ext*, which I call '*ext*(*A*, *t*, *C*(*P*))', is the class of red things, for some (*P*), it is also the class of *w*-emitters; see 5.3.

Both *den* and *ext* are extensional: if the object that some name denotes for some agent at some time is this table, then it picks out also the oldest piece of furniture in my rooms. Similarly, if all and only the red objects in the world have, at the moment, some strange disjunction of properties, then *ext*(Me, now, *C*(− is red)) picks out that strange class.

But though the functions are thus extensional, the *a priori* theory has to specify them somehow: and it specifies them in terms of some referring expression for objects and some predicate expression for extensions. In particular, if the predicate is (− is red), then if I am able to have beliefs about things being red, I will specify *ext*(*A*, *t*, (− is red)) for all agents and all times as the class of things that are red. This will be *a priori*. If I were to discover that

(*t*) (Something is red at *t*, iff it *w*-emits at *t*)

then I should know then that *ext*(*A*, *t*, (− is red)) picks out the class of *w*-emitters. But this would be *a posteriori* knowledge.

This is, of course, simply the manifestation at the sub-sentential level of Chapter 5's distinction between causal truth conditions and truth conditions *simpliciter*. There I said that someone who had beliefs about things being red would know that the belief that something is red is true iff that thing is red: that they would, in other words, represent to themselves the truth conditions of the belief by way of the very concepts that the belief contained. Here we see that if someone has the capacity for having beliefs about redness, then they will represent to themselves the extension of the concept of redness by way of that very concept.

Once we suppose that agents know the denotation of these singular elements; we can then use the apparatus of T-theory in the obvious way to generate an account of the truth conditions of representations; and we can thus guarantee that we can assign truth conditions to every representation given only a finite stock of axioms and satisfaction rules. We call the function from *C*(*R*) to the truth conditions of *R*, T, and its value for any *R*, T(*R*).

It should now be clear, given the account of T-theory in the last chapter, how the function T is definable in terms of *den* and *ext*. And because these functions are defined for speakers and times, which is an improvement on the sketch of the T-theory offered in Chapter 6, we shall be able to deal with token-reference. Thus,

A: An object *O* is in *ext*(*A*, *t*, *C*(− was red)) iff *O* is (atemporally) red at some time before *t*.

For singular terms, the relevance of token-referentiality is not so immediately obvious. But consider the sentence 'This is red'.[6] The belief that this sentence expresses has a computational component corresponding to 'this', which makes the belief about some object in the agent's vicinity. So $den(A, t, C(\text{this}))$ will have to denote one object before the agent; and on another occasion it may denote something else. Given the conventions about referring, there will be something about the context in which the agent utters 'this' which will tell us the value of $den(A, t, C(\text{this}))$. Let us call that object $O1$.

Then

$den(A, t, C(\text{this}))$ is $O1$

and

O is in $ext(A, t, C(-\text{ is red})$ iff O is red at t

will allow us to infer, using the structure of T-theory,

$T(A, t, C(\text{This is red}))$ is true iff $O1$ is red at t.

Given the general scheme,

For all A, for all t, $den(A, t, C(I))$ is A at t

we can derive the T value of the belief expressed, for example, by 'I am happy', as

$T(A, t, C(\text{I am happy})) \;=\; A$ is happy at t.

There is thus every prospect of getting from sentences to their truth conditions by way of the function which takes each sentence S to $C(S)$; and each $C(S)$ to $T(A, t, C(S))$. And this way we get truth conditions without the commitment that Davidson had to a purely truth-conditional theory of meaning.

7.6 SUMMARY

I have spent this chapter trying to say what people have to know if they are to know the declarative meaning of the sentences of a language. I claim that they have to know, for every sentence, S, and for each context, C, in which it might be uttered, which belief they would be expressing by uttering S in context C. I have also claimed that competent speakers have to know that it *is* a convention in the population of those who speak their language, that S, uttered in circumstances C expresses the belief in C that S.

6. It is worth observing that the proposal I am going to make deals with two of the odd features of 'this'. The mapping from 'this' (the word) to $C(\text{this})$, gives us an account of ostension; and the mapping from $C(\text{this})$ to the value for $den(A, t, C(\text{this}))$ deals with the fact that it is token-referential; i.e. the denotation of 'this' changes with context.

In saying what the convention is that members of a linguistic community are party to, I have suggested that it is a convention about what state of mind you wish those who hear you to believe you are in. That state of mind I call the assertibility condition for a sentence: if you are sincere you will utter sentences only when you believe they are assertible. That is, you will utter sentences only in contexts where you believe you are in the mental state that you intend others to believe you are in. This notion of assertibility is not the ordinary notion that Dummett and recent antirealists have made use of. For them an assertibility condition is a condition outside the agent which is such that if they believe it obtains they must assent to the sentence if they are sincere. I doubt that this is a useful notion; for the only specification I can think of of the assertibility conditions of a sentence in this sense is to say that the assertibility conditions of a sentence hold when there is evidence that the sentence is true. But Dummett wishes, if I understand him, to explain assertibility without recourse to the notion of truth: so this cannot be what he has in mind.[7] I do not intend to argue against Dummett's position; I wish simply to distinguish it from my own. I claim for my own use of the term 'assertibility' only the advantage that what is assertible is naturally taken as what it is proper to assert; and there is a good sense in which it is proper to assert only what a sincere person would be willing to assert. In the next section of this book I shall make use of my notion of assertibility to give an account of the semantics and logic of conditionals; an account which presupposes all the work of this chapter and the six before.[8]

7. Dummett's account of assertibility is criticised in my 1984a, 1984c, forthcoming.
8. Hugh Mellor has argued recently (1980c) that believing (to a high degree) that you believe (to a high degree) that S is consciously believing or asserting to S. Since my theory says that speakers who are sincere will assert only what they believe is assertible – and since what is assertible is what you believe to be so – this has the consequence that sincerity consists in asserting only what you consciously believe. I say nothing about consciousness in this book, but this consequence is a desirable one.

Part III *Conditionals*

8

Indicative conditionals

HASTINGS: If they have done this deed, my noble lord, –
GLOUCESTER: If! thou protector of this damned strumpet. Talks't
thou to me of 'if's? Thou art a traitor: – Off with his head!
(Richard III, Art III, scene iv)

8.1 SUBJUNCTIVE AND INDICATIVE CONDITIONALS

'If's and 'iff's abound in philosophical analysis, but the philosophical analysis of 'if's and 'iff's is a highly controversial matter. Still, I believe that, at least for *some* conditionals, the problem of analysis is now approaching a solution. In the next four chapters I say what I think that solution is for one class of conditional, the class that is usually called *indicative*.

That there are more conditionals in English than these is, I think, plain enough. In 3.3 I gave my main reason for thinking this: I suggested that there were two distinct jobs to be done by conditional beliefs, the states most naturally expressed in English by sentences beginning with 'if'. One job, that of the other major class, the *subjunctive* conditionals, was in deciding what to do, which shows up in the theory as computing expected utility. The other job, that of the indicatives, was in changing our minds, which shows up in the theory as conditionalisation. That these two jobs must be done by different beliefs follows from the existence of the class of Newcomb problems that led to the reformulation of decision theory in its *causal* version. We saw that if there were not two jobs, Jeffrey's theory would give the right answer: what I called subjunctive conditional beliefs and conditional beliefs would be able to stand in for each other, for they would be equivalent. Because of the Newcomb problems, we see that we need something other than the conditional probabilities to determine expected utility; but we still need the conditional probabilities as well, for conditionalisation.

Before I go on to say which beliefs indicative conditional sentences express, I want more precisely to distinguish the different syntactic forms of the sentences in which the two kinds of conditional belief show up in English.

We can begin with some basic definitions. Conditionals are sentences of the form

1: If *A*, then *C*,

where *A* is what I call the antecedent, and *C* is what I call the consequent. Sentences of this form can usually also be written '*C*, if *A*', and so the antecedent is not the first clause, but the one following the 'if'. I shall discuss singular conditionals, by which I mean those that do not lie in the scope of a quantifier; so that, in particular, there is no anaphoric connection, through pronouns and the like, between the *A* and the *C*.

Now, in one sense, the terms 'indicative' and 'subjunctive' do well enough to mark the relevant distinction. In indicative conditionals, usually, the antecedent and consequent are ordinary indicative sentences of English, which could be uttered on their own to indicate how things are. Thus, for example,

2: If John is coming, Mary is coming.

In subjunctive conditionals, on the other hand, the antecedent and consequent are not usually sentences at all. Thus, usually, we have something like

3: If John were coming, Mary would be coming.

Now subjunctive conditionals come in two classes, the first of which are (or are equivalent to) sentences of the form of 3; the second class are (or are equivalent to) sentences of the form of

4: If John had come, Mary would have come.

I think the latter are past-tense versions of the former, so that 4 is true iff 3 was true. But, as I say, I am concerned with indicative conditionals so I will not defend this claim; see, for such a defence, Dudman (1983*b*).

I say that these forms of sentence respectively do and do not have sentential components 'usually' advisedly. For indicatives, because English has lots of ways of abbreviating, and sentence 2 can be abbreviated as 'If John is coming, so is Mary' or 'Mary is coming, if John is', where consequent and antecedent, respectively, are not complete English sentences. But I think it is always possible to avoid this abbreviation and thus to find, for any singular conditional, an equivalent conditional, which does have full sentences in each position. For subjunctives, my reservations derive from the fact, exemplified in 4, that past-tense conditionals have antecedents like 'John had come', which *is* a sentence of English. Still, I think that this is because 'had' in English does (at least) two jobs; a thought which is confirmed by noticing that, where the subject is plural, you get the same feature in the 'were' conditionals; thus: 'If John and Mary were coming, so would Peter be'.

There is good evidence that both 'John had come' and

5: John and Mary were coming

have two meanings when they are embedded in conditionals, which depend on the tense of the other clause, and that neither occurs here under an interpretation which would allow it to be uttered on its own. Dudman (1983*b*) had made the case extensively and elegantly but two thoughts should make this plausible.

First, consider the frame 'If John and Mary were coming, —', and ask whether you do not think that its sense is different depending on whether it is completed by 'Peter is coming' or 'Peter would be coming'.

Secondly, with the same example, consider that both

6: If John and Mary were coming, Peter would be coming

and

7: If John and Mary were coming, Peter is coming

could be asserted together; and ask which one, along with 5, would allow us to draw the consequent as conclusion. Statement 7 does allow it; but 6 does not. So that, if from a conditional and its antecedent we can infer its consequent, 5 (in the interpretation it has when asserted alone) is not the antecedent of 6.

I have already given one reason for thinking that subjunctive and indicative conditionals are different. Here is another: the natural translations of sentences of the forms of 2 and 3 into some languages – some Aboriginal languages, for example[1] – do not share a common particle like 'if'. And once told this, we notice fairly swiftly that English has a related feature. The 'if' can always be dropped and the sentence word order inverted in subjunctive conditionals in English. So 3 is equivalent to

8: Were John to come, Mary would come.

But we cannot say what 2 says without an 'if'.

(Mary's coming is conditional on John's coming is a formal mode version of 3 not of 2.)

Despite this difference, it is natural to hold that there is some close connection between subjunctive and indicative conditionals. Both allow many of the same forms of inference for example; almost all those rules of inference I defend for the indicative hold in Lewis' subjunctive conditional logic, for example; see Adams (1977). Is it really likely, someone could ask, that this is contingent? (See, for example, Ellis (1984).) And, moving away from logical considerations, we have a tendency to think that whenever

9: If it is the case that *A*, it is the case that *C*

1. Steve Levinson, personal communication.

163

is asserted, and speakers learn that it has not come to pass that A, they are likely to assent, then, to

10: If it had been the case that A, it would have been the case that C,

as if 10 were the past tense both of 9 and of

11: If it were the case that A, it would be the case that C.

It is this connection between 9, 10 and 11, which had led to subjunctives being labelled 'counterfactual': they seem, especially the 'had been' ones, to be most apt when you do not believe the antecedent. It is now trite learning that the subjunctive is not always in this way counterfactual; see Anderson (1951). For

Had the butler done it, there would have been blood in the pantry

can be part of the detective's argument that the butler did it. Nevertheless, the connections in logic and the pattern of relations between sentences like 9, 10, 11 and not-A, might suggest that there is only one conditional, with the differences in the form of the verb reflecting different implicatures, say, about the likelihood of the antecedent.

That this is simply false, however appealing an idea it is initially, has been clear ever since it was noticed that

If Oswald had not shot Kennedy, nobody would have

and

If Oswald did not shoot Kennedy, somebody did.

If these were the same conditional of the form

$\neg$(Oswald shot Kennedy) $\rightarrow$ C

then they would appear to be inconsistent since, generally, as Ramsey (1978: 233) observed, 'If A, C' and 'If A, $\neg C$' are inconsistent. If these were the same conditional connective with different implicatures, then one could not be true when the other was.

Since the literature has concentrated on these Kennedy conditionals, it is as well to point out that there is nothing special about the past tense. Consider,

12: If Reagan is a Russian spy, no one knows he is

and

13: If Reagan were a Russian spy, someone would know he was.[2]

2. Both 12 and 13 obey *modus ponens*, so if they are jointly asserted we can infer, by *reductio*, that Reagan is not a Russian spy.

I suspect that most of us would assent to each of these claims. This sort of case completely rules out the possibility that subjunctive and indicative conditionals are related by the fact that the former is what is used when the antecedent is believed false. If they were, then, if we believed what the sentence 'Reagan is not a spy' asserts, we would assent to

14: If Reagan were/had been a spy, no one would know/would have known

But we would not, of course, since it is, as we have seen, inconsistent with 13.

So, to summarise, I have two main reasons for thinking that indicatives and subjunctive are distinct. First, there are two jobs for them to do and Newcomb's problems, like the Fisher Hypothesis (3.3), show that one kind of thought cannot do both of them. Secondly, the linguistic evidence, both in English and more generally, suggests it.

I shall discuss the relations between subjunctive and indicative conditionals from time to time later on; but only when it helps with my main task of elucidating the latter. Provided they are, as I have argued, distinct, we should be able to develop accounts of them separately.

From now on, then, unless I say so explicitly, by a 'conditional', I mean a *singular indicative conditional*; subjunctive conditionals will be called just that, and quantified conditionals will be distinguished, but not discussed.

For some time philosophers have tried to do without an analysis of these conditionals altogether, claiming that the material conditional, which is the indicative conditional only if a paper tiger is a tiger, will do. The case is no better for strict implication, material implication's modal relative, which has been offered as an analysis of some of our 'if's. For, as Anderson and Belnap (1975) have observed with passionate sarcasm, strict implication is not a form of conditional at all.

Fortunately there are signs that a new theory of the conditional is on the way. The first really important breakthrough, in my view, came with the publication, in 1965, of Ernest Adams' paper on the logic of conditionals.[3] Adams' proposal amounted to this: that we should look at the conditional not from the point of view of its truth conditions, but from the point of view of what I have suggested we call its assertibility conditions. Adams (1975), Stalnaker (1968), and more recently van Fraassen (1976) and Skyrms (1980a), have discussed and developed since then the consequences of a simple suggestion: that the assertibility of the conditional 'goes by' the conditional probability. But these developments have not gone on unresisted, and David

3. A precursor of this view is Finch (1957/8), which appears to have been strangled at birth by Jeffrey (1959/60).

Lewis, in particular, has carried on a heroic rearguard action in defence of the material conditional.

I begin this chapter, as a result, with a discussion of the classical account of the indicative conditional, which treats it as a material conditional. But my purpose in these remaining chapters is to show that one central semantic rule, and precisely the one originally floated by Adams and Stalnaker, can provide the core of an analysis of indicative conditionals. Discussing the material conditional allows me to introduce some of the main issues and to attack the main alternative theory.

Adams' exposition of his own theory does not, unfortunately, put it in the best light. Nor does it seem to be general enough to capture the whole class of indicative conditionals. I shall try to show how to do a little better. Stalnaker, even more unfortunately, has actually given up the idea that the conditional probability will do the job: I shall try to show that this is a pity. Van Fraassen has a different, and more 'metaphysical' account than mine of what is at fault in Lewis' arguments against the conditional probability theory. And, though Skyrms seems to me to have the matter substantially right, there is not as much detail in his treatment of conditionals as is necessary. It is time for someone to do a little 'underlabouring'.

In 8.2 I begin by giving an account of the material conditional and some of its defects as an account of the indicative conditional. I go on, in 8.3, to offer two positive reasons for accepting Adams' basic account for indicative conditionals. I then discuss and reject Lewis' defence of the material conditional, which begins by accepting Adams' rule but tries to derive it from the material conditional account. At the same time I show that a recent proposal in the same style, by Frank Jackson (1979), will not do either. That takes up 8.4 and 8.5. In Chapter 9 I argue that indicative conditionals are not truth-conditional at all; and I begin an informal account of a way in which we might do the logic of the conditional, granted that, if it is not truth-conditional, the classical account of entailment will not do. That completes my account of the general features of indicative conditionals, and prepares the way for the discussion of the logic of conditionals in Chapter 10. Chapter 11 proposes a more general view than Adams' Hypothesis as a solution to some of the limitations of his view; but it relies heavily on his basic insight, since his Hypothesis is a special, though central, case of the general theory.

8.2 MATERIAL CONDITIONALS

Philo, the Megarian pupil of Diodorus Cronus, is, so the Kneales tell us, the earliest logician to have suggested an analysis for conditionals (Kneale and Kneale, 1962: 128 *et seq.*). Sextus Empiricus reports that Philo said:

a sound conditional is one that does not begin with a truth and end with a false-hood . . . (Kneale and Kneale, 1962: 128)

And provided, 'sound' means 'true' it appears that this 'Philonian' conditional is the material conditional. We cannot reconstruct Philo's reasoning from the rather scanty materials provided by Sextus; but there are many intuitions which might lead someone to propose that:

MAT: 'If R, S' is true iff $\neg(R \ \& \ \neg S)$.

Success with a truth-functional approach to conjunction and disjunction, for example, might lead one to seek such a truth-functional analysis of the indicative conditional. And intuitions about inference lead very quickly to producing the material conditional's truth table.

To see why, let us begin with a standard account of validity.

V: An inference from the sentences in the set $[S_1, S_2, \ldots, S_n]$ to R is valid iff it is not logically possible that $(S_1 \ \& \ S_2 \ \& \ \ldots \ \& \ S_n \ \& \ \neg R)$.

It follows swiftly that if *modus ponens* – i.e.

MP: $R \rightarrow S$, $R \vdash S$

– is valid, then, if the conditional is truth-functional, it must be false if $(R \ \& \ \neg S)$. For suppose we have the line of the truth-table

$R \rightarrow S$
T ? F

we must write F under '$\rightarrow$'; for if we write T we should be allowing that it is possible that $(R \rightarrow S) \ \& \ R \ \& \ \neg S$. And then, by *V*, MP would be invalid.

To fill in the remaining lines we need only consider the following rule of inference:

DS: $(S \lor R) \vdash \neg S \rightarrow R$

(which is disjunctive syllogism). For if DS is valid, we must write T under the '$\rightarrow$' in the following truth-table, since it is a condition of this entailment's holding that whenever the disjunction is true, the conditional is.

$(S \lor R) \vdash (\neg S \rightarrow R)$
T T T   F T ? T
T T F   F T ? F
F T T   T F ? T

And since we are assuming that '→' is a truth-function, this gives us the three lines of the truth-table that we still need; i.e.

$$S \rightarrow R$$

T	T	T
F	T	T
F	T	F

We do not know what Philo's reasons were for proposing his analysis; but these are at least good arguments in its favour. There is one more, which played a large part in later Stoic discussions of conditionals, and it is this: the material conditional is the ideal connective for validating conditional proof. This rule of inference says (in the relevant form) that

CP: wherever $[S_1, S_2, \ldots, S_n] \vdash R, [S_1, S, \ldots, S_{n-1}] \vdash (S_n \rightarrow R)$.

That is, wherever R follows logically from a class of sentences $[S_1, S_2, \ldots, S_n]$, $(S_n \rightarrow R)$ is a logical consequence of the members of the class $[(S_1, S_2, \ldots, S_{n-1}]$. CP has often been found to be intuitive; and if it is correct, then, so it seems, given V as our account of validity, a conditional is necessarily true iff a material conditional is necessarily true. It would be possible to explain this intuition in other ways than on the assumption that the conditional is a material conditional. But that assumption is the obvious one to make.

Now it is notorious that, despite these arguments, the material conditional has some features which are counterintuitive in an account of the indicative conditional. The most familiar arguments against the material conditional analysis are the paradoxes of material implication; or, as I shall call them, for preference, the paradoxes of the material conditional.

One paradox is that

PMI: For any S and R: $S \vdash R \rightarrow S$.

And the other is

PMII: For any S and R: $\neg S \vdash S \rightarrow R$.[4]

The literature on this question is large: I wish only to rely on the claim that these results are counterintuitive and that an account of the conditional which did without them would be in that respect more plausible. What is interesting about these paradoxes is that they seem to be intimately connected with the forms of inference which I made use of in justifying the truth-table; disjunc-

---

4. The paradoxes are usually stated as paradoxes about implication, rather than about conditionals, but for my purposes this is obviously the form in which to consider them.

tive syllogism and conditional proof. Thus, given DS, we have:

1: S Premise
2: $\neg R \vee S$ DA, 1[5]
3: $R \rightarrow S$ DS, 2

This argument relies only on the relatively innocuous principle of the logic of disjunction, DA, and on DS. And it establishes the first paradox of the material conditional. For it shows that, for any S at all, and for any R, $(R \rightarrow S)$ is a consequence of S.

Finally, CP will allow us to derive both paradoxes very easily, assuming other relatively uncontroversial principles of sentential logic, none of which involves the conditional at all. Thus, for example, we can get the second paradox by:

1: $\neg S$ Premise
2: $\neg S \vee R$ DA, 1
3: S Hypothesis
4: R DB, $(2, 3)$[6]
5: $S \rightarrow R$ CP

This connection between DS and CP, on the one hand, and the paradoxes of the material conditional on the other, suggests that, however attractive these principles are, we ought not to assume them without further examination. And, indeed, once we look for counterexamples, motivated by this thought, they are not hard to find.

Take DS first. The simple proof I gave of the paradoxical result arose because we can always infer $(S \vee R)$ from S, even where S and R have nothing to do with each other at all. In cases where someone believes, say,

Mrs Thatcher lives in Downing Street

they may validly infer from this that

Either Mrs Thatcher lives in Downing Street or President Reagan lives in Dallas.

It is true that this would hardly be a reasonable thing to say simply on the basis of beliefs about Mrs Thatcher. But, on the other hand, there is no doubt that it is true, if Mrs Thatcher lives in Downing Street; and Gricean considerations,

---

5. DA is just the rule of the logic of disjunction:
   DA: From S infer $(S \vee R)$
6. DB is just the rule of the logic of disjunction:
   DB: From $(S \vee R)$, $(\neg S)$, infer R.

of a kind I consider later (8.4), suffice to account for the oddity of actually saying it in these circumstances.

Now if DS were valid we should be able to infer at once that

If Mrs Thatcher does not live in Downing Street, President Reagan lives in Dallas.

And this hardly seems something that follows from the fact that Mrs Thatcher lives in Downing Street; particularly because a parallel line of reasoning will get you to

If Mrs Thatcher does not live in Downing Street, President Reagan does not live in Dallas.

And no one will want to accept both of these supposed consequences.

Finally, so far as CP is concerned, one important objection to it just is the fact that it licenses us to infer that every conditional of the form $((S \,\&\, \neg S) \rightarrow R)$ is true; unless, with Anderson and Belnap (1975), we wish to deny that any R is always a consequence of $(S \,\&\, \neg S)$.[7] But if CP is valid, then DS must be also. For because DB

DB: $(S \,\vee\, R), \neg S \vdash R$

holds, CP will lead swiftly to DS.

1:	$S \,\vee\, R$	Premise
2:	$\neg S$	Hypothesis
3:	R	DB (1, 2)
4:	$\neg S \rightarrow R$	CP

If, now, we move away from the rules of inference which guided us to the material conditional in the first place, we can find large numbers of inferences sanctioned by it, which are absurd enough to be grounds for serious doubt as to the adequacy of Philo's account. To make the point, I need mention only a few of the many counterexamples that have appeared in the literature – see especially Adams (1975) and Cooper (1978) – which suggest that the indicative is not the material conditional.

One class of examples shows that the transitivity of the material conditional is not a feature of the indicative conditional. Thus, where

If Brown dies, Jones will win the election on Wednesday

If Jones wins the election on Wednesday, Brown will retire

---

7. I do not intend to discuss this alternative route out of the problem, though I have recorded the connections between my views on conditionals and on entailment in my 1981: Appendix 7.

we should be unwise to infer

If Brown dies, Brown will retire; see Cooper (1978: 183).

Another problematic rule of inference is what van Fraassen (1976) calls 'weakening', which allows us to infer $((S \ \& \ R) \rightarrow U)$ from $(S \rightarrow U)$. It would, for example, be unwise to infer

If John comes and Mary's baby dies, Mary will be happy

from

If John comes, Mary will be happy.

A final example, from Jeffrey (1981) should suffice. From

If, if we advance, they withdraw, then we will win

and

We will not advance

infer

We will win.

Jeffrey (1981: 75) calls this 'zapping them with logic'!

These few examples ought to discourage anyone who wants to go on with the material conditional, and there are plenty more where they came from.

One final example is worth describing in a little more detail. It is a case where contraposition – i.e.

CONTRA: From $(S \rightarrow R)$ infer $(\neg R \rightarrow \neg S)$ –

fails. It will provide us with a starting place in the next section, when we come to try to develop an alternative to the material conditional.

Suppose we are in a laboratory where a machine has been set up like this: it contains, behind a door in a panel, two urns, which we can call W and B, on a turntable. On the front of the panel is a button. If that button is pressed the turntable will turn through 90 degrees, either clockwise or anti-clockwise and the door will open. The turntable will go clockwise if, during the five seconds after you press the button there is an alpha particle emitted from a radium sample; and anti-clockwise otherwise. Suppose also that the half-life of the radium sample is such as to make the chances of a particle being emitted in that interval about 0.5. The urns are distinguishable externally only by a letter written on their bases, which is visible only if you lift them up. But they have different contents.

Urn B has 999,999 tiny white polystyrene balls in it and one black ball. Urn

W has 1,000,000 white balls. Now you press the button, and you wait for five seconds. Then you place your hand into the urn behind the door, which has now opened, and remove just one ball without looking to see what colour it is.

In this case it seems pretty clear that you should assent to both

B: If this is urn B, I am not holding a black ball

and

W: If this is urn W, I am not holding a black ball.

You ought to assent to B because there is only the very faintest chance of your getting a black ball out of urn B: a chance so remote that you will reasonably discount it. Just so, I discount the very faint possibility that the wooden stairs up to my room have been eaten through by termites, as I walk up and down stairs in the normal course of things. I will say that the stairs are safe (i.e. that if I walk on them I will not fall through them), even though there is a very remote possibility that they are not; and if that is the right thing to say, so, in our urn's case, is B. It is clear, on the other hand, that you will not assent to the contrapositives of both B and W. For the contrapositive of B is

B': If I am holding a black ball, this is not urn B

and of W is

W': If I am holding a black ball, this is not urn W.

And in fact you know very well that if you do not get a white ball, you will get a black one, and then the urn will certainly be urn B. So you believe

$B2$: If I am holding a black ball, this is urn B.

B' is clearly wrong, though its contrapositive is right. Contraposition, which holds for the material conditional, fails.[8]

For all these reasons I think we are obliged to look for analyses other than Philo's, despite its having been staple fare now for well over 2,000 years; and the last example provides the clue we need to tell us where to look.

---

8. If 1,000,000 balls is too few to discount the 1 in a million chance of getting a black ball, just suppose there are more.

    I am well aware that this example is not uncontroversial, even with this suggestion. For, some would say, if there are a million balls, B' and W' should both go subjective. Since I have already argued that subjunctives and indicatives of the form $(\neg A \rightarrow C)$ and $(\neg A \mathbin{\Box\!\!\rightarrow} \neg C)$ can be asserted together (see 8.1), I cannot agree with this. But the example is meant to be suggestive, not irresistible.

As I said in Chapter 1, the hypothesis about conditionals I am going to defend I call Adams' Hypothesis; for it owes its fullest development to Ernest Adams (1975). Adams' actual account is confused in various ways, and I shall improve on it. But the central idea is his. Return then to the case of the urns B and W.

Granted that in that set-up we should not assent to the contrapositive of a conditional which we do accept, it is worth investigating the beliefs that a rational person – call him 'Peter' – could be expected to have about the ball in the hand if he is convinced that the set-up is as I described it. Let us attend in particular to the probabilities Peter attaches to four beliefs:

   BB: the belief that he has a black ball in his hand

   WB: the belief that he has a white ball in his hand

   WU: the belief that the urn is urn W

   BU: the belief that the urn is urn B.

Presumably at least this much is true, if Peter is a rational agent (and supposing that we ignore the small degree of uncertainty attached to any contingent beliefs):

$$p(BB) = 1/2,000,000$$
$$p(WB) = 1,999,999/2,000,000$$
$$p(WU) = 1/2$$
$$p(BU) = 1/2.$$

A little further reflection suggests that he can also assign probabilities to conjunctions which have any of these beliefs or their negations as conjuncts. Thus, in particular,

$$p(BB \& WU) = p(\neg WB \& WU) = p(BB \& \neg BU) = 0$$
$$p(\neg BB \& WU) = p(WB \& WU) = p(WU) = 1/2$$
$$p(BB \& BU) = p(\neg WB \& BU) = p(\neg WB \& \neg WU) = 1/2,000,000$$
$$p(\neg BB \& BU) = p(WB \& BU) = 999,999/2,000,000.$$

Given this information, we can ask what facts about Peter's degrees of belief might be expressed by his asserting, as he is disposed to do, each of the conditionals:

   B: If BU, WB

W: If WU, WB

W': If BB, BU

$B2$: If $\neg WB$, $\neg WU$.

And we can say at once, for each of these conditionals, that, where the conditional is of the form (If S, R),

$\dfrac{p(S \ \& \ R)}{p(S)}$, is very close to 1.

This ratio is, of course, the conditional probability, $p(R/S)$, which I introduced in Chapter 3. Thus, for B, we have

$$\frac{p(BU \ \& \ WB)}{p(BU)} \ = \ 1{,}999{,}998/2{,}000{,}000.$$

For W we have

$$\frac{p(WU \ \& \ WB)}{p(WU)} \ = \ 1.$$

For $B2$ we have

$$\frac{p(\neg WB \ \& \ \neg WU)}{p(\neg WB)} \ = \ \frac{p(\neg WB \ \& \ \neg WU)}{1 - p(WB)} \ = \ 1.$$

And for W' we have

$$\frac{p(BB \ \& \ BU)}{p(BB)} \ = \ 1.$$

What is also important, however, is that for the conditional B', to which he is not disposed to assent, the conditional probability is low. For, for B', we have

$$\frac{p(BB \ \& \ \neg BU)}{p(BB)} \ = \ 0.$$

So that: where we are disposed to assent to the conditional, the conditional probability is high; and where we are not disposed to assent to it, the conditional probability is low. And this fact might lead us to propose the thesis I am going to defend, namely

Adams's Hypothesis: 'If A, C' is assertible iff $p(C/A)$ is high.[9]

9. This account, which I often call just 'AH', is restricted not just to indicative conditionals, but, more specifically to indicative conditionals for which $p(C/A)$ is defined. And a necessary condition for this is that A and C should have truth conditions: for probability is, as Lewis correctly observes (in Lewis (1976)), probability of truth. I shall take up this point again in the next two chapters. I leave the question of what to do when $p(A)$ is 0, and $p(C/A)$ is, therefore, undefined, until 10.2.

Remembering the account of assertibility of the previous chapter, we can say what this means. It means that if someone sincerely utters an indicative conditional they must believe their conditional probability of the consequent given the antecedent is high; i.e. near to 1. We will assert a conditional of the form of 'If A, C', then, only if we intend to express the belief that $p(C/A) > 1 - e$, where e is small and p is our own p-function.

Given the account of conditional beliefs of Part I, we can say that 'If A, C' expresses the belief $\langle B, A, t, (1 - e), \langle C(C), C(A), \text{COND} \rangle \rangle$, when uttered by A at t; but since, as we saw in Chapter 4, the agent's proof theory is reflected in the p-function, which reflects computational perfection, we can concentrate on the probabilistic features of the state. Simply put, the logical behaviour of a computational feature, like COND, shows up in the computationally perfect agent.

This case suggests that Adams' Hypothesis is at least worth examining, since, unlike the material conditional analysis, it suggests an explanation of why contraposition fails in this case. But we also need some more general reason for supposing that this hypothesis is right, and I propose to offer now two such reasons.

First, I shall show that there is good evidence that this hypothesis makes the right predictions about how people who assent to conditionals will react to the acquisition of new beliefs; secondly, I shall suggest an account of why we might expect there to be a connective whose use was governed by just this assertibility rule.

In Chapter 3 I spent some time establishing that we should accept conditionalisation as representing the way agents change their degrees of belief on the acquisition of evidence. Conditionalisation, recall, occurs when someone changes their degrees of belief from those in a function p, to those in a function p'; and where, for some partition, $[(S_1), (S_2), \ldots (S_n)]$, and for any representation (R)

$$p'(R) = \sum_{i=1}^{i=n} p(R/S_i) \cdot p'(S_i)$$

Granted that this is so, it follows, with Adams' Hypothesis, that where someone is disposed to assent to 'If S_i, R', then, were they to come to change their degrees of belief by conditionalisation on a set containing S_i, they would come to be disposed to assert that R, iff they would come to be disposed to assert that S_i.

For if $p'(S_i)$ is high, then the sum of the probabilities of the other members of the partition will be low; and the product $p(R/S_i) \cdot p'(S_i)$ will be approximately equal both to $p(R/S_i)$ and to $p'(R)$. The fact that conditionalising on a partition in which S_i occurs, where $p'(S_i)$ is high, produces a high $p'(R)$ iff $p(R/S_i)$ is high, is very familiar. Yet, so it seems to me, not enough attention has usually been paid to it. For conditionalisation is intended to represent what happens when an agent acquires direct evidence altering the probabilities of the representations in the set in which it originates. And it is surely true, that where someone believes that if *A*, *C*, they would, if they were to gain direct evidence that *A*, come to believe that *C*.

There are, then, good reasons, rooted in our account of decision theory, for supposing, with Adams, that the assertibility of conditionals is determined by the conditional probability. And once the idea is suggested, it will not seem surprising, I think, that we have a way, in English, of expressing the state we are in when we have a high conditional probability. We saw in Chapter 3 that conditional beliefs play an important role in conditionalisation. Granted that conditional beliefs are important, why should we not have a way of expressing facts about them; indeed, in view of the central role played by conditional probabilities and the beliefs that bear them, the surprise would surely be, if we did not?

8.4 LEWIS AND THE CONVERSATIONAL IMPLICATURE DEFENCE

The familiar arguments against the material conditional, and the less familiar arguments in favour of Adams' Hypothesis, AH, might seem to settle the issue against the material conditional. But there is one further line of defence available to its defenders. It is to claim that the counterexamples I offered are not invalid but in some other way infelicitous. The *locus classicus* of this sort of defence of the material conditional is Grice's 1968 William James Lectures at Harvard. There he suggested that what was 'unhappy' about the paradoxes of the material conditional, was not that the conclusion did not follow from the premise in each case, but that it would be a breach of a general constraint on normal conversation if we ever were to *use* these inference patterns. Such a 'pragmatic' defence of the material conditional has since been supposed by some to provide an answer to the case against the material conditional. And I want in this section and the next to show that this is not so. To do so, I shall consider the best-known recent Gricean defence of the material conditional, that given by Lewis (1976). Lewis undertakes there to accommodate the material conditional with AH. I shall argue that the defence fails. One failing is specific to Lewis' defence, another is fatal for a whole class of approaches, based on conversational implicatures. I shall then consider, in 8.5, an account of Jackson's, in terms of conventional rather than conversational implicatures, which escapes the general line of objection; and say why I am sceptical of his view as well.

Lewis begins by conceding that the assertibility of an indicative conditional of the form:

1: If A, then C

does 'go by' the conditional probability

2: $p(C/A)$.

So he agrees with Adams that if someone sincerely utters an indicative conditional they must believe the conditional probability of the consequent given the antecedent to be high. As I said at the end of Chapter 7, normally the assertibility of a sentence is determined simply by the probability of the belief it expresses: competent speakers represent themselves as believing they have a high degree of belief that S, when they utter S. This poses a problem for the material conditional account. For (using '$\supset$' for the material conditional):

3: $p(A \supset C) = p(\neg(A \ \& \ \neg C))$

and, therefore,

4: $p(A \supset C) = p(C/A) + p(\neg A) \cdot p(\neg C/A)$

(provided $p(A) \neq 0$). Generally, then, $p(A \supset C)$ isn't equal to $p(C/A)$; so that if the indicative conditional is a material conditional, its assertibility does not 'go by' its probability: and this exception to the general rule needs explaining.

Lewis' explanation runs as follows: the indicative conditional *is* a material conditional. But there is a general understanding governing normal conversation to the effect that one does not make pointless assertions. And, Lewis says, it is pointless to assert 'vacuous' material conditionals: conditionals believed largely because one thinks their antecedents are false. If we assert a conditional that is vacuous, we are liable to mislead; our audience will assume that we have not spoken vacuously and therefore suppose that we have better reason for asserting the conditional than we actually have.

This consideration detracts from the assertibility of $(A \supset C)$ to the extent that two conditions hold: first that the probability $p(\neg A)$ of vacuity is high; and second that the probability $p(\neg C \ \& \ A)$ of falsity is a large fraction of the total probability $p(A)$ of non-vacuity. The product

$$[5]: \quad \frac{p(\neg A) \cdot p(\neg C \ \& \ A)}{p(A)}$$

is therefore a suitable measure of diminution of assertibility. (1976: 306)

[5], of course, is just the difference between $p(A \supset C)$ and $p(C/A)$.

Two things in this splendidly brisk argument need special attention. First, Lewis' speedy derivation of 5; secondly, his claim that asserting conditionals whose antecedents we think false is 'vacuous'.

[5] is intended to measure the extent to which the conditional is believed because the antecedent is disbelieved. It should, therefore, reflect both the extent to which the antecedent *is* disbelieved – hence the factor $p(\neg A)$ – *and* the extent to which the conditional would not otherwise have been believed. How does Lewis derive the factor for the second component?

> The speaker ought not to assert the conditional if he believes it predominantly because he believes the antecedent to be false, so that its probability of truth consists largely of its probability of vacuous truth. (1976: 306)

Presumably there is some argument in here from the fact that $(A \supset C)$ is believed predominantly because $\neg A$ is believed, to the conclusion that the probability of truth of the material conditional 'consists mostly' of its probability of vacuous truth. I want to derive the enthymeme that is buried in this step.

The obvious thought is that there are different ways in which the material conditional can be true – vacuously, non-vacuously – and that, since these are the only two possibilities and they are mutually exclusive, the probability of truth is equal to the probability of vacuous truth plus the probability of non-vacuous truth. The measure of the extent to which it is believed true because it is believed vacuously true is thus the ratio of the probability of vacuous truth to the total probability.

There is a general principle here whose plausibility we might examine: namely that, where some S can be true in various mutually exclusive ways, $R_1, R_2, \ldots, R_n$, so that S is logically equivalent to $(R_1 \lor R_2 \lor \ldots \lor R_n)$, the measure of the extent to which S is believed true predominantly because some R_i is believed is

$$6: \frac{p(R_i)}{p(S)}$$

Since R_i entails S,

$$7: p(R_i) = p(R_i \ \& \ S)$$

so that 6 is in fact equivalent to

$$8: \frac{p(R_i \ \& \ S)}{p(S)} = p(R_i/S)$$

Is it plausible, for example, to hold that Mary believes S predominantly because she believes R_i, if R_i entails S, and Mary believes S, believes R_i, and has a high conditional probability of R_i on S? Not in general; for Mary will have a high conditional probability of R_i on S for any R_i and S both of which she believes. For if she believes that S and believes that R_i, then Mary will have a high subjective probability for $p(S \,\&\, R_i)$, and since $p(S/R) \geqslant p(S \,\&\, R)$, (provided $p(R_i) \neq 0$), Mary will have a high conditional probability of R_i on S. But surely Mary does not believe that the triangular closed-line figure she is contemplating has three sides largely because she believes that it has three sides and the Prince of Wales married Lady Diana, even though a cursory examination reveals that by this criterion we should have to say that she did?

It is just as well for Lewis that we do not need the general principle that seems to underlie the passage cited above. And when we examine the calculation that actually produces [5], we see that Lewis is in fact relying on a more plausible principle; namely

P: if S is believed predominantly because R is, $p(\neg S/\neg R)$ is high.

That, at any rate, is a principle that will get him the conclusion he wants. For, in the particular case of the material conditional believed largely because the antecedent's negation is believed, and substituting, therefore, '$(A \supset C)$' for 'S' and '$\neg A$' for 'R' in this principle, we get

9: $p(\neg S/\neg R) \;=\; p[\neg (A \supset C)/\neg(\neg A)]$

which is precisely what Lewis calls the ratio of the probability of falsity to the probability of non-vacuity. This is the second factor that Lewis needed to derive.

But Lewis cannot just help himself to this principle. Adams is entitled to it, because he believes that the assertibility of the indicative conditional goes by the conditional probability: $p(\neg S/\neg R)$ thus corresponds to the sentence

10: If $\neg R$, then $\neg S$,

and, plausibly, anyone who (reasonably) believes S predominantly because they believe R, will believe 10. But Lewis is trying to *derive* the conclusion that the assertibility of the material conditional should go by the conditional probability, and in showing it he is not entitled to assume it. If Lewis is right and the indicative conditional is a material conditional, then we should be able to conduct an argument which begins by looking to the truth conditions and passes, by way of considerations about assertion in general, to the concusion that the appropriate rule of assertion is AH. Lewis' argument relies on an account of what has to be true of the probability function of someone who believes S predominantly because they believe R; what such a person presumably believes is that if it is not true that R, it is not true that S. But then on Lewis' showing, that state of belief is captured in a p-function where

11: $p(\neg R \supset \neg S)$ is high.

And, unfortunately, if this were right, the factor in the equation corresponding to the fact that someone believes $(A \supset C)$ predominantly because they believe $\neg A$, would be

12: $p(\neg(\neg A) \supset \neg(A \supset C)) = p(A \supset \neg C)$

(and not the conditional probability $p(\neg C / A)$, as Lewis requires).

There is an obvious riposte here for Lewis. I have saddled him with a principle and with a bad argument for it. But there are good reasons for accepting the principle, P, reasons apparently independent of one's view about conditionals. The obvious reason for accepting that if someone believes S predominantly because they believe R, $p(\neg S / \neg R)$ should be high, is that someone who believes S predominantly because they believe R is someone who would not believe S if they did not believe R. But someone would not believe S if they did not believe R iff, if they acquired evidence that $\neg R$, which bore in no direct way on the truth of S, they would cease to believe that S. And that condition is satisfied by someone, as I argued in 8.3, if they have a high $p(\neg S / \neg R)$ and change their beliefs by conditionalising.

I think that this line of defence of the principle has much to recommend it. And I believe the principle P is roughly correct.[10]

But it raises a problem for Lewis. For if we accept the principle we must ask why it is that we have the strong intuition, on which I have already once relied, that if someone believes that if A, C and comes to believe A (while having no other direct evidence about C), they will come to believe C. For if we change our degrees of belief by conditionalisation; and if the conditional is a material conditional; this intuition is incorrect. It is easy to see why: if someone has a high degree of belief that if A, C, then on the material conditional account, $p(A \supset C) > 1 - e$; for some small e. But since this can be true when $p(C / A) < e$, for the same small e; and since, if the conditional probability is small, someone will not come to believe C by conditionalisation if they come to believe A, it follows that someone can believe $(A \supset C)$ and not be so disposed that if they came to have evidence that A they would come to believe that C.

It would be nice to find, then, a case where this condition obtains; where someone straightforwardly believes a conditional proposition and fails to come to believe the consequent when they come to believe the antecedent.

10. I say 'roughly' because, as Dorothy Edgington pointed out to me, it can be true that someone would not have believed S if they had not believed R, for other reasons than that they believe if $\neg R$, $\neg S$. (For example, the causal route that led to their believing that S might depend in some quirky way on their believing that R: suppose, e.g. that your brain goes into a certain state, R, when you believe that R, and that when your brain is in state F, you emit a pheromone which causes people to tell the truth. Then it might be that you would not have come to believe some state secret if you had not believed that R; because it were only because you believed that R and were thus in state F, that the normally reliable secret-keeper, told it you.) In such a case you might well not believe if $\neg R$, $\neg S$.

Provided the conditional is not *about* utterances it is plausible to hold that a good test for what someone would do if they came to believe A, while not having any direct evidence for C, is to consider what would happen if they were told by someone they are inclined to believe that A.[11] So what we want is a case where someone believes 'If A, C' but would not, if told that A, by a reliable informant, come to believe C. If the material conditional hypothesis is right, we know how to construct such cases; we simply find a case where the material conditional has high subjective probability and the conditional subjective probability is low.[12]

Now it is well known that it is difficult to find such cases. Anyone who has tried to teach sentential calculus to an intelligent student knows that it is a hard business getting people to accept that it is all right to believe a conditional purely on the grounds that its antecedent is false or its consequent true; yet, if these cases were plausible, they would be cases of the exactly the kind we are looking for. I cannot myself find cases where I think it plausible to suppose that someone believes that if A, C, where $p(C/A)$ is low.

However, Lewis might want to say that he has an account of this implausibility. For, he might say, granted that we have an explanation of why people do not *express* conditional beliefs except where the conditional probability is high, we might suppose that it would be at least unusual to find a case where we want to talk about someone's having such beliefs.

How successful this line of defence is depends on the view we take about another general issue; the issue, namely, of whether the relevant conversational implicature can be cancelled. For if Lewis' explanation is in terms of conversational implicatures, then it is a defining feature of them that they can be cancelled. It must be possible to produce cases where the normal inference sustained by the features of conversational exchange that generate the conversational implicature is not made, because it is understood that the conversational exchange is in some way abnormal. Thus, the conversational implicature from my utterance of a disjunction to the belief that I do not know which disjunct is true, is cancelled when, in a quiz game, I give a clue by saying, for example, 'She is Prime Minister of India or Sri Lanka.' Clearly in this context, no one is going to suppose that I do not know which of the places it is; for you understand that if I told you *that*, the game would come to an end.

11. I exclude conditionals about utterances because, if the conditional were of the form

    If A, someone will tell me that A

then, of course, this is not a good test for whether one believes it.

12. Ellis, in his unpublished 'Probabilities of Indicatives', has the best go I know of at producing such a case. But I think he is considering a subjunctive conditional wrongly expressed in the indicative.

It seems to me that by the test of whether it can be cancelled, the implicature that Lewis proposes from utterances of conditionals to high conditional probabilities, fails to be conversational. If it were, then we ought, in playing a game, to be able to say

If she is not Prime Minister of India, she is Prime Minister of Sri Lanka

when we know perfectly well that she is the Prime Minister of India and have a low conditional probability for

She is Prime Minister of Sri Lanka

given

She is not Prime Minister of India.

It seems obvious to me that we should say no such thing. But even if this case is not persuasive, if Lewis were right, it ought to be possible to find a way of cancelling the implicature in all cases; including, for example, the case considered earlier (8.2) of the urns. Intuitions in that case are sharper, it seems to me, and go decisively the wrong way in suggesting that the implicature is not cancellable.

For the moment, then, let me say that the argument by which Lewis moves from the claim that we avoid conditionals with vacuous antecedents to the claim that we have an account of the difference between the conditional probability, which determines assertibility, and the probability of the material conditional, is not as unproblematic as his presentation of it might suggest. To the general question of the possibility of cancelling conversational implicatures, I shall return when I discuss Jackson's proposals.[13]

I said that we needed to consider not only Lewis' derivation of [5], but also his claims about the vacuity of the antecedent. Lewis says that if the antecedent is disbelieved 'the probability of truth [of the conditional] consists mostly of its probability of vacuous truth' (1976: 306). But if the conditional is material, why distinguish between ways of being true, some vacuous, some not?

If we are to take our cue from Grice, we must appeal to general features of the conversational situation to explain vacuity. We must say that an utterance of a conditional when vacuous offends against some general constraint on conversational exchanges. What, then, is the general constraint in this case?

The obvious candidate is the Gricean maxim of quantity. What this requires – and this seems to be reasonable enough – is that we should make

13. As Dorothy Edgington has pointed out to me, there is a further problem with Lewis' argument: namely that there is no obvious reason why the factor $p(\neg A)$ and the factor $p(\neg C/A)$ should be multiplied together, rather than, for example, added. Still, if this were the *only* objection, I think it might be dismissed as nit-picking to make it.

the most informative relevant contributions we can. One way to capture at least part of what this means is to state the rule as follows:

R: Do not utter a sentence S in circumstances where, for some R,
  (a) R entails S, and S does not entail R
  (b) R is relevant, and
  (c) R is assertible.

Rules of this kind are rules that can be broken if we are not trying to be helpful, so that it is no objection to them that it is easy for competent speakers to ignore them. But this one is quite plausible. It accounts, for example, for the resistance we feel to uttering $(S \lor R)$ whenever we have evidence for S, and no special evidence for R. For $(S \lor R)$ is entailed by S, and is thus, in an obvious sense, less informative than it. So that even if R is relevant in the context, saying $(S \lor R)$ when you are in a position to say S is unhelpful if your interlocutor believes you are respecting the Gricean maxim.

Well, suppose this principle is in fact one on which we rely. Then we can now object to utterances of '$A \supset C$', where someone disbelieves A, on the grounds that there is something they believe – namely $\neg A$ – which entails (but is not entailed by) this material conditional, and which is presumably relevant if the conditional is.

We have here, then, a general principle which explains why the assertion of indicative conditionals is odd when all we know is that their antecedents are false; but which gives this explanation in a way that makes use of the 'fact' that indicative conditionals have the truth conditions of a material conditional.

This principle, however, though it does what Lewis needs, does much more; and, unfortunately, it does too much. Let us call conditionals believed largely because their antecedents are disbelieved, conditionals with vacuous antecedents; and conditionals believed largely because their consequents are believed, conditionals with vacuous consequents.[14]

Then the problem for Lewis is this: R rules out not only the assertion of conditionals with vacuous antecedents, but the assertion of conditionals with vacuous consequents also. For, if the conditional is a material conditional, C entails $A \supset C$; but $A \supset C$ does not entail C. Consequently an utterance of a conditional when the consequent is believed is a breach of the maxim – on the reasonable assumption that a sentence is relevant where a conditional containing it as consequent is relevant.

If we now applied the same line of reasoning as Lewis adopted for dealing with the vacuous antecedents, we should need to take away from the probability of the conditional, not only Lewis' factor, which reflects the extent to

---

14. This case corresponds to the first of the paradoxes of the material conditional, just as the case of vacuous antecedents corresponds to the first one.

which it has a vacuous antecedent and is believed because of this; but also a factor which reflects the extent to which it has a vacuous consequent and is believed largely because that consequent is believed. That factor is

$$p(C) \cdot p(\neg (A \supset C)/\neg C) \;=\; p(C) \cdot p(A/\neg C)$$

(applying, once more, the principle, P, that if S is believed predominantly because R is, $p(\neg S/\neg R)$ will be high).

It is obvious that if we took account of this factor as well, then the assertibility of the indicative conditional would not go by the conditional probability; for it is not in general true that

13: $p(C/A) \;=\; p(A \supset C) - p(\neg A) \cdot P(\neg C/A) - p(C) \cdot p(A/\neg C)$

The fact that it treats the vacuous antecedent and the vacuous consequent identically is thus an objection to the use of R as an account of the source of vacuity. But it will be an objection to any view that seeks to explain the vacuity of the conditionals with vacuous antecedents by way of the entailment relations of a conditional and its antecedent alone. For, as I have observed, just as $\neg A$ entails $A \supset C$, and $A \supset C$ does not entail $\neg A$, so C entails $A \supset C$, and $A \supset C$ does not entail C.

There is, in any case, as Jackson has pointed out (1979), an objection to the form of the principle of quantity as I stated it in R. For if R were right, it would always be a conversational infelicity to assert a disjunction when you believed only one disjunct; and it is not. I can very properly say that John or Mary is going to arrive soon, even though I think that it will in fact be John that comes, provided I have some reason for thinking that one or other of them will come over and above the fact that I believe that a *particular* one of them will come. Thus, if John and Mary are a couple, both of whom are punctual, and if I think there is a reason why one member of the couple will certainly come to the meeting, then I can say, as the second hand creeps round to the appointed hour, 'John or Mary will come soon', even though I think that, with the new baby to be fed, it is much more likely to be John.

It is not obvious how one should react to this fact. One possibility is suggested by what Lewis does in his paper. It is to say that what is going on in the case of the disjunction is that we are following the rule:

R′: It is permissible to assert some S, where you can assert R, which is equally relevant and entails (but is not entailed by) S, provided you do not believe S predominantly because you believe R.

This proposal has a certain appeal; for it follows from it that it is all right to assert 'John or Mary will come soon', where you believe John will come, provided p(John or Mary will come/John will not come) is high. And this conforms to our intuition that what is normally required is that we assert a disjunction $(S \lor R)$ only where we are also willing to assert 'If $\neg S, R$'. It is this fact, indeed, that probably accounts for the appeal of disjunctive syllogism.

But the trouble with this modified proposal is that it falls foul of the objection I made against R: it cannot distinguish between the case of the vacuous antecedent and the vacuous consequent, as is required for Lewis' argument.

I conclude that we have good grounds for thinking that any attempt to account for the vacuity of the conditional with vacuous antecedent, in terms of a form of the maxim of quantity, is liable to fall foul of the vacuous consequent. Lewis concedes in his paper that the case of the vacuous consequent shows that 'consideration of conversational pointlessness are not decisive'; but why, in the case of the vacuous antecedent, but not in the case of vacuous consequent, do they decide? If we cannot account for the vacuity of the conditional whose antecedent is disbelieved in a way that does not make the conditional with the vacuous consequent unacceptable also, Lewis' argument fails. It is not enough to say simply that conversational pointlessness is not decisive; in the absence of an account of what *is* decisive, we do not know why the assertibility of the conditional goes by the conditional probability.

8.5 JACKSON AND THE CONVENTIONAL IMPLICATURE DEFENCE

Frank Jackson, however, has set out on a line of defence of the material conditional that is not open to this objection, to which I now turn.

Just as 4 is the decisive equation for Lewis, so

14: $p((A \supset C)/A) = p(C/A)$

is decisive for Jackson. We shall see why when we have examined the general strategy of his argument.

Suppose that conditionals really do have the truth conditions of the material conditional. If I uttered conditionals just when I thought they were probable — just when their subjective probability of truth was high — I might sometimes quite properly utter a conditional just because I believed its antecedent false. But suppose I did this; and suppose I said to someone 'If John comes, Mary will', just because I thought John would not come. The most frequent use to which conditionals are put is in *modus ponens*. But in this case this policy would be one it would be well to avoid. For since all the evidence I have for the conditional is that its antecedent is false, any evidence that the antecedent is true should count not towards confirming the consequent, but to giving up the conditional. If we decided, then, that the real usefulness of conditionals was that they allowed *modus ponens*, we might restrict our use of them, in cases where we disbelieved the antecedent, to cases where the evidence we had gave grounds for believing that we should still think them true, even if we did not disbelieve the antecedent.

There is an obvious way to require that where a conditional is asserted, it should not be true that if its antecedent were believed *it* would not be believed; that is to require that the probability of the conditional, given its antecedent should be high. For, as pointed out in 8.3, the result of conditionalising on $[(S), (\neg S)]$, with a high $p'(S)$, will be a high $p'(R)$, in the new probability function p', iff $p(R/S)$ is high; and conditionalising on $[(S), (\neg S)]$ is just what reflects coming to have direct evidence that S.

It is now clear what the job of equation 14 is; it is to show that it follows from this plausible line of reasoning that we would have a use for a connective, '$*$', which was such that $(A * C)$ was assertible iff $p(C/A)$ was high.

Jackson observes that what appears to be happening here is an instance of a more general phenomenon. For there is, in English, a class of conventional markers of a relation between a sentence S, which is believed to be true, and some background sentence R, of 'robustness', where S is robust with respect to R iff $p(S/R)$ is high; if, simply put, you would go on believing S even if you came to believe R.

The phenomenon is fairly widespread: if, for example, someone says (Jackson, 1979: 575) 'He lives in Boston, or anyway somewhere in New England', then the function of the 'anyway' is to show that the conditional probability of (He lives in Boston $\vee$ He lives in New England) given that (He does not live in Boston) is high. Someone who utters this sentence sincerely would go on believing the disjunction even if they disbelieved the first disjunct. What 'anyway' does is tell you that the disjunction is believed robustly with respect to the negation of the first disjunct.

Jackson argues, plausibly, that there are many such markers of robustness in English: 'nevertheless', for example, signals the robustness of a belief in what is being asserted with respect to whatever has gone before. What Jackson claims is that 'If . . . , then . . .' in English is yet another instance of the same phenomenon: 'If A, then C' is assertible in English iff the speaker believes the material conditional, and this belief is robust with respect to its antecedent. Since $p(A \supset C/A) = p(C/A) \geqslant p(A \supset C)$, both these conditions are guaranteed if $p(C/A)$ is high.

It is important to see that this argument does not rely on a general rule of assertibility; Jackson is not requiring us to suppose, for example, that whenever it is true of a connective '$*$' that there is a common form of inference from $(S * R)$ and U to V, we should assert $(S * R)$ only where $p((S * R)/U)$ is high. So that it would be no objection to his argument to point out that

186

from this general principle there would follow constraints on the assertibility of conditionals that we do not conform to, as well as the constraints that we do. Jackson can agree that a similar line of reasoning based on *modus tollens*, might lead us to require that we assert a conditional only where $p((A \supset C)/\neg C)$ is high. For what he is arguing is not that the assertibility rule for the conditional follows from the truth conditions and a general conversational rule; what he is arguing is that the assertibility rule is a conventional and not a conversational constraint. Conversational constraints can be breached, as we have seen; but an implicature is conventional iff breaking it amounts to a breach of a semantic rule. Indicative conditionals are to be seen as being in this way like, say, 'but' sentences; 'but' has the truth conditions of 'and' plus an assertibility rule requiring that the R in 'S but R', should be in some way surprising in the context provided by S (along with the general background). Similarly, Jackson holds, 'if . . . , then . . .' has the truth conditions of '$\supset$' plus an assertibility rule which requires that $p(C/A)$ should be high. The argument in which 14 plays a part is thus an argument which is intended to show why we have a use for a connective with the truth conditions of the material conditional and the assertibility condition that the probability of the consequent given the antecedent should be high. Granted that it is useful, it should be less surprising that we actually have it.

This comparison of this account of the indicative conditional with the standard account of 'but' is worth examining. What does it mean to say that the truth conditions of

BUT: John is coming but Mary is not

are that John is coming and Mary is not?

One thing it clearly entails is that from the application of the normal assertibility rule – assert only what you take to be quite probably true – it will follow that it is a necessary condition for the assertibility of BUT, that p(John is coming and Mary is not coming) is high. This is only a necessary condition, because there is a further condition: the condition, namely, that there should be the right kind of contrast between the fact that Mary is coming and some prior expectation. It does not follow from this, however, that we can, for example, set up a logic for 'but'; for though the conjunction, for example, is entailed by 'John and Peter are coming and Mary is not', BUT does not obviously follow from it. If, for example, it is only surprising that Mary is not coming when John is, but not surprising that she is not coming when Peter, whom she hates when in John's company, is also, we may explain why John is coming but Mary is not by saying: 'John and Peter are coming, and Mary is, of course, not coming as a result.'

In the case of the conditional, we get, as we should expect, a similar pair of results. From the fact that the material conditional gives, on Jackson's account, the truth conditions of the indicative conditional, it follows that the normal assertibility rule makes having a high subjective probability for $p(A \supset C)$ a necessary condition for the assertibility of 'If A, C'; but this does not mean that we can use the truth conditions to give us anything like a logic for conditionals. For, for example, $(A \supset C)$ entails $(\neg C \supset \neg A)$, but, as we have seen, contraposition is not a principle that works for the indicative conditional.

It does follow from Jackson's view that sincere assent to the material conditional entails a commitment to the contraposed material conditional; but since, on his view, this is only a necessary condition for asserting the related indicative conditional; and since the further necessary condition that the related conditional probability be high is not guaranteed to hold, we cannot tell, from looking at the truth conditions, what indicative conditionals 'entail'.[15]

But there is also a striking disanalogy between the two cases. In the case of 'but', and, indeed, in Jackson's other cases, the rule for the implicature makes reference to some feature of a simple English sentence. In the case of 'He lives in Boston, or anyway in New England', it is the robustness of a *disjunction* with respect to the negation of a disjunct. In the case of 'but' it is the surprisingness of the second 'conjunct', in the context provided by the utterance of the first. In the case of the robustness of the conditional, however, the S whose robustness is defined is not a sentence of English at all. It is true that there are ways of producing something with the truth conditions of the material conditional in English: $(\neg A \lor C)$; $(\neg(A \& \neg C))$, for example. But the trouble with these forms is that Jackson's argument does not go so well with them: he says that we need some way of marking the robustness of $(A \supset C)$ with respect to its antecedent because we need to be able to rely on *modus ponens*. But substituting $(\neg A \lor C)$ in here makes the point very nicely that this looks like *petitio principii*. For, granted that there is no connective in English which has the truth conditions of the material conditional and *no* special assertibility rule, there is no such thing as *modus ponens* to motivate the search for a way of expressing robust belief that the material conditional is true. The inference from $(\neg A \lor C)$ and A to C is not *modus ponens*, but a familiar principle of disjunctive inference. Rules of inference are defined in terms of the form of the premises and the conclusion: if there is no material conditional in English, then there is no inference with it.

This disanalogy is connected with another. In the other cases of conventional implicatures of robustness, as when it is said that the speaker believes

---

15. In my 1984b, I show that if we ignored these objections and tried to do the logic with Jackson's proposal, we would get the wrong answers.

that '*S* or *R*' robustly, the reference to the sentence robustly believed is not inessential. It is at least a plausible claim that we must mention the truth conditions associated with 'or' in characterising the content of '*S* or anyway *R*'; and a similar point holds for the conventional implicature associated with 'but'. It is natural to say that the truth conditions of conjunction have something to do with 'but'-sentences, just because it is natural to see the assertibility rule for 'but' as made up of two parts: assert '*A* but *B*' only if

(a) you believe that *A* and *B*;

and

(b) there is the requisite kind of contrast between *B* and *A*.

Now I make this observation because, in the case of the conditional, it is not at all obvious that the reference to the material conditional is anything like essential. It is plausible to suppose that we can explain the assertibility conditions of 'but' statements by way of a rule which refers to truth conditions of conjunctions. We need the reference to these truth conditions because the meaning of 'but' can simply be broken up, so to speak, into two independent components.

In the case of 'if . . . , then . . .', as Jackson points out, it follows from the assertibility rule that he gives *alone*, that the indicative conditional is assertible only if the speaker believes the material conditional. For, from Lewis' equation 4,

$$4\colon p(A \supset C) \;=\; p(C/A) + p(\neg A) \cdot p(\neg C/A)$$

it follows that

$$15\colon p(C/A) \;=\; p(A \supset C) - p(\neg A) \cdot p(\neg C/A)$$

and from this it follows that

$$16\colon p(C/A) > 1 - e, \text{ only if } p(A \supset C) > 1 - e$$

since both $p(\neg A)$ and $p(\neg C/A)$ must be greater than or equal to 0.

We do not need two conditions to explain the meaning of 'If *A*, then *C*'; the simple assertibility rule does the whole job. This point is connected with the previous one: it is plausible to suppose that the truth-functional disjunction plays a role in our understanding of '*S* or anyway *R*', because we do have an understanding of that truth-function, and because it is hard to state the meaning of that operator naturally without mentioning 'or'; not least because, if we look more broadly at the matter, 'anyway', when it occurs in sentences without 'or', introduces an identical implicature of robustness with respect to some feature of those sentences also. Thus 'Anyway, *S*' implicates that *S* is believed robustly with respect to the negation of some set of contextually defined claims; usually claims earlier in the conversation. A smooth explanation of 'S or anyway R' ought to apply a general account of 'anyway', and Jackson's explanation of it does seem to be able to do just that.

But neither of these conditions applies in the case of Jackson's account of the material conditional: that conditional would need itself to be introduced before we could wield it in the explanation, and there is a perfectly natural explanation of how to use 'If . . . , then . . .' which makes no reference to the material conditional, or to robustness.

So far as I can see, the truth conditions on Jackson's view neither give the logic of the conditional, nor play any essential role in explaining the assertibility rule. In the case of 'but' and 'anyway' the truth conditions seem to be essential to explaining the assertibility rule. For the conditional, on Jackson's theory, they do not. In the absence of even this much role, the truth conditions are just so much idle machinery.

Jackson would say, of course, that he *had* given the truth conditions a role. The truth conditions of the material conditional play their part because the argument above is intended to show that we have a use for a form of words which expresses the fact that we are in a state in which we not only believe the material conditional but would continue to do so if we believed its antecedent true. But the state that we thus express is the state of: *believing the material conditional and being so disposed that we would continue to believe it even if we believed its antecedent true*; and it is not all clear why we should regard this fact as one which makes the truth conditions of the sentence we use to express this state those of the material conditional.

Even if, however, we think that these initial objections can be overcome, Jackson has not established that the indicative conditional has the truth conditions of the material conditional; *unless* it is conceded that $(S \lor R)$ gives the truth conditions of 'S or anyway R'; or that 'A but B' has the truth conditions of $(A \& B)$. Both of these claims it seems to me proper to deny. For if someone who utters 'S or anyway R' expresses the fact that they believe that S or R robustly with respect to $\neg S$, what makes it true that the truth conditions either of the sentence or the state that it expresses are that $(S \lor R)$? The truth conditions of a belief are the conditions that hold iff it is true. But the state expressed by 'S or anyway R' is not a belief at all. The point is plain too for 'A but B': the only *belief* that anyone expresses in saying 'A but B' is that A and B. But it does not follow from this that the truth conditions of the sentence 'A but B' are that A and B; that sentence does not just express a belief that A and B, it expresses also some complex fact about the agent's attitude to the holding of B when A is true and whatever else is presupposed in the context is true also. That is an interesting fact about the sentence, and an interesting fact about the agent's state: why should we treat that state as having truth conditions at all?

Jackson (1979: 573–4) takes it as uncontroversial that we should treat 'A but B' as having truth conditions: and this is, indeed, classical wisdom on the subject. I suggest that wisdom needs revising; what theoretical purpose is achieved by this proposal?

There is an analogy here with the epistemic modal 'may'. We sometimes want to express the fact, not that we believe that S to a sufficient degree to assert it outright, but that we do not disbelieve it. And then, of course, someone might say, there is a sentence form which does just this job, namely: 'It may be the case that S.' (This is developed in 11.5.) In explaining the role of this sentence we make essential reference to the truth conditions of the sentence S. For this sentence is assertible iff $p(S) > e$ – where e is small enough that if $p(S)$ were less than e, we should just say 'It is not the case that S.' And since probability is probability of truth, the state of believing that S to a degree greater than e is a state whose content is fixed, in part, by the truth conditions of S. But it simply does not follow from the fact that there is this reference to the truth conditions of the sentence S in our explanation of the modal sentence, that the truth conditions of S *are* the truth conditions of the modal sentence. It seems to me to be just a prejudice that all interesting semantics is to be done in terms of truth conditions.

Lewis' defence of the material conditional fails because, even if it is consistent with that view to hold, as his argument requires, that

P: if S is believed predominantly because R is, $p(\neg S/\neg R)$ is high

the explanation he gives, fails to distinguish, as it needs to, the cases of the vacuous antecedent and the vacuous consequent. Jackson's alternative view makes the truth conditions idle. But if that is so, and if the assertibility rule that all parties agree on is right, what do we want the truth conditions for? We can explain what people are doing when they utter conditionals by way of the assertibility rule, without reference to the material conditional. Why do we not rest content with that?

9

Truth and triviality

TOUCHSTONE: . . . Your 'if' is the only peace-maker: – much virtue
    in 'if'.

             (*As You Like It*, Act V, Scene iv)

9.1 OVERVIEW

AH: 'If A, C' is assertible iff $p(C:A)$ is high.

That is my claim. Once accepted, there is, as we have seen, good reason for
thinking that the indicative conditional is not a material conditional. Indeed,
since it is easy to see that no truth-function of two components has a
probability equivalent to the conditional probability, there is good reason for
thinking that the indicative conditional is not a truth-function at all. But the
fact that it is not a truth-function is not, in itself, evidence that it has no truth
conditions. The sentence-forming operator on sentences 'I believe that . . .' is
not a truth-function: but there is no reason to doubt that it determines truth
conditions, or to doubt that grasp of how those truth conditions are determined is part of a knowledge of what it means.

    Since, in general,

ASS: 'S' is assertible iff $p(S)$ is high, where S has truth conditions

it is tempting, given the strong evidence that Adams' assertibility rule is
correct, to look for a set of truth conditions for 'If A, then C', such that the
sentence is assertible iff it is believed to be probably true. So you might
suggest, as Jeffrey (1964), Ellis (1969) and Stalnaker (1970) at various times
have, that

PROPOSAL: For all p-functions, p, (Π): $p(A \rightarrow C) = p(C/A)$, if $p(A)$
$\neq 0$.[1]

Call a conditional which satisfies the condition (Π) *a probability conditonal for
P*; call a conditional a *probability conditional for a class of p-functions, p*, iff it is

---

1. This is not to be confused with what van Fraassen calls 'Stalnaker's thesis', which is the claim
   that '. . .$p(A/B) = p(B \rightarrow A)$ whenever $p(B)$ is positive. . .' (1976: 273), which I have rejected
   in claiming that conditionals are not truth-conditional and do not, therefore, have probabilities
   of truth at all.

a probability conditional for every member of that class; call it a *universal probability conditional* iff it is a probability conditional for all *p*-functions. Lewis' justly well-known 'triviality' proofs show that, given apparently reasonable assumptions, the PROPOSAL won't do; see Lewis (1976). The two proofs are called triviality proofs, because one shows that any language in which the conditional $(A \rightarrow C)$ is a universal probability conditional, will be a trivial language, where (the definition is Lewis'),

> TRIVIAL LANGUAGE: a language is *trivial* iff at most two possible and incompatible propositions can be expressed;

and the other shows that, any set of *p*-functions, which satisfies a closure condition I shall discuss, will consist entirely of *trivial p*-functions, if there is a probability conditional for the class; and here (once more following Lewis)

> TRIVIAL PROBABILITY-FUNCTION: a *trivial p*-function is one which assigns positive probability to at most two incompatible propositions; which is, in other words, at most four-valued.

Our language is not, in this sense, trivial; for consider the three sentences 'It is red', 'It is green' and 'It is purple', or, even more strikingly, the class of sentences of the form 'It is *x* miles as the crow flies.' So this result is apparently a *reductio* of the idea that indicative conditionals have their probabilities determined by the conditional probability; a *reductio*, then, of Jeffrey, Ellis and Stalnaker's modest PROPOSAL.

In the next few sections I want to argue that the triviality proofs, *in the forms they are standardly given*, though valid, should not be put to two of the uses they *have* been put to: namely, by Adams (1975) and myself (1981, 1984*b*), to showing that the conditional has no truth-value; and by Lewis (1976) and Jackson (1979, 1980/1) to arguing that their probability is not, despite ASS, what determines their assertibility.

It turns out that there is a crucial premise to the triviality proof offered by Lewis (1976), Skyrms (1980*a*), and (in the (1981) second edition of his logic text-book) Jeffrey, so I shall look at various possible defences of this premise, beginning, of course, with Lewis, who started it all. The bare formal bones are identical, so I give them in 9.2. Section 9.3 discusses Lewis' rationale for the crucial premise; 9.4 a weaker rationale, which might be thought to be implicit in Skyrms' account. Both Lewis' and Skyrms' rationales are rejected. Section 9.5 considers briefly Adams' triviality proof, which differs in its structure from Lewis', making objection to it also. I consider it only briefly because I think its essential strategy *can* be defended: and in 9.6 I report a proof, due to Carlstrom and Hill, which, in my view, captures that essential strategy.

I should say now, however, that I do not think that what I shall be saying gives any grounds for thinking that, perhaps, after all, conditionals *do* have probabilities in the way the PROPOSAL suggests. As I say, I end by offering one sort of triviality proof, due to Carlstrom and Hill, to which I have no objection; and more arguments (in 9.7 and 9.8) from the semantic behaviour of conditionals which tend to similar conclusions.

Part of the interest in showing what I think is wrong with Adams' and Lewis' proofs is that an examination of them confirms Adams' view that probability-structure assumptions – about the space of acceptable *p*-functions – are central to the development of a semantics which trades on probabilities. But I have to discuss the triviality proofs in supporting my claim that conditionals do not have truth conditions, since they are widely believed to be the best argument for this conclusion. I am not able to rely on the original proofs for a technical reason, because they depend on supposing that *p*-functions are not, as I believe they *are*, regular. But I am also keen to show that, despite my reservations, we really do have good reason to deny that indicative conditionals have truth conditions. The two most likely consequences to draw from the difficulties which arise for the PROPOSAL are either

(a) that indicative conditionals do not have truth conditions

or

(b) that they do, but that, for some reason, ASS does not apply to them. The most likely response, that is, is either Adams' (and mine) or Lewis' and Jackson's. I have shown in Chapter 8 why I think the right response is not (b); nothing I say here undermines what I say there on this question. Triviality, we shall see, is neither a simple, nor an unimportant matter.

9.2 THE PROOF ITSELF

We begin with the PROPOSAL that the conditional has a probability which is equivalent to the conditional probability, and that this probability obeys all the usual laws. We assume also that the substitution of a conditional for some atomic sentence of a tautology is a tautology, which it will be iff the conditional has truth conditions. We can then argue as follows; see Lewis (1976), Adams (1975: 34-5), Jeffrey (1981: 82-5), Skyrms (1980a: 169-70).

Suppose that $p(A \rightarrow C)$ exists, and that $p(A)$ and $p(C \ \& \ A)$ (and, thus, $p(C)$) are not 0. Then

$$\text{1: } p(A \rightarrow C) \ = \ P[[C \ \& \ (A \rightarrow C)] \ \lor \ [\neg C \ \& \ (A \rightarrow C)]$$

because $[(S \ \& \ R) \ \lor \ (\neg S \ \& \ R)]$ is tautologically equivalent to R, and we have as an axiom of the probability calculus that tautologically equivalent propositions have the same probability. From 1 we get

194

2: $p(A \rightarrow C) = p(C \,\&\, (A \rightarrow C)) + p(\neg C \,\&\, (A \rightarrow C))$

relying on the fact that the axioms tell us that where $(S \,\&\, R)$ is impossible, $p(S \lor R) = p(S) + p(R)$; and thence

3: $p(A \,\&\, C) = p(C) \cdot p([A \rightarrow C]/C) + p(\neg C) \cdot p([A \rightarrow C]/\neg C)$

relying on the general probability theorem that $p(S \,\&\, R) = p(S/R) \cdot p(R)$, where $p(R)$ is not 0. We now assume that

ASS1: $p([A \rightarrow C)]/C) = p(C/A \,\&\, C)$

and

ASS2: $p([A \rightarrow C]/\neg C) = p(C/A \,\&\, \neg C)$.

Both of these are of the form

DC: $p([A \rightarrow C]/B) = p(C/A \,\&\, B)$

and this is the crucial premise, to whose justification I return in the following sections.[2] Given DC we get

4: $p(A \rightarrow C) = p(C) \cdot p(C/A \,\&\, C) + p(\neg C) \cdot p(\neg C/A \,\&\, C)$

and thus

5: $p(A \rightarrow C) = p(C) \cdot 1 + p(\neg C) \cdot 0$.

From this, and the PROPOSAL that the probability of the conditional is equal to the conditional probability, we get

6: $p(C/A) = p(C)$.

This is pretty bad: in every system of degrees of belief, every pair of contingent sentences, C and A, in this language is statistically independent; for we assumed nothing special about them, save (implicitly, in invoking the equivalence of a conditional probability with a ratio of probabilities) that $p(A)$ and $p(A \,\&\, C)$ are not 0. In fact, as we can easily show, this leads to triviality.

For consider now any three propositions, C, D, E, which are all possible (and thus have probabilities greater than 0), but which are pairwise incompatible (so that $p(C \,\&\, D)$, $p(D \,\&\, E)$, $p(C \,\&\, E)$ are all 0). Let A be $(C \lor D)$. Then $p(A \,\&\, C) = p((C \lor D) \,\&\, C) = p(C)$ and $p(A \,\&\, \neg C) = p((C \lor D) \,\&\, \neg C) = p(D)$ are both positive; but $p(C/A)$ (which is $p(C)$ divided by $p(C \lor D)$) is not equal to $p(C)$, since $p(C \lor D) \neq 1$.[3] So, if 6

---

2. We only need to suppose DC to hold where $p(A \,\&\, B)$ is not 0, as it is here. I mention this because the derivation of DC in the next section is subject to this restriction. 'DC' is short for 'double conditionalisation', for a reason that 9.3 makes clear.

3. This would not follow if $p(E)$ were 0. For then $p(C)$ might be $p(\neg D)$, and then $p(C/A) = p(A)$.

is true, there are no three such possible but pairwise inconsistent propositions; and the language is, therefore, trivial. It is a short step from here to proving that all the p-functions are trivial also. For suppose, for purposes of *reductio*, that the p-function, p, had more than four values: then

there would be two different values of p, x and y, stricly intermediate between 0 and 1 and such that $x + y \neq 1$. But then if $p(F) = x$ and $p(G) = y$ it follows that at least three of $p(F \ \& \ G)$, $p(F \ \& \ \neg G)$, $p(\neg F \ \& \ G)$, and $p(\neg F \ \& \ \neg G)$ are positive; which is impossible. (Lewis, 1976: 302, notation altered)

And the reason this is impossible is that the language is trivial: hence there do not exist three such possible but pairwise incompatible propositions.

9.3 LEWIS' RATIONALE

The question to ask, of course, is what justifies DC. And for Lewis the answer is straightforward: what justifies it is that it follows from the claim that the class of p-functions which 'represent possible systems of belief' (1976: 302) is closed under conditionalisation: as I shall say, cond-closed. A class of p-functions is cond-closed (the definition is Lewis' (1976: 299)) iff

CC: For any p-function p in the class, and for all R, such that $p(R) \neq 0$, the p-function p', such that for all S, $p'(S) = p(S/R)$, is also a member of the class.

The first thing to do is to show that DC *does* follow. Consider some A and B, such that $p(A)$ and $p(A \ \& \ B)$ (and, therefore, $p(B)$) are all positive. If the class of p-functions is cond-closed, then there is also in the class a p-function p', such that, for any R, $p'(R) = p(R/B)$. Consider, then, some $(A \rightarrow C)$; from the PROPOSAL it follows that

1: $p(A \rightarrow C) = p(C/A)$

since $p(A) \neq 0$. And, since, p' is produced by simple conditionalisation on B,

2: $p'(A \rightarrow C) = p(A \rightarrow C/B)$.

From the definition of conditional probability it follows that

3: $p'(A \rightarrow C) = \dfrac{p'(A \ \& \ C)}{p'(A)}$

because $p'(A) = p(A/B) \neq 0$.

4: $p'(A \ \& \ C) = p(A \ \& \ C/B)$ (p' comes from p by simple conditionalisation) and

5: $p'(A) = p(A/B)$ (p' comes from p by simple conditionalisation).

Finally, applying the definition of conditional probability twice more, we get:

$$6: p(A \And C/B) = \frac{p(A \And B \And C)}{p(B)}$$

because $p(B) \neq 0$. Now from judicious substitutions into 2 to 7 it follows that

$$8: p(A \to C/B) = \frac{p(A \And B \And C)}{p(A \And B)}$$

and hence, by the definition of conditional probability, and remembering that $p(A \And B)$ is not 0, that

$$DC: p(A \to C/B) = p(C/A \And B)$$

of which, you will recall, both ASS1 and ASS2 are instances.

Lewis relies on Teller's (1973) defence of the claim that probabilities change by conditionalisation; see also 3.6. And it might be thought that the arguments given for the principle that probabilities change by conditionalisation make no special assumptions about conditionals and ought therefore to apply equally to them. And if probabilities change by conditionalisation then any p-function that could be reached by a series of conditionalisations from an acceptable p-function must also be acceptable. If this were right, then Lewis would be entitled to assume that the class of acceptable p-functions is cond-closed. I want to show, however, that Lewis' argument is not entitled to this premise. I argued in 4.5 that p-functions should be regular. Now Lewis' assumption of cond-closure is supposed to follow from the claim that probabilities change by conditionalisation. But in fact, as I shall now show, it follows only if p-functions are not, as I argued they should be, regular. Teller's argument (on which Lewis relies) is for the claim that probabilities change by generalised conditionalisation.[4] In his argument, however, Lewis uses simple conditionalisation. In holding that the class of p-functions is cond-closed, Lewis thus assumes that, for every S, there exists a p', such that $p'(S) = 1$. But if, for every S, there exists a p', such that $p'(S) = 1$, then, following regularity, every S is a priori. It is thus unsurprising that a language which is cond-closed is trivial, whatever view you take of the conditional: for every sentence in it is a priori true; except those which are a priori false. And so there cannot be three possible but pairwise incompatible sentences.

4. The defence of simple conditionalisation Teller offers is a 'heuristic' device, enabling us to see what is going on in the full proof of the generalised case.

The point is this: given regularity, simple conditionalisation follows from generalised conditionalisation iff every R in the language is *a priori* true. So the triviality results cannot be held against the thesis that the probability of the conditional is the conditional probability; for they follow without that thesis as a premise.[5]

I rely, I admit, very strongly on my claim that p-functions must be regular. If I am wrong about this, then the triviality results do indeed seem to be evidence that conditionals are not truth-conditional: evidence, that is, that there is no proposition whose probability is the probability that the conditional is true. For someone who denies that conditionals are truth-conditional need not be concerned by the triviality results. After all, they apply only to probabilities, and, on a non-truth-conditional account, though the conditional 'goes with' the conditional probability it does not have a probability. However, as Lewis points out, analogous triviality proofs could be given that made use of the concept of deducibility rather than truth, so that even if conditionals are not truth-conditional, it will be impossible both to accept cond-closure and to assume that the assertibility of the conditional obeys the same laws as the assertibility of truth-conditional sentences. But if conditionals do not have truth conditions, this need not be any cause for concern either. For the assertibility of truth-conditional sentences depends on their probabilities of truth; and if conditionals do not have probabilities of truth – because they are not ever either true or false – then there is no reason why their assertibility should obey the same laws as truth-conditional sentences. Indeed, later on I argue that it does not.

9.4 GIVING UP SIMPLE CONDITIONALISATION

The assumption of simple conditionalisation is also implicit in Skyrms' rationale for DC in the triviality proof. Skyrms justification for DC is that $p(R \rightarrow (B \rightarrow C))$ must be equivalent to $p'(B \rightarrow C)$ in the p-function got by conditionalisation on R; just as, so he thinks, $p(R \rightarrow S)$, in general, is equal to $p'(S)$ in the p-function obtained by conditionalisation on R. And, on this

5. Van Fraassen's objection to the triviality proofs takes a similar line, holding that CC entails an objectionable 'metaphysical realism' (1976: 274–5). I do not, however, object to what he calls 'metaphysical realism'; and his way of rejecting it means giving up conditionalisation (whether simple or generalised) as a model for change of belief altogether, substituting, presumably, something else, unfortunately not vouchsafed to us. Further, the only argument van Fraassen offers against CC seems to me to show only that it is unlikely to be the *only* way for changing our belief; but this is not an argument against CC, only an argument for thinking that the class of acceptable p-functions is even wider.

I have no further reason for not considering his detailed proposals further: most of his examples and intuitions have to do with subjunctive conditionals.

assumption, as we have seen, it does indeed follow that

DC: $p(A \rightarrow C/B) = p(C/A \,\&\, B)$

But the justification of DC in the previous section succeeds only if the conditionalisation involved is simple conditionalisation, not generalised conditionalisation. Where R is *a posteriori*, on the view I have been developing, we cannot conditionalise on $p'(R) = 1$, because $p'(R)$ cannot equal 1. We can only conditionalise on a high value of $p'(R)$, using the partition $[(R), (\neg R)]$. For the case of the non-conditional sentence S, this gives a result very close to the one Skyrms assumes. Thus, where $p(S/R) = k$, and $p(R)$ goes to $p'(R) = (1 - e)$, conditionalising on $[(R), (\neg R)]$ will give us $p'(S) = k(1 - e) + p(S/\neg R) \cdot e$; and if k is high, and e is small, then this will be high also. So that someone who believes that if R, S and comes to believe that R, will come to believe that S; where believing that R or believing that S is just having a high degree of belief that R or that S. But if k is small, and $p(S/\neg R)$ is large, then $p'(S)$ and $p(S/R)$ may be rather different. Thus, to take a case, if

$p(S/\neg R) = 0.99$

$p(S/R) = 0.01$

and e is 0.01, then

$p'(R) = 0.99$

$p'(S) = 0.0198$

which is almost twice $p(S/R)$. With the conditional there is no prescription for what must be true in the function p' achieved by generalised conditionalisation on the current p-function originating in the partition $[(R), (\neg R)]$, until we know what value to assign to $p(A \rightarrow C/R)$ and $p(A \rightarrow C/\neg R)$. The 'pre-formal' intuition on which Skyrms is relying is, I think,

SKYRMS: that someone believes a conditional iff the result of conditionalising on its antecedent will be a high probability for the consequent.

As I say, this does indeed follow from generalised conditionalisation, for truth-conditional consequents, and it *is* plausible, so we might try the same for conditional consequents. That is, we might look to see what has to be true of a p-function p for it to be the case that conditionalising on $[(R), (\neg R)]$ will produce a high value for $p'(U/S)$. For if the general principle SKYRMS holds for conditionals with conditional consequents also, this is what it is to believe that if R, then if S, then U.[6]

6. In Chapter 11 I rely on this fact to give a generalisation of AH, which copes with some non-truth-conditional consequents.

Now it turns out that it is possible to have a p-function p, such that the result of conditionalising with $p(R) = (1 - e)$, for small e, is a high $p(U/S)$, but where $p(U/R \ \& \ S)$ is not high. It is possible, then, on this analysis of the embedded conditional, to believe that if R, then, if S, then U, without believing that if R and S, then U. So that though the intuition SKYRMS is maintained with generalised conditionalisation, it does not follow from generalised conditionalisation that $p(R \rightarrow (S \rightarrow U))$ must be the same as $p(U/R \ \& \ S)$.[7]

I want now to consider whether the non-equivalence of $(R \rightarrow (S \rightarrow U))$ and $((R \ \& \ S) \rightarrow U)$ (which Skyrms (1980a: 175) calls 'Ellis's principle'), on an account which accepts SKYRMS but rejects simple conditionalisation, is a merit. I shall give reasons for rejecting this principle, and the derivation from simple conditionalisation is, as we have seen, not one a proponent of generalised conditionalisation needs to accept.

The entailment one way between these conditionals is the law of exportation:

EXP: $((R \ \& \ S) \rightarrow U) \vdash (R \rightarrow (S \rightarrow U))$

I have not offered a proposal about conditionals embedded in conditionals.[8] But given the minimal requirement that embedded conditionals can safely be used in *modus ponens* arguments we can show that EXP must not be accepted. For disjunctive syllogism

DS: $(R \ \& \ S) \vdash (\neg R \rightarrow S)$

and contraposition

CONTRA: $(R \rightarrow S) \vdash (\neg S \rightarrow \neg R)$

are unacceptable, on the PROPOSAL.[9] And if we were to accept EXP we should be obliged, as I shall now show, to accept both of these rules of inference also.

The reason is quite simple. Two valid rules of inference are

7. To see this we need only consider the trivial cases where $p(R) = (1 - e)$, so that conditionalising on $[(R), (\neg R)]$, where the new function has $p'(R) = (1 - e)$, is just the identity mapping. It is easy then to see that $p(R)$ and $p(U/S)$ can be high without $p(U/R \ \& \ S)$ being high; and, conversely, that $p(R)$ and $p(U/R \ \& \ S)$ can be high, without $p(U/S)$ being so. The former shows that there can be a p-function, such that conditionalising with $p'(R) = (1 - e)$, gives $p(U/S)$ a high value, even though $p(U/R \ \& \ S)$ is not high. And the latter shows that there can be a p-function in which $p(U/R \ \& \ S)$ is high, and such that conditionalisation with $p'(R) = (1 - e)$ does not give a high $p(U/S)$.

8. I shall argue later that there are not any indicative conditionals of the form $(A \rightarrow (B \rightarrow C))$ and $((A \rightarrow B) \rightarrow C)$; but, for the moment, let us see how far we can get with the assumption that there *are*.

9. I assume, as I did in Chapter 9.

CONSEQUENCE: (a) that S follows from T iff $p(T) \geqslant p(S)$, in all p-functions; *and* (b) that S follows from a set of premises iff it follows from their conjunction; see Adams (1966; 1975: Chapter 2), and 10.3.

DB: $(R \ \& \ S), \neg R \vdash S$

and

MT: $(R \rightarrow S), \neg S \vdash \neg R$

the familiar principle of *modus tollens*. We cannot accept EXP, because it gets us from DB to DS and from MT to CONTRA (provided we assume also that if

$(R \ \& \ S) \vdash U$

and $(R \ \& \ S)$ is not impossible,

$(R \ \& \ S) \rightarrow U$

is assertible).

If we apply this thought to DB, we get

$((R \ \& \ S) \ \& \ (\neg R)) \rightarrow S$

which has a conditional probability corresponding to it of 1, and is thus always assertible. By EXP, we should then have

$((R \ \& \ S) \rightarrow ((\neg R) \rightarrow S))$

always assertible. And from this and $(R \ \& \ S)$ it would follow by *modus ponens* that $(\neg R \rightarrow S)$; which is just disjunctive syllogism. An obvious parallel line of argument will get us contraposition.

There are, thus, reasons, quite independent of a preference for generalised conditionalisation over simple conditionalisation, for being suspicious of the triviality proofs.

9.5 ADAMS' PROOF

Adams' alternative derivation of the triviality results proceeds in a different manner. Rather than relying on CC, it assumes a different closure condition for the set of acceptable *p*-functions, namely:

TC: The class of acceptable *p*-functions includes every truth-function and every probability mixture of truth-functions.

What this means is most easily put in terms of possible worlds talk: for what it amounts to is that a *p*-function which assigns probability 1 to some possible world is an acceptable *p*-function;[10] and so is any *p*-function which distributes

10. For if this 'were really possible, then it should also be possible for these facts to become known as certainties: i.e. propositions known to be true should have probability 1, while those known to be false should have probability 0'. Adams (1975: 5–6).

probability over some finite set of worlds. So that, as usual, the probability of truth of any proposition is equal to the sum of the probabilities of the worlds in which it is true, and the sum of the probabilities of the worlds is 1.

Adams shows that given TC (truth-functional closure), triviality follows: it is, in fact, easy to see, in a rough way, why; see Adams (1975: 5–6). For

$$p(A \rightarrow C) = p(C/A) = f(p(A \& C), p(A))$$

where $p(A \rightarrow C)$ exists. So that, if truth-functions are acceptable p-functions and obey the same laws; and if $T(A \rightarrow C)$ exists,

$$T(A \rightarrow C) = T(C/A) = f(T(A \& C), T(A))$$

and then, since $T(A \& C)$ is a function of $T(A)$ and $T(C)$, $T(A \rightarrow C)$ would be a truth-function. But no truth-function '$*$' is such that $p(A*C)$ is such that $p(A*C)$ is the ratio of $p(A \& C)$ to $p(A)$.

This is not a *reductio* proof for the PROPOSAL, because the proposal does not strictly require that $p(A \rightarrow C)$ is a function of $p(A)$ and $p(A \& C)$; for, where $p(A)$ is 0, $p(A \rightarrow C)$ is not defined, and $T(A)$ is always either 0 or 1. But the more rigorous proof of Adams' (1975: 6–7) avoids this failing. I do not give that proof here, because I give in the next section a proof, due to Carlstrom and Hill, which captures the essential idea of Adams' proof, while not being open to the major objection I see to it: which is that Adams' proof too presupposes that p-functions are not regular.

For if TC holds, then, for every S, there is a p-function in the class which assigns S either 1 or 0; and from this it follows, by regularity, that every S is either *a priori* true or *a priori* false. And, as we already know, that is enough to entail triviality in the language and the class of p-functions, without any special assumptions about conditionals.

9.6 CARLSTROM AND HILL

Fortunately, Carlstrom and Hill provided, in their excellent (1978) review of Adams' *The Logic of Conditionals* (1975), a simple semantic triviality proof for a possible worlds interpretation, which does not, so far as I can see, rely on the questionable assumptions that underlie the standard triviality proofs.

We are trying to maintain that there is a way of assigning truth-values at worlds to conditionals which guarantees that, for every conditional $(A \rightarrow C)$, where A and C are not themselves either conditionals or embedded conditionals, the sum of the probabilities of the worlds in which $(A \rightarrow C)$ is true is equal to $p(C/A)$.[11]

---

11. Remember that talk of worlds here is a vivid way of putting a point about basic atoms; see 3.6.

Consider now three worlds X, Y and Z. In these worlds the truth values of $(A \to C)$, A and C, are as follows:

	$(A \to C)$	A	C
X:	T	T	T
Y:	T	Φ	θ
Z:	F	Φ	θ

where Φ and θ are truth-values, but it does not matter which. Since we know that $(A \to C)$ is not a truth-function – there is no truth-function of two propositions whose probability equals the conditional probability – it is presumably possible for A and C to have the same truth-value in two worlds where the conditional has different truth-values. It is pretty clear too that it is at least possible that $(A \to C)$ should be true when $(A \ \& \ C)$ is. But it is only these two assumptions we need to get to the conclusion that there are three such possible worlds.

Since each of these worlds is possible, it will have a probability between 0 and 1:[12] and every assignment of probabilities to the worlds X, Y and Z such that

$$0 < p(X) + p(Y) + p(Z) < 1$$

is permissible. So let us consider two possible p-functions, p and p': both of which assign to X a probability of about 0.5. However, p assigns Y a probability near 0.5, while p' assigns Z a probability near 0.5.

In the p-function p, $(A \to C) = $ (approx.) $p(X) + p(Y) = $ (approx.) 1; for the sum of the probabilities of all the other possible worlds is very low and it matters very little in which of them the conditional is true. In the p-function p', however,

$$p'(A \to C) \ = \ \text{(approx.)} \ p(X) \ = \ \text{(approx.)} \ = \ 0.5$$

(since at the world Z the conditional is false). Consider now the ratios of probabilities

$$\frac{p(C \ \& \ A)}{p(A)} \quad \frac{p'(C \ \& \ A)}{p'(A)}$$

which are equal to $p(C/A)$ and $p'(C/A)$ respectively. Whatever truth-values Φ and θ are, this ratio is approximately the same in each of the two p-functions. Yet the probabilities of the conditionals are clearly quite different. And this shows that we cannot have AH in such a possible world semantics; see Carlstrom and Hill (1978).

---

12. We thus avoid assuming TC; for we do not have to suppose that any *a posteriori* proposition has a probability of 0 or 1.

It is worth observing that this set-up allows us to produce a stronger result: and if we introduce a little terminology it is possible to see which assumptions it is that give rise to the *reductio*.

DEF 1: A partial truth-function of two truth-values, expressed by a connective '∗', is *strictly partial* iff there exists at least one ordered pair of truth-values such that, for a pair of sentences A and B, if A has the first value, and B has the second, '$A \ast B$' can be either true or false.

DEF 2: A *two-place probabilistic connective* is a connective '∗', such that, there exists a function, f, for which, for every p-function, p, $p(A \ast C) = f[p(A), p(C), p(A \ \& \ C)]$

With this language we can say that

THEOREM: No strictly partial truth-function of two truth-values is a two-place probabilistic connective.

To see that this is so, consider three worlds X, Y and Z. In these worlds the truth values of $(R \ast S)$, R and S, are as follows:

	$(R \ast S)$	R	S
X:	T	A	B
Y:	T	Φ	θ
Z:	F	Φ	θ

where A, B, Φ and θ are truth-values, and $\langle A, B \rangle$ may or may not be identical with $\langle \Phi, \theta \rangle$. The argument proceeds now exactly as before: we consider two p-functions, p and p'; one produced by summing up the probabilities, when $p(X) = 0.5$ and so (roughly) is $p(Y)$; and the other produced when $p(X) = 0.5$ and so (roughly) is $p(Z)$. Since '∗' is a probabilistic connective we are now trapped in a *reductio*. On the one hand, $p(R \ast S)$ must be the same in each of these two cases: for if '∗' is a probabilistic connective then, given the truth values of R and S (and thus of $(R \ \& \ S)$) in both worlds, we have fixed what $p(R \ast S)$ is, and it must be the same in p and p', because it is a function of the probabilities of R, S and $(R \ \& \ S)$, all of which are the same in p and p'. On the other hand, it also has to be different in each case, since $p(R \ast S)$ should be about 0.5 in p and about 1 in p'.[13] For three such worlds to exist '∗' has to be

13. The argument here is not quite rigorous: to make it so, assume both
  (a) that the pair of probabilities assigned to X and Y by p and the pair assigned to X and Z by p' are *identical*; *and*
  (b) that the probabilities assigned by these two p-functions to every other world are such that $p(R) = p'(R)$, $p(S) = p'(S)$, and $p(R \ \& \ S) = p'(R \ \& \ S)$.
  Note that this does not appear to commit us to TC.

(a) strictly partial, because otherwise there would not exist a pair of truth values $\langle \Phi, \theta \rangle$ for which $(R * S)$ can take both T and F;
and for the *reductio* to work, '$*$' must be

(b) a probabilistic connective, for which $p(R * S)$ is a function of $p(R)$, $p(S)$ and $p(R \ \& \ S)$.

It is, I hope, clear from this outline of a proof, that the combination of these two factors is what gives rise to the problem.

9.7 COMPOUNDS OF CONDITIONALS

The triviality proofs are rather abstract. Maybe something in the way they idealise is what gives rise to the problem. If we want to confirm our interpretation of them as showing that conditionals do not have truth conditions, some more concrete semantic evidence would be helpful. In particular, if conditionals have truth conditions, there ought to be nothing problematic about their behaviour when they lie within the scope of truth-functional connectives. If a sentence S has a truth condition, and the sentence R does also, there ought to be nothing difficult in saying what $(S \ \& \ R)$ and $(S \lor R)$ and $(\neg S)$ mean. So evidence that where S or R is a conditional sentence, the truth-function behaves in the normal way, would be evidence in favour of the view that they have truth conditions. Correspondingly, and in the absence of any alternative explanation, the fact that they do not behave normally when they lie within the scope of truth-functional connectives lends support to the view that they do not have truth conditions. I shall show in this section that conditionals, when compounded, behave quite differently from non-conditional sentences with truth conditions; and, having rejected a possible alternative explanation, I shall claim that the best evidence is that they have no truth conditions.

Let us begin with negation, and ask whether we can give an account of sentences of the form

It is not the case that if A, then C.

Stalnaker (1968) once suggested that the negation of

1: If A, C

is

2: If A, not-C.

The reason for thinking this is simple: if $(A \rightarrow C)$ has truth conditions, then the truth-function 'not' should apply to it in the normal way. In particular, it would follow, on the PROPOSAL, that, since, in general $p(S) = 1 \ -$

$p(\neg S)$, and $p(\neg C/A) = 1 - p(C/A)$, the negation of a conditional $(A \rightarrow C)$ should be $(A \rightarrow \neg C)$. So Stalnaker would be right. But we should then have conditional excluded middle: for every 'A' and 'C'

CEM: $(A \rightarrow C) \lor (A \rightarrow \neg C)$.

And the evidence is that this is false. Consider Schrödinger's cat: and suppose that there is a gun set up to fire at it iff a certain quantum event occurs, with a probability conditional upon that event of 0.5. That is

p(The cat dies/The event occurs) = 0.5.

Now suppose the event will occur, if at all, in five minutes' time. Does anyone want to say that one of the following sentences is true?

'If the event occurs, the cat will die.'
'If the event occurs, the cat will not die.'

It is true that we want to say

'If the event occurs, either the cat will die or it will not die.

But this is equivalent to

'If the event occurs the cat will die, or if the event occurs, the cat will not die'

only on the question-begging assumption of conditional excluded middle.

Some people think that these indeterministic cases are peculiar. But even in cases where indeterminism is not the issue, Stalnaker's proposal goes against the evidence. It is, of course true, that

3: John will not come. But even if he does, Mary will not

is a perfectly good way of 'contradicting' somebody's claim that

4: If John comes, Mary will.

But

5: It is not the case that if John comes Mary will

is also assertible when

6: If John comes Mary may not

is. And it seems perfectly proper to deny 4, even if we do not believe that if John comes Mary will not, just because it simply does not seem to us that if he does come she *will*. In other words, 5 is assertible just when 4 is not. And the rule for conditional negations that this suggests is that they are assertible just when the conditional is not assertible.

206

I think this rule pretty reasonable on the assumption that conditionals are not truth-conditional. For if conditionals have no truth conditions, the normal semantics of negation will not apply to them; at least not straightforwardly. To negate a sentence is to produce a sentence which is true iff that sentence is false; if conditionals do not admit of truth and falsity, any rule governing the assertibility of their negations will have to be some extension of that central rule. Stalnaker's rule is just one possible extension: and since the justification for the normal rule depends on S's having truth conditions, there seems no very good ground for extending it as Stalnaker does to indicative conditionals which are not truth-conditional. Of course, it will follow from my alternative rule that when $p(\neg C/A)$ is high, it will be proper to assert the negation of a conditional. For when

7: If A then not-C

is assertible,

8: If A, then C

certainly is not. But this will not be the only case in which the conditional's negation is assertible.

The correct rule

COND.NEG: '$\neg$(If A, then C)' is assertible iff 'If A, then C' is not assertible

is given by Pollock (1976) and Parry (1957).[14]

A defender of the view that conditionals are truth-conditional could, I suppose, insist at this point that Stalnaker's account of conditional negation was correct, and that my 'It is not the case that if A, then C' is not the negation of a conditional. For some reason, it might be alleged, 'It is not the case that . . .' operates on conditionals to produce a sentence which is assertible iff the embedded sentence is not assertible; while the application of 'real' negation on a conditional is reflected as 'If A, then not-C'. And it could be said in favour of this proposal that 'It is not the case that . . .' sometimes does operate in this way for non-conditional sentences. Thus, someone might just say, emphatically,

It is *not* the case that John is coming. He may still not come

and clearly not mean to assert that John is not coming – though it still needs

---

14. Dummett asserts that 'indicative conditionals of natural language can[not] . . . be negated . . .' (1973: 451). And, in a sense, this is correct. If we take the negation sign to be governed only by the normal truth-table, then it will not apply to non-truth-conditional structures. But 'not' need not be restricted in this way. 'It is not the case that S' need not only be a truth-function of 'It is the case that S'; it can still be governed by assertibility conditions even when S has no truth-value.

explaining why, for the conditional, the proposed interpretation is obligatory, while for non- conditional sentences it is not only not obligatory, but not even a natural alternative reading. In 11.5 I shall confirm this analysis with an account of the semantics of conditionals with 'may' in their consequents.

If it were only when they are negated that conditionals behaved oddly, we might, then, accept such a case for persisting in ascribing them truth conditions. But, if we now turn to the case of disjunction, we shall see that here too conditionals behave oddly.

The trouble with disjunctions of conditionals is simply that it is hard to make sense of them at all. This is surprising if conditionals have truth conditions, since, if they have truth conditions and 'or' is, as it seems to be, a truth-function, the application of the normal semantic rules ought always to give us a reading. But what are we to make of

Either if John comes, Mary will or if Peter comes, Martha will.?

There is one kind of counterexample to the claim that sentences of the form ((If A, C) or (if A', C')) do not make sense. But it is a kind of counterexample which reinforces the claim that conditionals do not behave normally under disjunction. Consider, for example

9: Either, if John comes, we will have fun, or, if James comes, we will go home.

Now there is no doubt that there is a reading for this sentence; but it is not a disjunction of conditionals at all. What we need to do, as is evidenced by the bracketing with commas, is to see it as a disjunction of non-conditional sentences, asserted along with a pair of conditionals which provide a specification of the circumstances in which each disjunct will be true. Thus what this sentence amounts to is the conjoint assertion of

(a) If John comes, we will have fun
(b) If James comes, we will go home
and
(c) Either John comes or James comes.[15]

Part of the evidence that this is not a really a disjunction of conditionals is easily given; if it were a disjunction then it would be assertible when one disjunct was. (This is a simple consequence of the normal disjunction rule:

DISJ: '$S \vee R$' is assertible iff $p(S \vee R) > 1 - e$.)

But 9 is not assertible when (a) is and (b) is not.

---

15. Like most disjunctive assertions, this one conversationally implicates that the speaker does not know which of them will come; see Chapter 8.

Once again there is a defence for truth condition theorists. They can say that the reason there is no reading for disjunctions of conditionals is that they strain our computational capacity. We cannot produce readings not because there are none, but because we cannot think them through. I mention this defence only because I have heard it offered. It seems to me to be open to the very serious objection that it would only be reasonable if there were never any readings of sentences whose surface form was of a pair of disjoined conditionals. But there is. And it is one that is, if anything, more computationally taxing than it would be to read it as a disjunction of conditionals, if they had truth conditions; for, as we have seen, it involves recognising the conjoint assertion of two conditionals and a disjunction. If this were regarded as a conjunction of the form

$$(A \lor A') \mathbin{\&} (A \to C) \mathbin{\&} (A' \to C')$$

then this seems to be at least as deeply computationally complex as any reading of it as a disjunction of the form

$$(A \to C) \lor (A' \to C')$$

would be.

The one exception to the claim that conditionals behave oddly when embedded is in the case of conjunction. But there is a very good reason why that should be so. For 'and' is not only a truth-function, it also marks the beginning of a new assertion, as I can exemplify in the next sentence. And there is no very easy way to tell in spoken English whether

John is coming and Mary is coming

is the assertion of a conjunction or the conjoint assertion of the two component sentences. Of course, in this case it does not matter: for though $p(A \mathbin{\&} C)$ can be slightly less than $(1 - e)$, when $p(A)$ and $p(C)$ are both equal to $(1 - e)$, such a reduction in probability of e, where e is very small, will not normally take us from the assertible to the un-assertible. (I take this matter up again in the next chapter.)[16]

In the case of 'or' and 'not', then, we get results which are surprising if the conditional is truth-conditional and not surprising if it is not: and the evidence from 'and' does not support a truth-conditional analysis. We need now to move away from the truth-functions, and consider the behaviour of conditionals embedded in conditionals.

16. Evidence that 'and' can actually introduce new speech-acts, so that its function is even more general than as a device for conjoint assertion, comes from the fact that we can say: 'To the left of the slide you will see the outline of the indifferent gonad. And don't you sit there smirking at the back of the class Smithers'.

But it will be easier to do this in the context of a generalisation of Adams' Hypothesis, which I shall offer in Chapter 11. So far, at least, the evidence all supports or is consistent with the view that indicative conditionals have no truth conditions; and it is to the consequences of this fact that the next chapter is devoted.

9.8 A FINAL ARGUMENT

Let me end by offering a further, simple, argument for the view that the PROPOSAL leads one very quickly into difficulties. First, note that the proposal entails (what most conditional logics allow) that

EQUIVALENCE: $A \& A \rightarrow C \dashv\vdash A \& C$[17]

(where '$\dashv\vdash$' is logical equivalence). To show that it entails this equivalence we need to say what account of logical consequence we assume when we are using probabilistic connectives: I suggest that we follow Adams' account of consequence in supposing that U follows from premises R and S iff $p(U) \geqslant p(R \& S)$ in all acceptable p-functions; see Chapter 10. *Modus ponens*, which is, after all, the rule of inference by which we recognise a conditional, follows pretty obviously; and that gives us EQUIVALENCE in the forward direction; to get the backwards direction, notice that if $p(A \& C) = k$, $p(C/A) \geqslant k$.[18]

Now the 'proof'. We suppose $(A \rightarrow C)$ has truth conditions *and* a probability equal to $p(C/A)$. If it has truth conditions then $p(A/A \rightarrow C)$ exists: it is just the ratio of $p(A \& (A \rightarrow C))$ to $p(A \rightarrow C)$, (provided, as we may assume, $p(A \rightarrow C)$ is not 0). Suppose, for the purpose of *reductio* that $p(A/A \rightarrow C)$ is not equal to $p(A)$. This is just the condition that the conditional is not statistically independent of its antecedent: and it seems a modest requirement that A and $(A \rightarrow C)$ can be independent of each other; for neither entails the other and each is consistent with the other, and any pair of propositions satisfying that condition would usually be held to be potentially statistically independent in the p-function of a reasonable person.

Given this assumption it follows almost immediately that the PROPOSAL is false. For if the probability of A given $(A \rightarrow C)$ is not equal to $p(A)$, it must be either greater or less than $p(A)$. Suppose that it is greater. Then

---

17. This rule, incidentally, distinguishes the logics of indicative and subjunctive conditionals. For, provided you are not sure the world is deterministic, it can be true that A and C will happen without its being the case that C would happen if A were to happen; see Lewis (1918a: 24–8).
18. Presumably we do not need to worry about cases where $p(A)$ is 0 and $p(A \rightarrow C)$ is undefined; for in those cases
    (a) A is *a priori* false (and so, by standard assumptions, anything follows from it); *and*
    (b) we should not, anyway, want to make the inference in either direction if A were *a priori* false, except, perhaps, in a *reductio*; in which case (a) applies.

1: $p(A/A \rightarrow C) > p(A)$

2: $p(A \& (A \rightarrow C)) > p(C) \cdot p(A \rightarrow C)$ (def. of $p(/)$)

But, by EQUIVALENCE, and the probability theorem that if S and T are logically equivalent $p(S) = p(T)$;

3: $\dfrac{p(A \& C)}{p(C)} > p(A \rightarrow C)$

and so, by the definition of conditional probability, once more,

4: $p(C/A) > p(A \rightarrow C)$

which is inconsistent with the PROPOSAL. An argument of the same form will obviously lead to the same conclusion if $p(A/A \rightarrow C)$ is less than $p(A)$.

Give up the PROPOSAL, and with it the claim that conditionals have truth conditions, and this problem need never arise.[19]

Suppose I am right, then, and conditionals do not have truth-values. What, in terms of the account of truth in Chapter 5 does this mean?

If conditionals do not have truth-values, there is nothing in the world, no fact, to correspond to them. So, in particular, conditional facts can play no role in causation. But that means there will be no input claims connecting conditional facts with conditional beliefs, and no output claims connecting utilities of conditionals with acts of bringing about conditional states of affairs; in fact, there will not be any conditional utilities and desirabilities at all. For, for a belief to have a truth condition it must be possible to act on it, as TRUTH requires. But to act on a belief it has to be possible to think that whether or not it is *true* is *causally* independent of what you do. For a desirability to have a truth condition, it has to be possible to try to bring it about that what is desired is true.

In the absence of connections of these kinds with the outside world, a representation has no truth conditions.

So: we cannot have evidence for a conditional belief (only evidence for other beliefs which causes us to have high conditional probability); and we cannot perform conditional acts, whose aim is to bring it about that if A happens, C does.

These claims are likely to seem more surprising than they need to because, as I have argued, English has two distinct conditionals. I have been discussing indicative conditionals, which express conditional beliefs. For subjunctive conditionals, which express subjunctive conditional beliefs, all of these claims are false. Evidence that a subjunctive conditional is true can come from looking: we can see that a blade is sharp, that is, that it would cut us if we

19. Brian Ellis taught me this argument.

were to tun our fingers along it. And we can try *and* succeed in bringing about subjunctive conditional states of affairs: handcuff John to Peter and we have made it true that Peter would come, if John did.[20]

9.9 CONCLUSION

If, like me, you think that p-functions should be regular, the original triviality proofs need not worry you. But the arguments of the last three sections, including Carlstrom and Hill's version of the triviality proof, *are* reasons for rejecting the view that conditionals have truth conditions, *if* you accept AH, which has found much favour. There are, as van Fraassen has shown (1976), ways of avoiding the triviality results if you do not suppose that *all* the laws that hold for the probabilities of simple truth-valued sentences hold for the probabilities of conditionals. But if conditionals have truth-values, why should their probabilities of truth behave differently from those of other truth-valued sentences? I think the best policy is to accept Adams' demonstration that you can have a disciplined account of the semantic behaviour of a conditional which does not depend on assigning it truth conditions (1965, 1966, 1975); especially since, as we shall see in the next chapter, Adams has also shown how to give an account of inference with indicative conditionals without assigning them truth conditions. I find this result quite congenial. For if there is one thing that has seemed to me dubious since my introduction to the material conditional in sentential logic, it is the claim that all indicative conditionals are either true or false.

---

20. If you are sceptical about these last two claims, you might be tempted – as I was – to try to provide a probabilistic semantics for the subjunctive conditional, supposing that there is some p-function, other than the agent's actual p-function, for which $p(A * C) = p(C/A)$. But if this were right, then subjunctives would be possible only in trivial languages; and our language is not trivial. Furthermore, this would commit you to conditional excluded middle, for subjunctive conditionals; which is only valid if determinism is logically true. Since determinism is not even contingently true, this would be an error.

10

Logic without truth

> *Hypothesis*: in a situation where a reasoner must reason from some-
> what uncertain or fallible premises, he should want to reason in accord
> with principles that lead from probable premises to probable
> conclusions – because he wants to arrive at probable conclusions.
>
> (Adams, 1975: 1)

10.1 ADAMS AND THE VALIDITY OF CONDITIONAL INFERENCES

From the fact that indicative conditionals have no truth conditions, conventional wisdom will have us inferring that they have no logic. On a standard
definition, which I relied on in 8.2, a sentence S follows from a class P of
premises iff it is not logically possible for the members of P to be *true* and S
to be *false*. But this way of thinking surely concedes too much to one modern
conception of the function of logical theory. For on the traditional conception
logic is the study of reasonable argument; and indicative conditionals show up
in arguments both good and bad, so that something needs to be said about
how we tell which is which. A theorist of argument who said nothing about
indicative conditionals, just because they have no truth-values, would be
avoiding a central and familiar class of cases. Indeed, we might well respond
by denying that someone whose theory cannot tell us that *modus ponens* is an
acceptable form of argument and affirming the consequent is not, understands
what an argument is at all.

In this chapter I want to explain the way in which Adams has suggested
we can use his semantic proposal to give an account of reasoning with
conditionals. Adams' strategy in the face of conditionals without truth-values,
is to try to formalise an alternative intuition about reasonableness of inference,
which applies to truth-conditional and non-truth-conditional sentences alike.
The informal idea is this:

> PR: 'If an inference is reasonable, it cannot be the case that on any occasion
> the assertion of its premises is justified and the non-vacuous denial of its
> conclusion is justified.' (Adams, 1965: 177)[1]

---

1. The stipulation about non-vacuity is a consequence of Adams' holding a slightly modified
version of AH, which holds that a conditional is assertible iff either $p(C/A)$ is high *or* $p(A) = 0$.
When the second disjunct of this criterion is satisfied, he says that the assertion of the

Adams offers two formalisations of PR: one corresponding to the case where justification means that $p(S) = 1$ ('strict' justification), and the other to the case where justification means $p(S) \geqslant (1 - e)$ and e is small ('probabilistic' justification). For strict justification we have the strict reasonableness criterion:

SRC: For any class of sentences $(S_1, S_2, \ldots, S_n)$ and any sentence R, the members of the class of the S_i are the premises of a reasonable inference to R iff

(i) (p) $((p(S_i) = 1)$ entails $(p(R) = 1))$.

For probabilistic justification we have the probabilistic reasonableness criterion:

PRC: For any class of sentences $(S_1, S_2, \ldots, S_n)$ and any sentence R, the S_i are the premises of a reasonable inference to R, iff

(e) $E(d)$ (p) $(((i)p(S_i) \geqslant (1 - d))$ entails $(p(R) \geqslant (1 - e))$,

where $e, d \neq 0$. (1965: 185–6).

Adams' strategy is to show that we can delineate strictly the class of 'inferences' involving the conditional that satisfies PRC.

It is worth enquiring why Adams chose to work with PRC. In particular, why not SRC? The answer is that the strict reasonableness criterion is, in two ways, rather uninteresting. First, since Adams thought that the assertion of a conditional is justified iff either the conditional probability is high or the probability of the antecedent is 0, it follows that the assertion of a conditional is strictly justified iff the material conditional is certain. For the Lewis equation, which holds when $p(A) \neq 0$,

$$p(A \supset C) = p(C/A) + p(\neg A) \cdot p(\neg C/A),$$

tells us that, if $p(A) \neq 0$, the probability of the material conditional and the conditional probability are identical iff $p(C/A) = 1$. And if $p(A)$ is 0, $p(A \supset C)$ is certain. Consequently an inference involving conditionals has premises that are strictly assertible, iff a corresponding inference with the material conditional replacing all indicative conditionals also has premises which are strictly assertible. Now Adams shows that inferences satisfy the SRC iff the premises tautologically imply the conclusion. So that an argument which includes indicative conditionals as premises or conclusion satisfies the

conditional is vacuous. I think that the notion of vacuity here is unhelpful. The paragraph where he discusses the matter (1965: 176) is strewn with confusions, and I shall discuss these later, in 10.2. We shall miss nothing, for the moment, if we ignore Adams' introduction of talk of vacuity.

214

SRC iff the premises of a corresponding argument, in which material conditionals replace conditonals, tautologically entail the conclusion. So if we were to use SRC, the conditional would have exactly the inferential behaviour of the material conditional; and since the conditional is not, given AH, a material conditional, we should like this fact, presumably, to be reflected in its inferential behaviour.

The second reason why SRC is uninteresting is that in everyday argument we rarely work with premises of which we are certain. On my view, in fact, we are certain only of what is *a priori* true, and it would be absurdly restrictive to be unable to look at inferences with *a posteriori* premises. If inferential behaviour is to represent justified moves from sentences we believe, not certainly, but strongly enough to assert them, then a criterion something like PRC is essential; see Adams (1965: 190–4, Section 14).

PRC is set up, as I have observed, by analogy with the criterion for entailment: but there is an immediate difference between PRC and the criterion for entailment. For PRC is supposed to formalise the idea that an inference is reasonable iff it is not possible for the premises to be assertible and the conclusion deniable. And whereas truth and falsity, in the criterion for entailment, are the only two possibilities – for normal purposes we can assume excluded middle – assertibility and deniability (which is the assertibility of the negation) are not the only possibilities. In many circumstances it is proper to assert neither S nor its negation; we just do not know whether or not S. Now Adams says (1965: 185) that the condition, PR, that if all the premises are assertible, the conclusion must not be deniable, is equivalent to the rather different

PR': that if all the premises are assertible, the conclusion must be assertible.

The general requirement is that it should not be the case that there be a situation under which all the formulas in S [i.e. my S_i] are assertible but A [my R] is non-vacuously deniable. We will actually formulate a slightly stronger requirement: namely, that in any situation in which all of the formulas of S are assertible, A must also be *assertible* (not just not deniable), though it can be shown that this apparently stronger requirement is actually equivalent to the weaker one. (1965: 185).

But it is not. For though PR and PR' *are* equivalent when 'assertible' means 'strictly assertible', they are plainly not when looser degrees of assertibility are in question. Take a pattern of inference that involves no conditions at all: say from S and R to $(S \& R)$. Let a sentence be assertible iff its probability is greater that $(1 - e)$, for some small e. It will be deniable, then, where its probability is less than e. Then, if S is assertible and R is also, $(S \& R)$ is not deniable so long as e is less than $1/3$; but we can only be sure that $(S \& R)$ is assertible, given that S and R both are, if we know that $p(S/R) =$

$p(R/S) = 1$; which, of course, it may not be. Yet this pattern of inference conforms to PRC.

Since Adams' two readings, PR and PR′, do not coincide, it is important to see exactly what PRC *does* amount to. The answer is this: an inference satisfies PRC iff there is some probability $(1 - d)$, where d is greater than 0, such that if all the premises have at least this probability (and all the conditional premises have corresponding to them conditional probabilities of at least $(1 - d)$ also), then the conclusion will be assertible; i.e. the conclusion will have probability greater than or equal to $(1 - e)$. (Of course, d will be a function of e and the logical form of the inference.)

Now the trouble with this is that in many cases which satisfy PRC, d will be less than e. We shall have to have considerably more confidence in the premises than would suffice simply to make them assertible, if we want to be sure that the conclusion is assertible also. For the inference from both conjuncts to a conjunction, if we want to guarantee that the conclusion is assertible, we must make sure that the premises have probabilities of at least $(1 - (e/2))$; if, that is, we know nothing about the conditional probabilities. PRC does not, then, establish that if the premises are assertible, the conclusion will be. But it turns out that it does not even guarantee that if the premises are assertible, the conclusion will not be deniable. To see this we need only consider a version of the lottery paradox.

Adams shows that all inferences which are tautologically valid satisfy PRC. Take a set of sentences about the n tickets in a lottery.

LOTTERY: Ticket 1 will not win $= T_1$
Ticket 2 will not win $= T_2$
Ticket 3 will not win $= T_3$
. . .
Ticket n will not win $= T_n$

and the sentence

R: $((T_1 \,\&\, T_2 \,\&\, \ldots \,\&\, T_n) \supset$ None of the tickets will win$)$.

The inference from the various T_i and R to

None of the tickets will win

is tautologically valid. But we can be in a position to assert all of the sentences T_i and R (reading it as a material conditional) and also be in a position to assert the negation of the conclusion, namely

One of the tickets will win,

provided n is large enough.[2] Every premise sentence is assertible, but the conclusion is deniable. Yet the inference satisfies PRC.

Since PRC does not correspond to the intuitive principle PR, which it is supposed to formalise, nor to the principle PR', which Adams asserts to be equivalent to it, it is most unclear that the results Adams has proved with the PRC have the significance he claims for them. So that while I think that there are good reasons for accepting AH, Adams' earliest exposition of the logic of the conditional is flawed by the fact that PRC does not adequately formalise his informal criterion of adequacy for inferences involving conditionals. The flaw is not fatal and I shall remedy it in 10.4. In particular I shall show that PRC is more attractive than Adams' informal exposition of it, and I shall suggest we should accept it.

In the course of showing that PR, PR' and PRC are not equivalent, I made use of a version of the lottery paradox, to show that tautological implication can fail to satisfy both PR and PR'. (Of course, an inference that does not satisfy PR' will not satisfy PR.) This result should make us pause: for if the informal criterion rules out inferences where the premises *entail* the conclusion, this surely undermines its plausibility. It is certainly important to realise that the fact that the premises of a valid argument entail its conclusion does not guarantee that the argument satisfies PR. Until that is clear, the lottery paradox remains paradoxical, and many questions in epistemic logic (such as why it seems possible to believe the premises of a valid argument, while rationally not believing the conclusion) remain shrouded in mystery. But we must also realise that argument, as logicians standardly deal with it, is not a matter of discovering what must be said, so much as a matter of examining what must be so; confusion on this matter might lead us misguidedly to give up entailment because entailments do not satisfy PR. Examination of what must be so has to do with truth, however, and if indicative conditionals do not have truth conditions, there is no question of what must be so in respect of them.

When I say that logic is standardly concerned with what must be so — with logical truth — I do not mean to underestimate the significance of the development of techniques of natural deduction, with their emphasis on the actual process of proof; nor the important attempts, in work on entailment, for example, to clarify the epistemology of logic. Modern logic has a much greater claim to be called a theory of argument than had the logic of *Principia Mathematica*. But what I want to insist is that logicians are, and in my view

2. Having said I reject the material conditional, my use of it here perhaps bears comment: though not an indicative conditional, the material conditional is a perfectly good sentential connective, read with $(A \supset C)$ equivalent to $(\neg(A \& \neg C))$.

quite rightly, primarily concerned with the question of truth-preservation, rather than with the preservation of assertibility; this tendency is manifest, for example, in modal logic where, since validity plainly cannot be settled in terms of truth in the actual world, 'truth conditions' are sought in worlds that might have been.

We saw in Part I what the role of logical truth and validity was in determining what computations are available to an agent. So that the notion of a logic in which truth-preservation is central has a natural place in the view of language and mind I have been developing. If the lottery paradox reminds us that there is more to real arguments than the preservation of truth, it should not lead us to give up the notion altogether.

At this point, then, there seem to be two options: on the one hand we could accept that, since conditionals cannot be true and false, they have no logic. On the other hand, we could reject the standard characterisation of the proper concerns of logic, and try to reformulate criteria for reasonableness in argument that do not rely on relations of truth. The latter was, as we have seen, Adams' route.

Adams' work on the conditional is part of a wider project of charting the way in which the probability of a conclusion may diminish through the course of a logically valid argument. And that project is both interesting and important; see Adams and Levine (1975). It is obviously important in the application of logic. And it is also important in the theory of meaning, since, given the rule that assertibility goes by subjective probability, and the connection between logics and computational capacity, results of this kind close the gap between logic and discourse, by showing us which arguments will actually lead people from sentences to which they are disposed to assent, to others to which they will be disposed to assent also. Such an account will be one of the steps between a theory of meaning and an explanation of the actual linguistic behaviour of agents. But all this is implicit in the structure of the p-function and the general account of meaning given in Chapter 7; and though it is interesting to draw what conclusions we can from work of this kind, it is reasonable to see such results as derivative from the logic and as belonging to what we might call a theory of discourse; by which I mean a theory of actual speech-acts and the way people use them.

So that if all there is to be said about indicative conditionals, from a semantic point of view, is that they are assertible iff the conditional probability is high, then we may feed this fact into the theory of discourse: and it will be misleading to regard any of the results achieved as matters of logic, where logic is conceived of as the theory of truth-preservation in arguments.

This is misleading; but not dangerously so. For so long as we keep clear about the distinction between truth-preservation and probability-preservation, the inclusion of the latter within the scope of logic might be a worthwhile change in the division of intellectual labour.

I think that Adams' Hypothesis *is* all there is to say in a general way about the assertibility of indicative conditionals with truth-valued antecedents and consequents, give or take the dots on i's and crosses on t's that take up the remaining pages of this chapter. So I suggest we take a middle way between our two options: accepting that the conditional has, in the strictest sense, no logic, but trying to describe in detail those extensions of its basic rule of assertibility that are necessary to provide a full account of the role of the conditional in actual discourse, including, of course, argument. As a preliminary to this, we need to examine the scope and the limitations of Adams' Hypothesis.

10.2 IMPOSSIBLE ANTECEDENTS

The first step towards making Adams' Hypothesis more precise is to extend it to cases where a conditional has an antecedent with 0 probability. On my view, every representation with 0 probability is *a priori* false – as I shall say 'impossible' – since in considering the way probabilities should behave, we are considering the behaviour of computationally perfect agents, whose p-functions are regular. The problem arises because of the familiar fact that the conditional probability cannot be given by

$$\text{COND: } p(C/A) \ = \ \frac{p(C \ \& \ A)}{p(A)}$$

when $p(A) = 0$; since, where the denominator is 0, the fraction is undefined. As a result, if the conditional's assertibility goes by the conditional probability, we have a problem defining the relevant function.

There are two different kinds of approach to the definition of conditional probability, and consequently two slightly different forms in which the problem may arise. In some probability axiom systems, $p(C/A)$ is defined by COND. That is how I introduced conditional probability. In such a case there is no conditional probability when $p(A)$ is 0; and AH, as stated so far, rules the assertion of such conditionals out because there is no conditional probability, and thus no conditional probability to be high. There would never be any reason, on this account, to assert a conditional whose antecedent is thought to be certainly false.

This purely technical result is hardly a good enough reason on its own for denying assertibility to conditionals with impossible antecedents. Indeed Adams, taking the bull by the horns, suggested in 1965 that *all* such conditionals are assertible. Given his view that '$A \rightarrow \neg C$' is the negation of

'$A \rightarrow C$', this has the unhappy consequence that a whole class of mutually inconsistent sentences is assertible. We have rejected Adams' account of conditional negation, but we still have these conditionals as a kind of 'contrary' each of the other, so the result is no happier for us.

In other axiom systems (for 'Popper-functions'), the conditional probability is taken as primitive and COND is a theorem, provided $p(A) \neq 0$. In such systems absolute probability can be defined by

PROB: $p(A) = p(A/T)$

where T is any sentence that is certain, so that

(S) $(p(T/S) = 1).$[3]

In such a system, the question arises as to what criteria there can be for ascribing conditional probabilities where $p(A) = 0$. If we are using generalised conditionalisation to represent changes of p-function, then the probability of any R, where the originating representations are S_1 to S_n, goes to

$$\sum_{i=1}^{i=n} p(R/S_i) \cdot p'(Ri)$$

If we are using conditional probabilities in the course of charting changes of p-function, we will be interested in how probabilities conditional on sentences whose probability is 0 affect the process. Consider, for that purpose, some S_k, such that $p(S_k) = 0$. The probability of any R conditional on S_k will enter into the determination of the new probability $p'(R)$ only in the product $p(R/S_k) \cdot p'(S_k)$. But since, *ex hypothesi*, $p'(S_k) = 0$, the conditional probability $p(R/S_k)$ can take any value at all while leaving the resultant $p'(R)$ unaffected. For the purposes of epistemology, then, probabilities conditional upon impossible representations are of no use. A similar result is available for using conditional probabilities in calculating expected desirability. Because the d-value of a representation with probability 0 is undefined, there is no way in which the product

$d(R \ \& \ S) \cdot p(S/R)$

can enter into the calculation of the desirability of R on a partition of which S is a member.

If we do adopt $p(\ / \ )$ as a primitive, then, we can allow the conditional probability on R to take on any value at all, when $p(R/T)$ (for tautology T) is 0. How are we to decide which value?

---

3. For the sentential and predicate calculi this condition is satisfied by all and only the theorems; see Field (1977).

As usual we should be guided by theoretical convenience when the options are open. And, since the conditional probability plays no role in generalised conditionalisation when the sentence conditionalised upon has probability 0, we might define it in such a way as to maintain the simplest form of Adams' Hypothesis. So we need to consider whether conditionals with impossible antecedents are ever assertible, and, if so, when, and to assign to the conditional probability a value that will give the right results. I shall suggest that, where $p(R) = 0$, $p(S/R)$ should be 0 or undefined also.

We need then to consider facts about the assertibility of conditionals with 0 probability antecedents. Where someone assigns a representation 0 probability, it is, for them *a priori* false. But since people are not computationally perfect, they may fail to assign 0 probability to representations which would have 0 probability in the p-function of a computationally perfect agent. Suppose, however, Mary does assign 0 probability to a representation, R. We must ask now whether, in these circumstances, she would assent to a sentence of the form 'If R, S'. And it seems pretty clear that the answer is: No.

No one who grasped that it is *a priori* false that

John is and is not coming

would assent to

If John is and is not coming, then Mary is coming

or even, I suggest, to

If John is and is not coming, then John is coming.

Adams points out that

indicative conditional statements are seldom made in the knowledge that their antecedents are false . . . they are usually made in subjunctive mood. (1965: 176).

This remark is followed by a passage containing a series of muddles. Adams says that it is doubtful whether ordinary usage provides criteria for the justification of a conditional's assertion when the antecedent's probability is 0.[4] But once it is acknowledged that indicative conditionals are seldom used in these circumstances, it is odd to insist that they are all assertible; odd too to

---

4. What Adams actually says is misleading because it suggests that he may mean that subjunctive conditionals have no criteria in ordinary usage. But I think my reading is the right one:

   Where conditionals are stated [in the knowledge that their antecedents are false] . . . they are usually put in the subjunctive mood. It is doubtful if ordinary usage prescribes criteria . . . for the justification of . . . such conditional assertions (grammatically they are unjustified, but this is a different sense of justification . . .) (1965: 176).

   Incidentally, Adams must also mean grammatically *justified*, and not *un*justified.

regard the ensuing logical laws as 'awkward', since they follow from what is acknowledged to be an arbitrary stipulation.

We need to look more carefully at Adams' observation that conditionals are *'seldom'* used in the *'knowledge'* that their antecedents are false. The implicit identification of knowledge with the limit subjective probability of 1 is, of course, one that I would challenge. What matters is not whether the antecedent is known to be false, but rather whether the agent recognises that it is necessarily false. If a person does so recognise it, there seems to me no doubt that they will not assert the indicative conditional.

If someone does not believe the antecedent of a conditional to be impossible, then, of course, there is nothing to stop them assenting to it. We can thus account for the fact that such sentences as

If (2×167) is 324, then so is (167×2)

do get asserted. For we may imagine that someone could assign such a sentence a high conditional probability, just because they did not realise that its antecedent was false *a priori*. It is no more difficult to account for the fact that people regularly do assent to conditionals with impossible antecedents, on my view, than it is to account for the fact that they assent to sentences which are impossible; in the *p*-functions of computationally imperfect agents *a priori* falsehoods can have positive probabilities.

We are able then to give the right assertibility rule for conditionals with impossible antecedents, either by defining that conditional probability as a ratio, which is either undefined or defined as 0 when the antecedent probability is 0; or by having conditional probabilities as primitive and assigning them 0 when the representation conditionalised upon has 0 probability. Though I introduced conditional probabilities originally by way of the first of these approaches, I have no objection to the second.

There has been a great deal of controversy in the literature on conditionals about what to do with the case of the impossible antecedent. It seems to me a virtue of my approach that the account of why such conditionals appear to be sometimes assertible is just a special case of a general picture in which what is *a priori* false (or unassertible) is sometimes believed by computationally imperfect agents. We do not have to tinker with the *p*-function to give an account of these cases; compare van Fraassen (1976).

10.3 PROBLEMS OF INFERENCE

With this question settled, we can turn now to some of the problems connected with the application of AH in the analysis of our use of conditionals in argument. We need to begin by being clear what 'inference' means here.

As we discovered in 10.1 when considering Adams' criteria for acceptable inferences, we accept for the purposes of sentential logic many rules of inference which allow us to get from premises which are assertible to conclusions which are not: the lottery paradox is but a spectacular example of this. Yet, as I observed, even the simple rule that allows us to go from two premises to their conjunction can take us from premises which are both assertible (setting assertibility at $(1 - e)$), to a conclusion whose probability is $(1 - 2e)$, and, therefore, on the account of assertibility of Chapter 7, to a conclusion which is not assertible. This may not worry us much in short chains of reasoning – whatever value e has it must be very small – but such uncertainties can add up.

Now one reason for Adams' use of PRC is that, for a language without the conditional, all and only tautological entailments satisfy PRC. And we all feel there is some intuitive plausibility in the rules of natural deduction systems for sentential languages, at least where conditionals are read as material conditionals; and we are all inclined to use at least some of them in everyday argument.

We all feel, that is, of such rules as *modus ponens*, that if someone is entitled to assert the premises, they are entitled to assert the conclusion: indeed we feel they are obliged to assent to the conclusion even if they do not actually assert it. In fact, if we look at the rules of most natural deduction systems, we find that the most plausible of them are rules of inference from one or two premises to a conclusion: and I shall show in a moment that all such one or two premise inference rules for the sentential calculus have an important property:

IR: if conditionals are read as material conditionals, and if the premises for the application of the rule are assertible, the probability of the conclusion (in a computationally perfect agent) will always be at most slightly less than that necessary to make it assertible.

Given that this is so, it seems reasonable to suppose that we are willing to use in everyday argumentation principles which have this property; and we can then extend the rules we will accept by generalising IR to inferences involving indicative conditionals. A natural notion of theoremhood on this view is that something is a theorem iff it is always assertible; that is, it is assertible with no assertible premises at all.

This procedure is more *ad hoc* than Adams': he shows that all and only tautological entailments with the conditional read as a material conditional satisfy the PRC, and then goes on to extend the use of PRC to cases where the conditional is read according to AH. And he does this by the very natural procedure of assuming that we should place the same constraints on the conditional probability for conditionals, as PRC places on the absolute probability for non-conditional sentences. I adopt the less formal procedure because it seems to me that, since we accept in every day use rules of inference which can lead from premises which are assertible to conclusions which are not only not assertible, but actually deniable, our practice is best represented as what it is: namely, from an epistemic point of view, rather risky. (I shall, at any rate, resurrect PRC in 10.4.) But unless we can see that the rules of inference we normally use satisfy a more intuitively acceptable constraint than PRC, our practice is made by the lottery paradox to seem totally absurd. If we can see that the rules of inference we use conform to the intuitively more acceptable IR we can also see that the source of the problems of which the lottery paradox is typical, is that the multiple application of principles which are not in themselves totally unreasonable, can lead to unreasonable conclusions: the risks mount up. We can also see that the source of these problems is that the relation 'is a reasonable inference from' is not what we might call additive: where this means that it does not follow from the fact that every member of the set S is a reasonable inference from the set R of sentences, that the conjunction of S's members is a reasonable inference from the set R. Put in more familiar language what this amounts to is that rational belief does not satisfy the conjunctive closure principle (Kyburg, 1970).[5] If we are *not* clear that this *is* the source of our problems we may be inclined to lose confidence in individual rules of inference because, when linked together, they may lead to epistemic catastrophe. And that would deprive us of many useful principles of argument.

It is often said that deductive inference, unlike inductive inference, is not 'ampliative'; the conclusions do not 'go beyond' the premises. This is, of course, true if we consider the question from the point of view only of truth-values. But from the point of view of probability, deductive inference is certainly often, in another sense, ampliative: for the conclusions of a deductive argument may make stronger claims than the premises, in the sense of being less probable than any of them. The conclusion of a deductive argument may never be 'less true' than the least true premise (where the only way of being less true than true is to be false); but it may certainly be less probable than the least probable premise.

With this in mind we can now consider how to establish IR. We do not need to consider any particular rules of inference, because we can use standard results about p-functions over languages of the form of the sentential calculus; see, for example, Field (1977: 383). For we know that, for any R, and any set $[S_1, S_2, \ldots, S_n]$ of sentences, if the conjunction of the S_i is C, then

$$[S_1, S_2, \ldots, S_n] \vdash R \text{ iff } p(R) \geqslant p(C).$$

5. That is, the principle that if S and R are in the set of things it is rational to believe, (S & R) is also.

224

For inferences with one premise, this means that if the premise is assertible, the conclusion will be, provided the premise tautologically entails the conclusion. For inferences with two premises, and since

$$p(S) \geq (1 - e), \, p(R) \geq (1 - e) \vdash p(S \, \& \, R) \geq 1 - 2e$$

it follows that if both premises are assertible, the conclusion will have a probability of at least $(1 - 2e)$; and since e is small, it would seem carping to deny assertibility to a conclusion that satisfied this condition.

I propose, on this basis, to say that we accept rules of inference from one premise to a conclusion iff the conclusion must be assertible when the premise is; and from two premises to a conclusion iff the assertibility of both premises guarantees that the probability of the conclusion is at least $(1 - 2e)$. That, essentially, is what IR says, and it is all we need for the rest of this section.

Applied to indicative conditionals read according to AH, this would explain why we do not accept the inference corresponding to the sentential calculus tautological entailment:

$$\neg R \vdash (S \supset R)$$

namely

From $\neg R$ infer 'If S, then R'.

For it is perfectly possible for $p(\neg R)$ to be greater than $(1 - e)$, when $p(R/S)$ is less than $(1 - e)$. Indeed, it is possible for $p(R/S)$ to be 0, when $p(\neg R) > (1 - e)$. A similar analysis can be applied to

$$S \vdash (R \supset S)$$

and these two can be recognised as the paradoxes of the material conditional. We can also account easily for the fact that we accept both *modus ponens* and *modus tollens*.[6]

I have already shown that, on AH, neither disjunctive syllogism nor contraposition are sound principles. To show this I relied on the fact that the premise of each of these forms of argument could be assertible and the conclusion not; thus assuming implicitly the treatment of inference in the one premise case that I have just been advocating. And, since $p(S/R)$, $p(U/S)$ and $p(\neg U/R)$ can all be high, the rule of inference

TRANS: $(R \rightarrow S), (S \rightarrow U) \vdash (R \rightarrow U)$

which logicians have been misled by the transitivity of entailment into accepting, is not valid either.[7]

6. The algebra is too easy to be worth reproducing; but see my 1981: Appendix 6.
7. A counterexample to transitivity for the indicative conditional was given in 8.2.

And since the addition of DS, TRANS or CONTRA to the rules of inference sanctioned by AH and IR, would mean, as Adams has argued (1965: 189), that the indicative conditional would have the inferential behaviour of the material conditional,[8] we can understand why the material conditional has so enduring an appeal.

Adams' Hypothesis gets standard valid rules of inference for the conditional right, without being committed to the invalid ones we detected for the material conditional. But it shares with the material conditional a rule of inference which some have found counterintuitive. I call it the conjunction–conditional inference:

CC: $(A \ \& \ C) \vdash (A \rightarrow C)$

This rule is familiar, just because it holds for the material conditional, and has often been held to be at least highly artificial. Thus there is something odd about someone's saying that Mary will come, if John does, because they believe that Mary and John will both come. But we can surely give a Gricean account here of the counterintuitive feel of this inference. In Chapter 7 I suggested that a version of the Gricean maxim of quantity would explain why the inference from a sentence to a disjunction of which it is a disjunct seems unnatural. That principle was:

Do not utter a sentence S in circumstances where, for some R
   (a) R entails S, and S does not entail R
   (b) R is relevant, and
   (c) R is assertible.

This rule would certainly account for the fact that the utterance of the conclusion of CC in circumstances where the premise was assertible would normally be a breach of a conversational maxim. For $(R \ \& \ S)$ entails $(R \rightarrow S)$ but not conversely, according to IR; and $(R \ \& \ S)$ is presumably relevant in most cases where $(R \rightarrow S)$ is.[9]

---

8. This is only strictly true on the further assumption that all conditionals with impossible antecedents are assertible.
9. The alternative conversational rule (which Jackson prefers):

   R': It is permissible to assert some S, where you can assert R, which is equally relevant and entails (but is not entailed by) S, provided you do not believe S predominantly because you believe R,

where someone believes S predominantly because they believe R iff they have a high $p(\neg S / \neg R)$, could only apply in this case, if

   $p(\neg (R \rightarrow S) / \neg (R \ \& \ S))$

was defined. But since $(R \rightarrow S)$ is not truth–conditional, this conditional probability does not exist.

One final thing to be said in favour of CC is this: whenever a conditional and its antecedent are both assertible, the conjunction of antecedent and consequent is assertible also. There cannot, therefore, be an objection to holding that a conditional's assertibility is consistent with the assertibility of the conjunction, since, whenever the antecedent is true, they are always both assertible if *modus ponens* is valid.

AH and IR together have made it possible for us to give satisfactory accounts of intuitions about inferences with indicative conditionals. In the next section I turn to the full account of Adams' logic of indicative conditionals.

10.4 ADAMS' LOGIC

All the principles that Adams uses in the natural deduction system I shall be giving shortly satisfy IR, the principle I suggested in 10.3 for testing the adequacy of rules of inference with conditionals. But Adams' criterion of adequacy was PRC. If we are to decide whether to accept the claims of his system, we must make up our minds finally about this. The criterion IR applies only to one or two premise inferences: it says that an inference from one premise is valid iff the assertibility of the premise guarantees the assertibility of the conclusion; and that one from two premises is valid iff the assertibility of both premises guaranteed that the probability that determined the assertibility of the conclusion was greater than $(1 - 2e)$. Let us introduce the notion of the uncertainty of a sentence.

> UNCERTAINTY: The uncertainty of a truth-conditional sentence S is $(1 - p(S))$; and the uncertainty of a conditional $(A \rightarrow C)$ is $(1 - p(C/A))$.

We can now restate the criterion I used for one and two premise arguments as follows: where n is 1 or 2,

> GIR: an inference is reasonable iff the assertibility of the n premises guarantees that the uncertainty of the conclusion is at most (ne), (where, as before, a sentence S is assertible iff $p(S) > (1 - e)$, for a suitable small e).

Now I specifically restricted n to one or two premises because we needed only to consider inferences with one or two premises. But what is there to be said in favour of GIR – the *generalised* form of IR – for any finite number n of premises?

The feature which will make GIR most appealing to logicians is that for the sentential calculus, all and only entailments (i.e. tautologically valid inferences) satisfy it. But it has a number of other highly intuitively attractive features. First of all, it allows for the fact, which all of us respect in our everyday arguments, that the more premises we rely upon in an argument, the less secure we are in our conclusion. GIR says that the uncertainty of the conclusion (i.e. 1 minus the probability of its negation, where it is truth-conditional) has a higher possible maximum, the more premises we add. Hume put this very nicely:

'Tis certain, that when an inference is drawn immediately from an object, without any intermediate cause or effect, the conviction is much stronger, and the persuasion more lively, than when the imagination is carried through a long chain of connected arguments, *however infallible* the connection of each link may be esteemed.

(1888; 144; my italics)

What GIR allows us to do, however, is to define the maximum uncertainty of the conclusion as a function of the number of premises, given any particular level of assertibility, set by a choice of e.

Secondly, where the number of premises, n, is small, GIR reduces to the proposal that we should be able to be sure, of any acceptable inference, that if the premises are assertible, the conclusion will be highly probable; so highly probable, in fact, that, given the small size e must take, in any plausible model, it would not be too far wrong to say that the assertibility of the premises effectively guaranteed the assertibility of the conclusion. Of course, as we have seen, as the number of premises gets larger this gets less and less adequate as an approximation (remember the lottery paradox): but then we have already seen that where the number of premises is large we are less secure in the conclusion – the 'persuasion' is 'less lively' – even where we regard the argument as formally valid. Many philosophers with whom I have discussed this matter appear to think that the longer a proof is, the more likely we are to have made a mistake, and that this explains Hume's observation. This is no doubt true; but GIR, I think, offers a better account for inferences with *a posteriori* premises, explaining why the persuasion is less lively even where we have checked the argument's form. The length of a proof and the number of premises are, of course, two different matters; but, in practice, they are often positively correlated.

There is a third thing to be said for GIR. Where an inference satisfies it we know immediately one way of reducing the maximum possible uncertainty of the conclusion: namely to gather evidence that raises the probability of the premises. That is a desirable property in an inference; one that GIR guarantees. In his later work, Adams has focussed on this feature of his criterion of adequacy for inferences, and made it central. In his 1975 book he says, while developing what is just the old criterion of inference PRC in new dress, that a class of sentences probabilistically entails another iff it is possible to ensure an arbitrarily high degree of certitude in the conclusion of an inference, by making sure of the premises (1975: 56). The discussion of probabilistic entailment in the book is largely formal, however, and I have preferred to discuss the earlier and more extended informal exposition. It is worth observing one formal corollary of the notion of probabilistic entailment, however, which Adams demonstrates in the book: inferences that do not satisfy PRC have the property that 'it is not possible to assure *any* degree of certainty in the conclusions, no matter how certain the premises are required to be' (1975: 45). This is surely more reason to find PRC (and, therefore, GIR) attractive.

GIR thus seems to me initially attractive. Adams has shown that GIR is satisfied by all and only the inferences which satisfy PRC.[10] I mentioned, when I introduced IR in 10.4, that it was related to PRC. In fact, for the language of the sentential calculus, extended to include a conditional connective, it is equivalent to a special case of it, where the number of premises, n, is one or two.

Given the equivalence of GIR and PRC it follows that all and only tautological entailments of the extended sentential calculus language, L, satisfy GIR; since this is true of PRC (Adams, 1966). This language, L, is an extension of the language of the sentential calculus. Adams uses only the truth-functional connectives '$\neg$', '&' and '$\vee$'; but I shall use '$\supset$' and '$\equiv$' as well, for material implication and material equivalence, introduced, we may suppose, by way of standard equivalences. He adds to such a language the connective '$\rightarrow$' and adds to the normal wffs any wff of the form '$P \rightarrow Q$', where P and Q are truth-functional wffs. He also makes use of the necessarily true wff T. Where a wff, A, follows from a set of premises S, with members S_1 to S_n, by PRC, I write '$S \vdash A$'.

I also adopt, from now on, the convenience of speaking of the conditional probability as if it were the probability of the conditional. This allows the treatment to be totally general, instead of requiring us to state truth-conditional and non-truth-conditional results separately. Up until now, in this book, I have consistently spoken of the conditional probability corresponding to or determining the assertibility of a conditional sentence, in order to achieve the same effect. This clumsy circumlocution was intended to allow us to keep in mind that I was not assuming that the conditional had a probability of truth, only that its assertibility went by the conditional probability. Now that this is firmly established, no harm will come from speaking as if the conditional probability were the probability of a conditional, as Adams does throughout his formal paper. I have been keen to keep the distinction so far largely because Adams does not seem fully to have grasped it. Sceptics are urged to check that nothing in what follows hangs on any confusion that might have resulted.

10. This follows, as I show in my 1981: Chapter 10, from some meta-theorems in Adams (1966).

We can turn now to Adams' natural deduction system: remembering that T is the constant true sentence; and using P, Q, R, for any truth-functional compound of atomic sentences. To a system of natural deduction for the sentential calculus without the conditional add the following rules:

Premises		Conclusion
1: $\vdash (P \equiv Q)$, $(P \to R)$,	infer	$(Q \to R)$
2: $T \to P$ and *vice versa*.	infer	P
3: $\vdash (P \supset Q)$,	infer	$(P \to Q)$
4: $(P \to Q)$, $(R \to Q)$,	infer	$((P \vee R) \to Q)$
5: $((P \vee Q) \to R)$, $(Q \to \neg R)$,	infer	$(P \to R)$
6: $(P \to (Q \,\&\, R))$,	infer	$(P \to Q)$
7: $(P \to Q)$, $(P \to R)$,	infer	$(P \to (Q \,\&\, R))$
8: $(P \to Q)$, $((P \,\&\, Q) \to R)$,	infer	$(P \to R)$

That is Adams' system.[11]

The language over which these rule of inference are defined includes no embedded conditionals. But I do not see that this is a serious objection to it. Conjunctions of conditionals can be handled simply by treating each conditional as a separate premise, following the proposal that asserting a conjunction of conditionals is equivalent to asserting both of them. Disjuncts of conditionals we have no use for; and embedded conditionals create special problems. It is true that there is a rule for negated conditionals, and it might seem, therefore, that at least sentences of the form '$(\neg (A \to C))$' should be admissible. Adams, of course, has no need for such a move, since he believes that the negation of a conditional is a conditional with the same antecedent and the consequent negated. But that is a bad reason for refusing negated conditionals a place in your logic, since, as we have seen this is just not true. There are, however, better reasons for excluding it. For, as I suggested in 9.7,

It is not the case that $(A \to C)$

is equivalent to

If A, then it may be that $\neg C$.

11. In the course of 10.2 I defended the claim that conditionals with necessarily false antecedents are never assertible. Adams' conditional differs in that respect only from the one I have defended. In my 1981: Chapter 10, I show how to modify the natural deduction system to deal with this slight difference.

This suggests that conditional negation had better be handled in a modal conditional logic.[12] So I do not think Adams' system should be objected to on the grounds that it does not countenance negated conditionals. As for embedded conditionals, these will be considered in the next chapter.

Using this system we can get all the PRC-consequences of a finite set of premises: and since PRC and GIR are equivalent, we can get all (and only) the GIR-consequences.

This system organises our analysis of the indicative conditional, interpreted according to AH. So far as it goes, then, Adams' theory, trivially modified, seems to me a great leap forward. But it does not go far enough. Of particular importance is the question what consequences his semantic account has for the inductive logic of conditionals. And, for this purpose, it is essential to develop a theory of quantified conditionals. Field (1977) has made a start here by developing the idea of an extension of a language, and regarding values for 'probabilities' for quantified sentences as constraining the possible probability assignments to sentences in the extended language. Roughly, to believe that $(x) (Fx)$ is to be so disposed that the addition of a new singular term, a, to your system of representations will produce an extension of your p-function in which $p(Fa)$ is high. This seems to me a natural development of Ramsey's (1978) account of general beliefs as habits of singular belief. On a view like this, universally quantified conditionals would presumably be represented as constraints on assignments of conditional probabilities in extensions of the language, just in the way that simple universal judgements of the form $(x) (Fx)$ constrain the assignments of unconditional probabilities. Such a development would have one welcome consequence: since singular conditionals do not respect contraposition, there is no obvious reason why universal ones should. And the paradox of the ravens would cease to worry anyone that had not ceased to worry about it a long time ago (Hempel, 1965).

10.5 CONDITIONAL LOGIC

If I am right, and I think I have offered a range of reasons for thinking that I am, then we have in Adams' work the core of a new and better theory of the conditional. It is antirealist – in the sense of not assigning truth conditions – and it answers Lewis' implicit challenge to substantiate its feasibility in detail. Whether the account could be given a possible world interpretation is an interesting question. There is no *prima facie* reason why it should not: for

---

12. It turns out, on my account of conditionals of the form

  If A, then it may be the case that C

 that they are assertible iff $(\neg (A \rightarrow C))$ is; see 11.5.

possible worlds theories do not have to be realist. No one who like Kripke's account of modality, for example, has to hold that all possible worlds really exist: and, since, if they do not, modal statements need not be construed realistically – there might be literally nothing in virtue of which they were *true* – it follows that giving a possible world semantics leaves open the question of metaphysical realism.

What we can say for possible worlds approaches is that they cannot be constructed in the way Stalnaker originally proposed (1968). For Stalnaker's semantics has conditional excluded middle as a theorem:

CEM: $(A \rightarrow C) \lor (A \rightarrow \neg C)$

since he holds, wrongly as we have seen, that $(A \rightarrow \neg C)$ is the negation of $(A \rightarrow C)$; see also van Fraassen (1976). Yet Stalnaker's theory correctly rejects weakening, contraposition and transitivity,

WEAK: $(A \rightarrow C) \vdash (A \ \& \ B) \rightarrow C$

CONTRA: $(A \rightarrow C) \vdash (\neg C \rightarrow \neg A)$

and

TRANS: $(A \rightarrow C), (C \rightarrow C') \vdash (A \rightarrow C')$.

Lewis' theory, in his book *Counterfactuals* (1973), is not intended to cover the indicative conditional at all; but it is interesting to see that, over those inferences that involve no embedded conditionals, Lewis' semantics and GIR give the same logic (as Adams (1977) has shown), modulo the assumption, which both Lewis and Adams make, that conditionals with impossible antecedents are always assertible.[13]

This is, however, no reason to be indifferent between the two accounts; any more than the fact that exchanging 'T' and 'F' in all the truth-tables and giving an account of validity in terms of preservation of falsity will give the same sentential calculus, should encourage acceptance of this as an alternative account of inference. For one thing, the restriction to unembedded conditionals is completely arbitrary in Lewis' semantics, but quite natural, as we have seen, in Adams'. Lewis presumably holds that the fact that he can give an account of embedded conditionals is a virtue in his theory; but, if we believe Adams' Hypothesis is true for unembedded conditionals, we can show that this virtue is bought at a high price. For Carlstrom and Hill's triviality proofs show that Lewis' theory, though it gives the right logic, could not give conditionals the same semantic behaviour as AH. Lewis' language is not

---

13. Lewis, of course, thinks they are all true as well: Adams seems now to be uncertain about how to treat impossible conditionals (Adams, 1975).

trivial, and so cannot allow that the conditional's probability is its probability of truth. It follows, of course, that a Lewis conditional might sometimes have, say, a high probability when the conditional probability is low; and *vice versa*. And from this it will follow that a Lewis conditional can be assertible when an Adams conditional is not.

11

Generalising the probabilistic semantics of conditionals

> A state of information justifies our assertion of 'if P, then Q' just in case we can recognize that its enlargement into a state of information justifying the assertion of P would *eo ipso* transform it into a state of information justifying the assertion of Q.
>
> Wright (1976: 236)

11.1 OVERVIEW

Adams' Hypothesis is extremely restrictive. Not only will it be confined to indicative conditionals, but, it will only cover indicative conditionals for which $p(C/A)$ is defined. And a necessary condition for this is that A and C should have truth conditions. For we defined $p(C/A)$ thus

$$p(C/A) = \frac{p(C \ \& \ A)}{p(A)} \ ;$$

and $p(C \ \& \ A)$ and $p(A)$ are defined standardly only where $(C \ \& \ A)$ and A have truth conditions. Probability, as I have often repeated, is probability of truth.

The problem, of course, is that there are many conditional forms whose antecedents or consequents do not have probabilities of truth: and it follows that we cannot give an account of them. We cannot, notably, treat embedded conditionals on Adams' view, since, if $(A \rightarrow C)$ has no truth conditions, neither $p(B/A \rightarrow C)$ nor $p(A \rightarrow C/B)$ will be defined. We might try to define non-standard p-functions in which the conditional probability *is* defined on pairs of non-truth-conditional sentences. But there is, in the context of our general account, no rationale for doing so.

Embedding is not, however, the only problem: any conditional with indicative antecedent, whose consequent has no truth-value, will escape Adams' Hypothesis. So, in particular, AH offers no treatment of what I call the 'semi-indicative' conditional, of which

SI: If John is here, Mary may be here

is an exemplar, either.

I seek, therefore, in this chapter, to give a more general account of the semantics of conditionals with indicative antecedents; and, from now on, that is what I denote by the unqualified term 'conditional'. My proposal will give Adams' rule as a special case, and it will therefore allow us his logic for conditionals with truth-conditional antecedents and consequents. But it will also allow us to give an assertibility rule for conditionals with conditional consequents; and it will allow us to treat semi-indicatives in what I take to be the natural way, as having in their consequents sentences of the form 'It may be the case that *C*.'

I begin, in 11.2, by setting up my proposal, and offer, in 11.3, reasons for thinking that AH follows from it. In 11.4, I show how it allows us to treat conditionals with conditional consequents. I admit that it does not give a straightforward account of conditionals with conditional antecedents, though I show that it does give some sort of story for them, and I offer a reason for thinking that this is not such a bad result. For, as I argue, there is some evidence that there are no embedded indicative conditionals in English, that sentences which appear to be of this form are not. In 11.5, I report, and then endorse with modifications, a proposal of Ian Hacking's which tells us what the assertibility conditions of 'It may be the case that *C*' are, and then show that combining it with the generalised account of conditionals produces a semantics which conforms to some intuitions about semi-indicative conditionals. Section 11.6 consists of some concluding observations.

It is a merit, I believe, of the proposals I have to make that they offer explanations of a wide range of logical and semantic phenomena, and that they allow us to deal with the interaction between 'if . . . then . . .' and other structures without appeal to *ad hoc* subsidary hypotheses. But these proposals are made tentatively, especially in relation to embedded conditionals (11.4). On these questions, the last word has not been said.

11.2 RAMSEY CONDITIONALISATION

It is a familiar idea, which goes back at least to Ramsey, that we should understand conditionals like this:

> RAMSEY: someone believes a conditional $(A \rightarrow C)$ if every way of adding A directly to their stock of beliefs would lead to their believing C; see Ramsey (1978).

It is obvious, of course, that this will not do by itself. For one way of adding A directly to my stock of beliefs would be to add A and not-C at the same time, and that would mean that we never believe $(A \rightarrow C)$. But the force of 'directly' here is to rule out the addition to our stock of beliefs of anything other than the belief that A, a task which is relatively straightforward if the class of a person's beliefs is conceived of as a set of accepted sentences, and the conditional in question is one whose antecedent is not believed false. Where the antecedent *is* believed false, such deductive approaches characteristically try to restrict ways of adding *A* without circularity to ways that do not leave not-*C* in the deductive closure of a person's beliefs.[1]

This is not a strategy that suggests itself in a framework which uses subjective probabilities. For to acknowledge that beliefs have degrees, is to acknowledge that there is at least some difficulty in characterising someone's beliefs as consisting of a set of accepted sentences. I do not accept that it is raining in Philadelphia, yet I rather suspect that it may be; and, though 'It is raining in Philadelphia' is not amongst my beliefs, the fact that I partially believe it is one of the things that affects what I will come to believe when someone tells me it is raining in New York. In fact, as I argued in Chapter 4, it is more natural to characterise someone's total belief state by a subjective *p*-function, which captures not only beliefs but partial beliefs. And then there is no set of accepted beliefs, the addition to which of *A*, would entail *C*. Rather, what we normally call 'belief' is equated with a high degree of partial belief; and how high is enough will depend on our purposes.

Even in this probabilistic framework, the issue of what it is to add directly the belief that *A* to a person's total belief state remains problematic. We will want to represent change of beliefs by conditionalisation; but it does no good to say that someone believes that $(A \rightarrow C)$ iff they would come to have a high $p(C)$ on any direct rational revision of their degrees of belief in which $p(A)$ approached 1. For, once more, we must answer the problem I posed for deductivism: why should one rational revision not be to come directly to have a high $p(A)$ and $p(\neg C)$ at the same time?

The obvious answer is the same here as before: to add $(A \ \& \ \neg C)$ is to add more than *A*. What RAMSEY requires us to do is to consider the consequences of adding *just* the belief that *A*. Call that evidence necessary to add just the belief that *A*, 'minimal' evidence that *A*. Then, I suggest, we may rely on the following intuition about conditionals with truth- conditional antecedents and consequents:

INT: somebody believes a conditional $(A \rightarrow C)$ iff coming to have minimal evidence that *A* would lead to their believing *C*.

And so what we need is a characterisation of kinds of revision that change $p(A)$ minimally; the analogue of the deductivist's addition of just *A* to the accepted set of sentences. If $p(C)$ would be high in every probability function produced by minimal revision of a person's current probability function, which led to a high $p(A)$, they believe that $(A \rightarrow C)$.

---

1. See Goodman (1947), where heroic attempts are made to deal with subjunctive conditionals in this way.

There is another problem with combining RAMSEY with an attempt to characterise the consequences of the addition of the belief that A in terms of deductive closure; and it is centrally related to my task in this chapter. It is that deduction is classically conceived of in terms of truth-preservation. It follows that on any 'deductivist' interpretation of RAMSEY, we shall not be able to achieve the extension of our theory to conditionals with non-truth-conditional components. But this problem too arises on the probabilistic approach: for a p-function assigns values only to truth-valued sentences. And it is to deal with this fact, that I make the central proposal of this chapter. I suggest that we should exchange RAMSEY for a more general view, which is (where A and C are both truth-conditional) roughly equivalent to it.

I propose then that:

COND: somebody is entitled to assert a conditional $(A \rightarrow C)$ iff coming to have minimal evidence warranting the assertion of A would lead to their being entitled to assert that C.[2]

It is plausible, I think, that where A and C have truth conditions, COND is equivalent to RAMSEY. For to have minimal evidence warranting the assertion of A is to have evidence for believing that A, if the following is true:

ASS: S is assertible iff the speaker believes that the truth conditions of S hold.

And that is just the view of assertibility I urged in Chapter 7.

For COND to be any use, we need, now, to say, what it is to have minimal evidence warranting the assertion that A, for any A. And I approach this problem, by considering what minimal evidence for asserting that A is, where A is truth-conditional.

II.3 MINIMAL EVIDENCE

How we characterise *minimal* evidence depends on how we characterise the process of acquiring evidence in general. With simple conditionalisation, we recall, coming to believe that A, is coming to have $p(A) = 1$, and rational revision occurs by adjusting every $p(C)$ to $p(C/A)$. With simple conditionalisation we have an easy analogue of the deductivist's case; for adding *just* A will be conditionalising on A. The reason why conditionalising on $(A \& \neg C)$ is not acquiring *minimal* evidence that A, is that $(A \& \neg C)$ properly entails A – and is thus logically and evidentially stronger than it, ruling out more possibilities. We can say that

2. I think this proposal was suggested to me by the passage from Wright (1976) which provides my epigraph.

MINIMAL: minimal evidence that A is evidence which warrants the belief that A, and which does not properly entail any evidence that is sufficient to warrant the belief that A.[3]

If A has truth conditions and simple conditionalisation represents acquiring evidence, then AH follows immediately from COND. For what justifies asserting A is having $p(A) = 1$; and, simple conditionalisation will give a $p(C)$ of 1, when we acquire a $p(A)$ of 1, iff $p(C/A)$ is 1.

Unfortunately for the simple life, there are, I have said, decisive objections to this view; see 4.6. So we need to generalise the notion of minimal evidence. It needs to be minimal in two ways.

First, what we want is evidence that is sufficient to raise $p(A)$ to $p'(A) = (1 - e)$, but no more. Since raising probability occurs by conditionalisation, we want to consider conditionalisation on a partition of evidence, $[E_1, \ldots, E_n]$, such that

$$\sum_{i=1}^{i=n} p(A/E_i) \cdot p'(E_i) = 1 - e.$$

Secondly, we want to raise the probability of A to $(1 - e)$, but not to raise the probability of anything else, unless we must. The idea, then, is that the changes of probability must be *consequences* of coming to believe that A to degree $(1 - e)$; and the way to capture that, is by requiring that the partition in which the change originates, contains A.

Let us say that if we conditionalise on a partition containing A, to produce a p-function in which $p'(A) = (1 - e)$, that we have conditionalised A to $p'(A) = (1 - e)$.

If we conditionalise A to $p'(A) = (1 - e)$, we have acquired minimal evidence that A. COND says that if every way of acquiring minimal evidence that A produces belief that C, we are in a position to assert 'If A, C'.

We do not need to require that minimal evidence that A produce $p'(C) = (1 - e)$; for $p'(C)$ does not have to be raised to the same level as $p'(A)$ for 'If A, C' to be assertible. But $p'(C)$ must be large and close to $(1 - e)$. Unsurprisingly, it turns out that

(a) If we conditionalise A to $p'(A) = (1 - e)$, we get $p'(C) > (1 - e)^2$, iff

(b) $p(C/A) > (1 - e)$.

And $(1 - e)^2$ is always close to $(1 - e)$, when e is small. So: someone believes $(A \to C)$, where A and C have truth conditions, iff $p(C/A)$ is high. COND, then, entails AH. Given the triviality proofs, this means that COND does not allow us to give a truth-conditional account of the conditional, but, as shown

---

3. This suggestion was made by an anonymous reviewer for the *Journal of Philosophical Logic*.

in the previous chapter, we are able, given Adams' work, to develop a logic for conditionals whose constituents are truth-valued.

But what can COND do for us when the constituents of a conditional are not truth-valued?

11.4 EMBEDDED CONDITIONALS

Let us begin by making clearer what the problem is that embedded conditionals raise for AH.

If conditionals of both indicative and subjunctive forms could be embedded in each other and themselves quite freely, then there would be conditionals of each of the following forms:

1: $A \rightarrow (B \mathbin{\square\!\!\rightarrow} C)$

2: $A \mathbin{\square\!\!\rightarrow} (B \mathbin{\square\!\!\rightarrow} C)$

3: $A \mathbin{\square\!\!\rightarrow} (B \rightarrow C)$

4: $A \rightarrow (B \rightarrow C)$

On AH, the first two of these will raise no problems, provided subjunctive conditionals have truth conditions, as I think they do. Nothing I have said rules out that we should have a $p(B \mathbin{\square\!\!\rightarrow} C/A)$, if $p(B \mathbin{\square\!\!\rightarrow} C)$ exists, so 1 is all right; and whatever the correct semantics for '$\mathbin{\square\!\!\rightarrow}$', 2 seems likely to be acceptable also. However, 3 and 4, raise problems: 3, because subjunctive conditionals probably need truth-valued consequents; 4, because indicative conditionals, on AH, certainly must have them.

Now there are, as it happens, in English, no grammatical sentences of the form of 3. Thus,

*If John were to come, then, if Mary comes, so will Peter,

is simply defective; which, given that subjunctives require truth-valued consequents, confirms the view of AH, that indicatives do not have truth conditions. The problem case, then, is 4. So much for conditional *consequents*.

For conditional antecedents, we would have a similar roll-call:

5: $(A \mathbin{\square\!\!\rightarrow} B) \rightarrow C$

6: $(A \mathbin{\square\!\!\rightarrow} B) \mathbin{\square\!\!\rightarrow} C$

7: $(A \rightarrow B) \mathbin{\square\!\!\rightarrow} C$

8: $(A \rightarrow B) \rightarrow C$

Here again, the first two cases raise no problems for AH; 5 because we can conditionalise on a subjunctive conditional, because it has a truth-value, 6 because it is not an indicative conditional. The potential problem cases are 7 and 8; but, once more, sentences of the form of 7 do not exist, just as AH, with the assumption that subjunctive conditionals need truth-valued components, would predict.

Thus,

*If, if John is coming, Mary is coming, Peter would come

is simply not an English sentence. So we only have to deal with 8.[4]

Certainly *some* sentences of this form make sense. Dummett denies not only, as we saw in 10.7, that conditional negation makes sense but also that conditionals can 'appear as antecedents of more complex conditionals.' (1973: 451) But this is too strong a claim. It is certainly true that indicative conditionals with indicative conditional antecedents are rare and often difficult to understand; still,

If, if Mary comes tomorrow, James will be happy, then James is in love

is not unintelligible, and something must be said about what it means.

In this case, a truth-conditional view of the conditional would have distinct theoretical advantages, since it would allow us to say that

$$(A \rightarrow B) \rightarrow C$$

is assertible iff

$$p(C/(A \rightarrow B)) > 1 - e.$$

4. A word of warning may be needed here about what will and will not count as examples of embedded conditionals. In dealing with embedded conditionals, it is important not to be misled by the fact that, in English, a conditional in which the two main verbs are in the continuous aspect, is sometimes not of the form

If A, C

at all. Thus

If John comes, Mary comes

is, in effect of the form,

(t) (If John comes at t, then Mary comes at t).

I do not deal in this book with the operation of quantifiers when conditionals lie within their scope. But I am inclined to think that it is easier to make sense of embedded conditionals where the embedded conditional is in fact of this form. For whatever reason this is true, it does not damage any claims I now make about conditionals of the forms

If, if A, B, then C

and

If A, then, if B, then C

which are to be understood as being about sentences of this form outside the range of quantifiers.

On a non-truth-conditional view, of course, this conditional probability does not exist: and there is no obvious way of extending Adams' Hypothesis to deal with the embedded conditional.

Similarly if $(B \to C)$ has truth conditions, $p(B \to C/A)$ exists, and will give us the assertibility condition for

If A, then if B, then C.

This apparent advantage is rather less than it might at first appear. For a truth-conditional view has to explain why so many embedded conditionals are hard to make sense of. The explanation that embedded conditionals are particularly computationally taxing is no more convincing than it was with the disjoined conditionals of Chapter 9. So there are problems on both sides, and not such a preponderance on mine as to settle the question in favour of conditionals having truth conditions. So, though AH cannot, as I have said, apply directly to embedded conditionals if we could show that COND could handle conditionals without assigning them truth conditions, then even the existence of some intelligible embedded conditionals will not count in favour of the truth-conditional view.

Consider, therefore, what COND implies for conditionals with conditional consequents. To get an account of what it is to believe something of the form of 4, if COND applies to conditionals whose consequents are conditionals, we need only suppose that what goes for the probability of a non-conditional consequent, goes for the conditional probability corresponding to a conditional consequent. So that the relevant version of COND would say that:

someone is entitled to assert a conditional $(A \to (B \to C))$ iff coming to have minimal evidence warranting the assertion of A would lead to their being entitled to assert that $(B \to C)$.

It follows that, where A, B and C have truth conditions, $(A \to (B \to C))$ is assertible iff the agent will have a high $p'(C/B)$ in the p-function p' derived from their current p-function by conditionalising A to $p'(A) = (1 - e)$, for small e. The value of $p'(C/B)$ after so conditionalising will be

$$p'(C/B) = \frac{(1 - e) \cdot p((C \ \& \ B)/A) + e \cdot p((C \ \& \ B)/\neg A)}{(1 - e) \cdot p(B/A) + e \cdot p(B/\neg A)}$$

and this, as we saw in 9.4 footnote 7, does not reduce to $p(C/(A \ \& \ B))$. We thus avoid having the theorem

$$(A \ \& \ B) \to C \dashv\vdash A \to (B \to C)$$

which did the damage in the triviality proofs.

But consider the case where $p(B \; \& \; \neg A)$ is 0. In this case, the factors of e, in both numerator and denominator, reduce to 0. And in this special case $p'(C \; \& \; B) = p(C/(B \; \& \; A))$. This simple case will allow us to test out some intuitions about the adequacy of this account of what it is to believe a conditional with a conditional consequent.

It is, as I have said, rather difficult to come up with plausible embedded indicative conditionals. That, indeed, is part of my evidence for the view that conditionals are not truth-conditional. But here is one which satisfies the condition that the negation of the antecedent is inconsistent with the antecedent of the conditional embedded as the consequent:

If it is an element, then, if it is sodium, it will burn yellow.

This conditional seems to be assertible. And, if my account is correct, it ought also to be assertible that

If it is an element and it is sodium, it will burn yellow.

which reduces, since being sodium entails being an element,[5] to

If it is sodium, it will burn yellow.

And, of course, I believe each of these last two conditionals. This case has, then, come out according to our intuitions. But we should need to examine other cases to see if we could come up with counterexamples.

There are other special cases we might investigate. It would be tempting for example to investigate what happens in the case where $p(A \; \& \; B) = 0$. Intuitions here are somewhat strained, however, by the fact that in such a circumstance, as when, for example, we have:

If John is coming, then if he had stayed away, I would be happy

the consequent in the resultant conditional is not an indicative conditional at all. Still, if this is of the form

(John comes) $\rightarrow$ (John stays away $\rightarrow$ I am happy)

then what our hypothesis says is that this is assertible iff

p(I am happy/(John does not come and John stays away))

is high; a condition which holds iff

If John does not come, I shall be happy

is assertible; and this is, at least, plausible.

The conditional with conditional antecedent is rather harder to fit into this sort of framework. It is, perhaps, to the advantages of my view, that such conditionals are the hardest embedded conditionals to find. It is true that there

5. This is an application of Adams' rule 1; see 10.4.

are conditionals such as

If, if you drop it in a minute, it will break, then it is fragile.[6]

But it is hard to find a case where this is a more natural thing to say than

If you drop it in a minute and it breaks, then it is fragile.

The reason there is a problem with this case, of course, is that in order to apply COND, we should need to be able to make sense of the idea of conditionalising on a conditional. But we only can make sense, given GC, of conditionalising on non-conditional sentences.[7]

This is not to say that COND says nothing about $((A \rightarrow B) \rightarrow C)$, only that, in the framework I have developed, it is not clear at the outset what the significance is of what it says. We know, from COND, that

someone is entitled to assert a conditional $((A \rightarrow B) \rightarrow C)$, iff coming to have minimal evidence warranting the assertion of $(A \rightarrow B)$ would lead to their being entitled to assert that C.

But what is it to have minimal evidence warranting the assertion of $(A \rightarrow B)$?

The issue is not straightforward. It must be part of the content of the view that conditionals do not have truth conditions, that we cannot perceive that they are true; see 9.8. If conditionals have no truth conditions, there simply are no states of the world, interaction with which can constitute perception that if A, then C. Intuition confirms this result: it is true that one can come to believe a conditional because one hears it uttered. But there has always been thought to be a difficulty about perceiving conditional facts: I know what it is to see that Mary is arriving in a hat, and I know what it is to see that John is happily dancing. But what is it to perceive that if Mary arrives in a hat, John will dance happily?

Even if we cannot perceive 'conditional facts' (because there are none), it does not follow that we cannot have evidence warranting the assertion of something of the form $(A \rightarrow B)$. Quite to the contrary; I have just given a

---

6. I insert the 'in a minute' to stop the reading as

If (t) (if you drop it at t, it will break at t), then it is fragile.

See footnote 4

7. Skyrms has suggested that we might deal with this case by looking to second order probabilities. Instead of the question what effect conditionalisation on $(A \rightarrow B)$ would have on our p-function, we could ask what would be the effect of second-order conditionalisation on the proposition that the first-order conditional probability is high. Since what value a conditional probability has is a question which has a true answer, we should here be conditionalising on a truth-conditional sentence. I have not discussed second-order probabilities in this book, and so I cannot take this proposal further, but this is an interesting approach (Skyrms, 1980a: Appendix 3). I think it is not likely to be necessary, however, if, as I argue later, there may be no such embedded conditionals.

theory which tells us what such evidence is — it is evidence which leads to our having a reasonable p-function in which $p(B/A)$ is high. But $((A \rightarrow B) \rightarrow C)$ will be assertible, on COND, only if *every* way of acquiring some evidence *minimally* will produce a high degree of belief that C. And *minimal* evidence for $(A \rightarrow B)$ is a notion that applies only where we can apply the notion of a partition of which $(A \rightarrow B)$ is a member. But that requires the conditional to have truth conditions. Since, as I have argued, $(A \rightarrow B)$ has no truth conditions, we can explain the very great difficulty we have in interpreting some conditionals with conditional antecedents.

What now needs explaining, of course, is we do sometimes say such things as

'If that plate will break if you drop it now, then it is fragile.'

And I suggest the reason why we have this form is that we have a surrogate for minimal evidence that the antecedent is true, in this case, which is simply hearing it reliably asserted. (Strictly, of course, being told is never minimal evidence: for beliefs about the utterance are acquired at the same time.) If we did not have a language, we should only be able to have truth-valued evidence (where $p(C/A)$ is not 1) or semantic grounds (where it *is* 1), that raised $p(C/A)$ to near 1. But because we have a language we are sometimes disposed to alter our $p(C/A)$ just because we have heard 'If A, C' uttered by a reliable source. In cases where this happens the possession of a disposition to assent to $((A \rightarrow B) \rightarrow C)$ manifests itself in adjusting $p'(C)$ to a high value when we assent to $(A \rightarrow B)$.

But it seems to me that many cases where conditionals superficially of the form of 8 occur are cases where the antecedent conditional is not indicative but subjunctive in force, so that the conditional is in fact of the form of 5. And, since I suppose that subjunctive conditionals *do* have truth-values, the treatment of conditionals of this form will be completely straightforward.

I have made these suggestions on the assumption that these embedded conditionals occur in English. If they do, then COND offers this much account of them. But what it suggests is not very satisfactory; and I want now to argue that all sentences which appear to be of the forms of 4 and 8 may in fact be of the forms of 1 and of 5 respectively. And if this is right, the suggestions I have been making, by way of COND, for embedded indicative conditionals, will turn out to be unnecessary. The arguments I am going to make depend very much on my not having been misled by cases, since they are frankly untheoretical. But the cases I offer will at least provide some support for the view that indicative conditionals do not embed in the only ways that raise a problem for the conjunction of AH (which COND entails) and the claim that conditionals do not have truth conditions.

Take 4, then, first. Superficially, the following sentence is of the form of 4.

9: If the C.I.A. is efficient, then, if President Reagan is a Russian spy, there is a file on him the Pentagon.

Now I believe the C.I.A. is efficient; so, since *modus ponens* holds for the conditional, I should be able to detach the consequent.

10: If Reagan is a Russian spy, there is a file on him in the Pentagon.

But I believe no such thing. If, as I doubt, Reagan is a spy, the only reason he is still President is that there is no such file. What I *do* believe is

11: If Reagan were a Russian spy, there would be a file on him in the Pentagon.

The conditional

12: If the C.I.A. is efficient, then, if Reagan were a Russian spy, there would be a file on him in the Pentagon

I *can*, therefore, assent to, along with believing the C.I.A. is efficient.

What does this show? It shows that if embedded conditionals in the indicative obey *modus ponens* (and they do), then I cannot believe 9 *and* that the C.I.A. is efficient, because I believe

13: [Even] if Reagan is a Russian spy, there is no file on him in the Pentagon.[8]

I conclude that 9 is not of the form it appears to be.

Because I believe 11, I am inclined to think that what 9 expresses is the thought properly expressed by 11. Because normally tenses in conditionals are in accord between antecedent and consequent (so that both are either indicative or subjunctive), I suggest we may be misled into saying 9.

This is only one case. Perhaps someone can find a convincing counter-example. But until then, I will stick with the claim that $(A \rightarrow (B \rightarrow C))$ is not the form of an English sentence.

A similar argument can be made for the view that sentences superficially of the form of 8 are in fact of the form of 5.

Consider

14: If, if Reagan is a Russian spy, there is no file on him in the Pentagon, the C.I.A. is inefficient.

---

8. I share the view, recently defended by Jonathan Bennett, that 'even' if conditionals are just conditionals within the scope of the force of 'even'; so I do not think the fact that we have a tendency to put it in here marks anything more than the fact that (roughly it's surprising that the conditional is assertible. See Bennett (1982).

I believe both 13 and 11; but I also believe that

15: If, if Reagan were a Russian spy, there would be no file on him in the Pentagon, then the C.I.A. is inefficient.

Now suppose, however, that I still think

16: The C.I.A. is efficient.

Then, if indicative conditionals obey *modus tollens* (and they do), and subjunctive conditionals do also (which, so far as I know, everyone agrees they do), then from 14 and 16 I can infer

17: It's not the case that, if Reagan is a Russian spy, there is no file on him in the Pentagon;

and from 15 and 16, that

18: It is not the case that, if Reagen were a Russian spy, there would be no file on him the Pentagon.

But 18, assuming conditional excluded middle, is equivalent to 11, which I believe, and is, on any plausible view, consistent with it; while 17 is inconsistent with 13, which I believe also.

Once again, this suggests (but does not, I agree, entail) that we do not have a sentence of the right form in 14, and that its real form might be 15. In this case too, we can explain why we have conditionals which are superficially of this form, by supposing that it is the desire to conform to the rules of tense accord between antecedent and consequent, which leads us into error.

Not only, therefore, do we have, in the triviality proofs, the strongest theoretical ground for doubting that indicative conditionals embed, but also the apparent linguistic counterevidence can, at least in some cases, be explained away; and, once this evidence is accounted for, the rest of the linguistic evidence suggests a non-truth-conditional view.

I have suggested that COND does say something about conditional consequents, but nothing about conditional antecedents. But I have also suggested that the evidence that these embedded conditionals occur in English is not good. Embedded conditionals do not provide a good testing ground for the merits of COND over AH; let me turn now to a case where COND has decisive advantages.

11.5 SEMI-INDICATIVES

Consider, then, semi-indicatives: conditional sentences with an indicative antecedent and a consequent whose main auxiliary is 'may'. My exemplar, you recall, is:

SI: If John is here, Mary may be here

whose logical form may be written

SI': $(A \rightarrow (\text{possibly } C))$.

The first thing to say is that the relevant sense of possibility is not logical possibility. In a sentence such as 'John may come', which is equivalent to 'It is possible that John will come', more than mere logical possibility is at stake.

In fact, I believe the relevant sense of possibility has been well characterised by Ian Hacking: it is what he calls L-possibility; see Hacking (1976a, 1975b). The criterial feature of L-possibility is that L-occurrences of 'possible' can intelligibly be replaced by 'probable'. Thus 'It is possible that . . . ' is an L-occurrence, because 'It is probable that . . . ' makes perfectly good sense. All other kinds of occurrence are, Hacking thinks, M-occurrences, where 'possible' can intelligibly be replaced by 'permissible'; thus 'It is possible for pigs to fly' is an engagingly mistaken M-occurrence because 'It is permissible for pigs to fly' is an engagingly silly, but intelligible, sentence.

L-possibility, according to Hacking, works like this:

a state of affairs is possible if it is not known not to obtain, and no practicable investigations would establish that it does not obtain. (1967a: 149)

This, at any rate, is Hacking's working hypothesis. Now, as he points out, this definition is not the first one that suggests itself. L-possibility is pretty obviously what we call 'epistemic possibility'; and the definition of *that* that suggests itself is simply that a state of affairs is possible iff we do not know that it does not obtain. There is no question of considering what would be the result of practicable investigations. But, to use an example which Hacking offers, if the mate on a salvage ship thinks that it is possible that the crew will find the treasure in a certain bay, we will say that he was wrong if we find that the hulk they were looking for went aground 30 miles away in another bay. We say it was not possible, because we know the hulk was not there, and 'practicable investigations' would have shown that it was not.

Conversely, there are cases where 'practicable investigations' would not reveal that what 'does not obtain' does not obtain.

Consider a person who buys a lottery ticket. At the time he buys his ticket we shall say that it is possible that he will win, though probably he will not. But retrospectively it would be absurd to say that it only *seemed* possible that he would win.

(1967a: 148–9.)

And, as we see, Hacking's explanation of this, built into the working hypothesis, is that no practicable investigations at the time – 'short of waiting to see who actually wins', as Hacking puts it – could have established that he would not win. So far, so good: we have some facts and an explanation of them. But the explanation is not quite right.

For *L*-possibility in the present tense, exhibits a curious feature in its assertibility conditions:

L-POSSIBLE 1: 'It is possible that *A*' is assertible iff the speaker does not know that not-*A*.[9]

And this is true even where the speaker knows that if he or she carried out 'practicable investigations' he or she could now discover whether or not *A*. It is because *L*-possibility has this feature that the conception of epistemic possibility as what is not known to be false is initially attractive.

I think I can suggest a modification of Hacking's account that will do the trick. Begin with the past tense rule of assertibility:

L-POSSIBLE 2: '*A* was possible at *t*' is assertible iff the speaker believes that it was not possible for someone to know at *t* that not-*A*.

Like Hacking, I rely on the fact that the 'possible' in the *analysans* is *M*-possibility; so the account is not circular. (For 'it is permissible for someone to know' makes sense; and 'it is probable for someone to know' does not.) Is there a simple way of connecting this assertibility rule with the rule, *L*-POSSIBLE 1, for the present tense? For, after all, it looks at the moment as if we just have separate cases: one for the present, one for the past. In fact, I think, we can produce a more unitary account.

In the present-tense case, a sentence is *L*-possible iff it is epistemically open for the speaker: iff the speaker does not know that it is false. In the past tense, it was possible iff it was epistemically open from the best perspective the speaker could have occupied at the time.[10] In assessing the sentence 'It is possible that *A*' people judge whether, relative to their present cognitive

---

9. It has to be 'know' and not 'believe' here. For otherwise, when I buy a lottery ticket I should not be able to say that it is possible that I will win: I believe I will not. But I *can* say that it is possible that I will win, because, though I believe I will not win, I do not know that I will not win. This fact is relevant to Michael Slote's claim that the correct rule for assertion is not assert what you believe, but assert what you know; see Slote (1979). There are not many cases where this difference matters: usually, if you have rational grounds for believing to a high degree that *S*, then, if *S* is true, you know that *S*; but not always. Some counterexamples to ASS (such as the claim that it is not assertible that I will not win in the lottery, even if I believe it) are consequences of this. I think Slote is right that what matters for assertibility is not belief but knowledge. But I have not restated the account of assertion in terms of knowledge, both because to do so would have involved a substantial discussion in the theory or knowledge, and because, so far as the discussion of the conditional in Chapters 8, 9 and 10 was concerned, nothing hung on it.

10. 'The best perspective the speaker could have occupied' means 'the best perspective in which it would have been possible for the speaker to have been': and this 'possible' is an occurrence of '*M*-possibility' also.

position, it is ruled out that A. If it is not, A is possible. In assessing 'It was possible that A' a speaker needs to find some past cognitive position from which to assess whether it was ruled out that A. There would be no point in assessing this from the perspective of someone who knew all the truths about that time: for then epistemic possibility would collapse into truth. Nor is there any point in assessing the question from the perspective of someone who knew about that time everything the speaker now knows: for then, 'It was possible that A' would collapse into 'It is possible that it was the case that A'. So in assessing past tense statements of possibility, speakers consider what would have been epistemically open for someone who knew everything about the past position that they know, *except those things they could not have known at the time*.[11]

We are now in a position to explain an important fact about L-possibility: namely that there is no future L-possibility, 'It will be possible that A' is not the form of an English sentence. We can see why if we seek to generalise L-possibility on the analysis of it I have just given. For in order to find a future tense, we should need to be able to find a cognitive position from which to assess whether or not A is epistemically open. And, if 'It will be possible that . . .' is not to collapse into 'It is possible that it will be the case that . . .', this cognitive position needs to be distinct from the speaker's current position. Since anything that can be known at some time, t, can be known after t — this is just a fact about our conception of the relation between knowledge and time; see Mellor (1982) — the future perspective from which we assessed such a future possibility would have to include all our present knowledge. But we cannot assess what will be epistemically open from a future cognitive position which includes all we know now and more: for we do not yet know what the more will be.

Because the analysis essentially depends upon reference to the cognitive perspective of the speaker, it cannot be stated in terms of truth conditions rather than assertibility conditions. So L-POSSIBLE 1 and 2 must stand as our account of L-possibility.

We can now apply the account to the semi-indicative conditional, if, as I have claimed, its logical form is

SI': $(A \rightarrow (\text{possibly } C))$.

and the 'possible' is L-possibility. Since we are working in the present tense we need only consider

L-POSSIBLE 1: 'It is possible that A' is assertible iff the speaker does not know that not-A.

---

11. Once again, the 'could' here is M-possibility.

I shall now show that this entails a slightly different condition. And to do this, I need to say a little about the proper analysis of the concept of knowledge, bearing in mind that we are to apply L-POSSIBLE 1, which is stated in terms of the speaker's knowledge.

Knowledge requires something more than just a justifiably high degree of true belief, as Gettier has taught us, and I do not wish to discuss what this something more is. I shall suppose that it has something to do with the belief's justification depending causally in the right way on the facts. Since we are working with assertibility rules, I shall state this proposal by giving the assertibility conditions for 'A knows that S': the conditions under which we utter sentences of that form. So: we say that A knows a truth-conditional sentence S iff

(a) A believes that S,
(b) we believe that S,
(c) we believe that A's belief is justified *and*
(d) we believe that A's justification depends in the appropriate way on the truth of S; see Grandy (1980).

Speakers have to believe that they know that S if they are to be justified in asserting that S. But, as is easily confirmed, conditions (a) and (b) in the analysis I have just given of when someone may believe that A knows that S, collapse into a single condition when A is that someone; and, since rational agents have degrees of belief iff they believe they are justified in having them, condition (c) is redundant also. The analysis thus reduces to this:

KNOW: A believes that A knows that S iff A believes that S and A believes that A's grounds for believing this are the appropriate grounds.

Sincere speakers assert only what they believe is assertible: and from KNOW and L-POSSIBLE 1 it follows that

L-POSSIBLE 1': 'It is possible that A' is assertible for S iff *either*
(a) S does not believe that not-A, *or*
(b) S does believe that not-A, but does not believe that this belief is justified in the appropriate way.

Where A has truth conditions (and believing that A is having a high degree of belief that A), condition (a) reduces to the condition that $p(A)$ is not low; so that we have

L-POSSIBLE 1'': 'It is possible that A' is assertible for S iff *either*
(a) S's $p(A)$ is not low, *or*
(b) S's $p(A)$ is low, but S does not believe that this degree of belief is justified in the appropriate way.

So much then for the case with truth conditions.

Given COND, we should have for the conditional
SEMI-INDICATIVE: 'If A, possibly C' is assertible for S iff *either*
(i) the result of coming directly to believe that A is to have a $p(C)$ that is not low *or*
(ii) the result of coming directly to believe that A is to have a $p(C)$ that is low, but S does not believe that this degree of belief would be justified in the appropriate way.[12]

Consider now a case where $p(C/A)$ is low, but the semi-indicative is still assertible. Hacking has already given us one. For where I know that a lottery is fair and has n tickets; and if $n > 1/e$, p(I will win/I buy a ticket) is low, but 'If I buy a ticket, I may win' is assertible; assertible, I claim, because the result of my coming to know that I have bought a ticket will not be that I know that I will not win. For here I should have a high degree of justified belief without knowledge.

This proposal has the properties we want: usually a sentence like 'If John comes, Mary may' will be asserted when the speaker simply does not have a high $p(\neg C/A)$. And this conforms to the view that is widespread in the literature that we say 'If John comes, Mary may' just when we will not say 'If John comes, Mary will not.' However, there are exceptions, to this general rule, exceptions which rely on condition (ii). Thus suppose there are enough tickets in a lottery for me to have a very high degree of belief that if I buy a ticket, I will not win. Then $p(C/A)$ is high; but, as Hacking originally pointed out, this degree of belief, though justifiable, is not justified in the way that is appropriate for knowledge. For I could only claim to know that I would not win if I bought a ticket, if I had a reason for thinking the lottery unfair. It is a good guess that your ticket will not win in a fair lottery: but it is not knowledge.

11.6 CONCLUSION

Adams' rule is the first well understood assertibility rule in philosophical semantics. I think we should be led by its successes to look for more. In this chapter, I have built on his assertibility rule and offered two more. But it is worth observing, finally, that the interest of such rules lies, in part, in the contrast with semantic rules stated in terms of truth conditions. Much recent discussion of assertibility conditions derives from Dummett's 'antirealist' claim that we should perhaps substitute assertibility conditions for truth conditions in general; see Dummett (1973), Wright (1976). This notion of

12. (i) is true iff $p(C/A)$ is not low; for $p'(C) = p(C/A)$.

assertibility is not the one I have been working with here: for, as I pointed out at the end of Chapter 7, the antirealist notion of an assertibility condition is of a condition whose obtaining provides epistemic warrant for the sentence asserted. Dummett's and Wright's assertibility conditions are thus to do with the justification of the belief expressed by a sentence and not directly with the justification for asserting it. But realists may be interested in a more modest role for assertibility conditions – in my sense – which are not derived, by way of ASS, from truth conditions. Realism need not be the claim that all declarative sentences can be given truth conditions; it requires only the view that truth conditions account for the central class of cases. The proposals in this chapter presuppose a realist treatment of the antecedents and consequents of unembedded conditionals, *and* a realist view of the sentences within the scope of the epistemic modality. What could be more central than that?

Epilogue

I have tried in this book to use the general account of the nature of belief, given in Part I, to ground an account of meaning, given in Part II; and to use the theory of meaning, and, in particular, the notion of assertibility that it entails, in Part III, to explain the semantics of some indicative conditionals. I have produced only a small part of the full theory of beliefs: nothing about second-order probabilities; little about the reference relation between singular representational elements and the world; mere intimations – promissory notes – about quantification. The account of meaning, too, needs developing: to deal with speech-acts other than assertion, for example, and, more generally, with conversational and conventional implicature. And there is much more to be said about conditionals: subjunctives, in particular. All these are matters well worth pursuing. And, I conjecture, the study of each of the unresolved problems in the theory of meaning will benefit, as I think the study of conditionals has, from an approach that begins with the nature of beliefs and moves out to the semantics of sentences that express them.

The main argument for the theory I have developed is that we need its features to do the job we do every day of explaining each other's action . . . including, of course, out utterances. I claim, in fact, that, except for a technical precisification and, no doubt, some errors of mine, it *is* your theory also. And so I should expect you to find much that I have said resonating in many places with thoughts you have had before. I have relied on the excellent philosophical literature that has grown up around these questions, and this approach to them. And even if what I have said has no resonance with your views, I would urge you to consider seriously that literature, to which I have offered many signposts: for even if I have not got it right, I am sure that our theory is something like this, and in those writings you will find routes around my errors. For if there is one thing of which I am morally certain it is that Cartesianism is wrong, and that functionalism, of some sort, is a better alternative than behaviourism. And, in a sense, I have only been concerned to give an account of the relation of language, mind and world which steers that middle course.

Bibliography

Adams, E. W. 1965 On the logic of conditionals. *Inquiry* 8.

　1966 Probability and the logic of conditionals. In *Aspects of inductive logic.* ed. J. Hintikka and P. Suppes, Amsterdam, North-Holland.

　1975 *The logic of conditionals.* Dordrecht, Reidel.

　1976 Prior probabilities and counterfactual conditionals. In *Foundations of probability theory, statistical inference and statistical theories of science.* ed. W. L. Harper and C. A. Hooker, Dordrecht, Reidel.

　1977 A note comparing probabilistic and modal logics of conditionals. *Theoria* 43.

Adams, E. W. and Levine, H. P. 1975 On the uncertainties transmitted from premises to conclusions in deductive inferences. *Synthese* 30.

Anderson, A. R. 1951 A note on subjunctive and counterfactual conditionals. *Analysis* 12.

Anderson, A. R. and Belnap, N. D. Jr 1975 *Entailment; the logic of relevance and necessity.* Volume 1. Princeton, New Jersey.

Anderson, J. 1952 Hypotheticals. *Australasian Journal of Philosophy* 30.

Anscombe, G. E. M. 1969 Causality and extensionality. *Journal of Philosophy* 66.

Appiah, A. 1981 Conditions for conditionals. Unpublished Ph.D. Thesis, Cambridge.

　1982 Conversation and conditionals. *Philosophical Quarterly* 32.

　1984*a* Antirealism unrealised. *Philosophical Quarterly* 34.

　1984*b* Jackson on the material conditional. *Australasian Journal of Philosophy* 62.

　1984*c* An argument against antirealist semantics. *Mind* 93.

　forthcoming *For truth in semantics* Oxford, Basil Blackwell.

Armstrong, D. W. 1968 *A materialist theory of the mind.* London, Routledge & Kegan Paul.

　1973 *Belief, truth and knowledge.* Cambridge.

Baker, A. J. 1967 If and ⊃. *Mind* 76.

Bennett, J. 1974 Counterfactuals and possible worlds. *Canadian Journal of Philosophy* 4.

　1976 *Linguistic behaviour.* Cambridge.

　1982 Even if. *Linguistics and Philosophy* 5.

Bigelow, J. C. 1976 If-then meets the possible worlds. *Philosophia* 6.

Biro, J. I. and Shahan, R. W. eds. 1982 *Mind, brain and function.* Brighton, Harvester Press.

Blackburn, S. ed. 1975 *Meaning, reference and necessity.* Cambridge.

Block, N. 1978 Troubles with functionalism. In *Perception, cognition and issues in the foundations of psychology.* Minnesota Studies in the Philosophy of Science Volume 9. ed. C. W. Savage. Minneapolis, University of Minnesota Press.

Block, N. ed. 1980 *Readings in philosophy of psychology.* Volume 1. London, Methuen.

1981 *Readings in philosophy of psychology.* Volume 2. London, Methuen.

Bolton, N. ed. 1979 *Philosophical problems in psychology.* London, Methuen.

Braithwaite, R. B. 1932/3 The nature of belief. *Proceedings of the Aristotelian Society* 33.

Brandt, R. and Kim, J. 1963 Wants as explanations of actions. *Journal of Philosophy* 60.

Brown, R. and Rollins, C. D. eds. 1969 *Contemporary philosophy in Australia.* London, Allen & Unwin.

Butler, R. J. ed. 1966 *Analytical philosophy.* Oxford.

Carlstrom, I. F. and Hill, C. S. 1978 Rev: Adams, E. W. *The logic of conditionals. Philosophy of Science* 45.

Chandler, H. S. 1978 What is wrong with addition of an alternate? *Philosophical Quarterly* 28.

Chisolm, R. 1946 The contrary-to-fact conditional. *Mind* 55.

Clark, M. 1971 Ifs and hooks. *Analysis* 32.

1974 Ifs and hooks: a rejoinder. *Analysis* 34.

Cohen, L. J. 1971 Some remarks on Grice's views about the logical particles of natural language. In *Pragmatics of natural language.* ed. J. Bar-Hillel. Dordrecht, Reidel.

1977 Can the conversationalist hypothesis be defended? *Philosophical Studies* 31.

Cooper, W. S. 1968 The propositional logic of ordinary discourse. *Inquiry* 11.

1978 *The foundations of logico-linguistics.* Dordrecht, Reidel.

Dale, A. J. 1972 The transitivity of 'if, then'. *Logique et Analyse* 15.

1974 A defense of material implication. *Analysis* 34.

Davidson, D. 1963 Actions, reasons and causes. *Journal of Philosophy* 60.

1967 Truth and meaning. *Synthese* 7.

1973 In defence of convention T. In *Truth, Syntax and Modality.* ed. H. Leblanc. Amsterdam, North-Holland.

1974 Belief and the basis of meaning. *Synthese* 27.

1975 Thought and talk. In *Mind and language.* ed. S. Guttenplan. Oxford.

1976 Reply to Foster. In *Truth and meaning: essays in semantics.* ed. G. Evans and J. McDowell. Oxford.

Davidson, D. and Harman, G. 1972 *Semantics of natural language.* Dordrecht, Reidel.

1975 *The logic of grammar.* Encino, California, Dickenson Publishing Company.

Davidson, D. and Suppes, P. 1957 In collaboration with S. Siegel. *Decision making: an experimental approach.* Stanford.

Dennett, D. 1978 *Brainstorms.* Brighton, Harvester Press.

Descartes, R. 1968 Meditations on the first philosophy . . . In *Discourse on method and the meditations.* trans. F. E. Sutcliffe. London, Penguin.

Dudman, V. R. 1983*a* Tense and time in English verb clusters of the primary pattern. *Australasian Journal of Linguistics* 3.

1983*b* Conditional interpretations of if-sentences. Unpublished m.s.

Dummett, M. 1973 *Frege: philosophy of language.* London, Duckworth.

1975 What is a theory of meaning? In *Mind and language.* ed. S. Guttenplan. Oxford.

1976 What is a theory of meaning? Part II. In *Truth and meaning: essays in semantics.* ed. G. Evans and J. McDowell. Oxford.

Edwards, J. S. 1974 A confusion about 'if . . . then'. *Analysis* 34.

Edwards, W. 1960 Measurement of utility and subjective probability. In *Psychological scaling: theory and applications.* ed. H. H. Gulliksen and S. Messick. New York, John Wiley & Sons.

Eells, E. 1982 *Rational decision and causality.* Cambridge.

Ellis, B. 1969 An epistemological concept of truth. In *Contemporary philosophy in Australia.* ed. R. Brown and C. D. Rollins. London, Allen & Unwin.

1979 *Rational belief systems.* Totowa, New Jersey, Rowman & Littlefield.

1984 Two theories of indicative conditionals. *Australasian Journal of Philosophy* 62.

Evans, G. and McDowell, J. eds. 1976 *Truth and meaning: essays in semantics.* Oxford.

Feigl, H. 1967 *The mental and the physical.* Minneapolis, University of Minnesota Press.

Feigl, H., Scriven, M. and Maxwell, G. eds. 1958 *Concepts, theories and the mind-body problem.* Minnesota Studies in the Philosophy of Science Volume 2. Minneapolis, University of Minnesota Press.

Field, H. 1977 Logic, meaning and conceptual role. *Journal of Philosophy* 74.

1978 Mental representation. *Erkenntnis* 13.

1978 A note on Jeffrey conditionalization. *Philosophy of Science* 45.

Finch, H. A. 1957/8 An explication of counterfactuals by probability theory. *Philosophy and Phenomenological Research* 18.

1959/60 Due care in explicating counterfactuals: a reply to Mr. Jeffrey. *Philosophy and Phenomenological Research* 20.

Fodor, J. A. 1976 *The language of thought.* Brighton, Harvester Press.

1978 Computation and Reduction. In *Perception, cognition and issues in the foundations of psychology.* Minnesota Studies in the Philosophy of Science Volume 9. ed. C. W. Savage. Minneapolis, University of Minnesota Press.

1981 The mind-body problem. *Scientific American* January.

Gazdar, G. 1979 *Pragmatics: implicature, presupposition and logical form.* London, Academic Press.

Gibbard, A. and Harper, W. L. 1978 Counterfactuals and two kinds of expected utility. In *Foundations and applications of decision theory.* ed. C. A. Hooker, J. J. Leach and E. F. McLennen. Dordrecht, Reidel.

Gibbins, P. 1979 Material implication, the sufficiency condition and conditional proof. *Analysis* 39.

Gomberg, P. 1978 Does 'possible' ever mean 'logically possible'? *Philosophia* 8.

Goodman, N. 1947 The problem of counterfactual conditionals. *Journal of Philosophy* 45.

1973 *Fact, fiction and forecast.* Indianapolis, University of Indiana Press.

Grandy, R. E. 1980 Ramsey, reliability and knowledge. In *Prospects for pragmatism.* ed. D. H. Mellor. Cambridge.

Grice, H. P. 1975 Logic and Conversation. In *The logic of grammar.* ed. D. Davidson and G. Harman. Encino, California, Dickenson Publishing Company.

Gulliksen, H. H. and Messick, S. eds. 1960 *Psychological scaling: theory and applications.* New York, John Wiley & Sons.

Gunderson, K. ed. 1976 *Language, mind and reality.* Minnesota Studies in the Philosophy of Science Volume 7. Minneapolis, University of Minnesota Press.

Guttenplan, S. ed. 1975 *Mind and language.* Oxford.

Hacking, I. 1967a Possibility. *Philosophical Review* 76.

　　1967b Slightly more realistic personal probability. *Philosophy of Science* 34.

　　1975a *Why does language matter to philosophy?* Cambridge.

　　1975b All kinds of possibility. *Philosophical Review 84.*

Harman, G. 1978 Is there mental representation? In *Perception, cognition and issues in the foundations of psychology.* Minnesota Studies in the Philosophy of Science Volume 9. ed. C. W. Savage. Minneapolis, University of Minnesota Press.

Harper, W. L. 1974 A note on universal instantiation in the Stalnaker-Thomason conditional logic. *Journal of Philosophical Logic* 3.

Harper, W. L. and Hooker, C. A. eds. 1976 *Foundations of probability theory, statistical inference and statistical theories of science.* Volume 1. Dordrecht, Reidel.

Harrison, J. 1968 Unfulfilled conditionals and the truth of their constituents. *Mind* 77.

Hazen, A. and Slote, M. 1979 'Even if'. *Analysis* 39.

Hempel, C. G. 1965 *Aspects of scientific explanation and other essays in the philosophy of science.* New York, Free Press.

Hintikka, J. and Suppes, P. 1966 *Aspects of inductive logic.* Amsterdam, North-Holland.

Hobbes, T. 1839 *Elements of philosophy. The first section, concerning body.* In *The English works of Thomas Hobbes of Malmesbury.* ed. Sir W. Molesworth, London, John Bohn.

Hooker, C. A., Leach, J. J. and McLennen, E. F. eds. 1978 *Foundations and applications of decision theory.* Dordrecht, Reidel.

Hornsby, J. 1980 *Actions.* London, Routledge & Kegan Paul.

Hosiasson-Lindenbaum, J. 1940 On confirmation. *Journal of Symbolic Logic* 5.

Hume, D. 1888 *A treatise of human nature.* ed. C. A. Selby-Bigge. Oxford.

Jackson, F. 1977 A causal theory of counterfactuals. *Australasian Journal of Philosophy* 55.

　　1979 On assertion and indicative conditionals. *Philosophical Review* 87.

　　1980/1 Conditionals and possibilia. *Proceedings of the Aristotelian Society* 81.

Jeffrey, R. C. 1959/60 A note on Finch's 'an explication of counterfactuals by probability theory'. *Philosophy and Phenomenological Research* 20.

　　1964 'If.' *Journal of Philosophy* 61.

　　1965 *The logic of decision.* New York, McGraw-Hill.

　　1981 *Formal logic: its scope and limits.* (2nd edn) New York, McGraw-Hill.

　　1983 The logic of decision. (2nd edn) Chicago.

Johnson-Laird, P. N. and Wason, P. C. eds. 1977 *Thinking: readings in cognitive science.* Cambridge.

Kempson, R. M. 1975 *Presupposition and the delimitation of semantics.* Cambridge.

Kneale, W. and Kneale, M. 1962 *The development of logic.* Oxford.

Knox, J. Jr. 1971 Material implication and 'if . . . then'. *International Logic Review* 3.

Kripke, S. 1972 Naming and necessity. In *Semantics of natural language.* ed. D. Davidson and G. Harman. Dordrecht, Reidel.

Kyburg, H. Jr. 1961 *Probability and the logic of rational belief.* Middletown, Connecticut, Wesleyan University Press.

　　1970 Conjunctivitis. In *Induction, acceptance and rational belief.* ed. M. Swain. Dordrecht, Reidel.

1978 Subjective probability. *Journal of Philosophical Logic* 7.

Leblanc, H. 1957 On logically false evidence statements. *Journal of Symbolic Logic* 22.

Lehmann, S. K. 1979 A general propositional logic of conditionals. *Notre Dame Journal of Formal Logic* 20.

Levi, I. 1978 Newcomb's many problems. In *Foundations and applications of decision theory*. ed. C. A. Hooker, J. J. Leach and E. F. McLennen. Dordrecht, Reidel.

Lewis, D. 1966 An argument for the identity theory. *Journal of Philosophy* 63.

    1969 *Convention: a philosophical study*. Cambridge, Massachusetts, Harvard University Press.

    1970 Completeness and decidability of three logics of counterfactual conditionals. *Theoria* 37.

    1972a Psychophysical laws and theoretical identifications. *Australasian Journal of Philosophy* 50.

    1972b General semantics. In *Semantics of natural language*. ed. D. Davidson and G. Harman. Dordrecht, Reidel.

    1973 *Counterfactuals*. Oxford, Basil Blackwell.

    1975a Languages and language. In *Language, mind and reality*. Minnesota Studies in the Philosophy of Science Volume 7. ed. K. Gunderson. Minneapolis, University of Minnesota Press.

    1975b Causation. In *Causation and conditionals*. ed. E. Sosa. Oxford.

    1976 Probabilities of conditionals and conditional probabilities. *Philosophical Review* 85.

    1977 Possible-world semantics for counterfactual logics: a rejoinder. *Journal of Philosophical Logic* 6.

    1980 Veridical hallucination and prosthetic vision. *Australasian Journal of Philosophy* 58.

    1981a Causal decision theory. *Australasian Journal of Philosophy* 59.

    1981b Logic for equivocators. *Nous* 16.

Loar, B. 1980 Ramsey's theory of belief and truth. In *Prospects for pragmatism*. ed. D. H. Mellor. Cambridge.

Luce, R. D. and Raiffa, H. 1957 *Games and Decisions*. New York, Wiley.

Mackie, J. L. 1973 *Truth, probability and paradox: studies in philosophical logic*. Oxford.

    1975 Causes and conditions. In *Causation and conditionals*. ed. E. Sosa. Oxford.

Marcus, R. B. 1953 Strict implication, deducibility and the deduction theorem. *Journal of Symbolic Logic* 18.

Margolis, J. 1967 Entitled to assert. *Synthese* 17.

Maxwell, G. 1978 Rigid designators and mind–brain identity. In *Perception, cognition and issues in the foundations of psychology*. Minnesota Studies in the Philosophy of Science Volume 9. ed. C. W. Savage. Minneapolis, University of Minnesota Press.

McCawley, J. D. 1974 If and only if. *Linguistic Inquiry* 1974.

McGinn, C. 1979 Action and its explanation. In *Philosophical problems in psychology*. ed. N. Bolton. London, Methuen.

McKay, A. and Merrill, T. eds. 1976 *Issues in the philosophy of language*. New Haven, Connecticut, Yale University Press.

McKay, T. and van Inwagen, P. 1977 Counterfactuals with disjunctive antecedents. *Philosophical Studies* 31.

Mellor, D. H. 1971 *The matter of chance*. Cambridge.

1974 In defence of dispositions. *Philosophical Review* 82.

Mellor, D. H. ed. 1980a *Science, belief and behavior*. Cambridge.

1980b *Prospects for pragmatism*. Cambridge.

Mellor, D. H. 1980c Consciousness and degrees of belief. In *Prospects for pragmatism*. ed. D. H. Mellor. Cambridge.

1982 *Real time*. Cambridge.

1984 Computational psychology. *Proceedings of the Aristotelian Society Supplementary Volume* 58.

Myhill, J. 1953 On the interpretation of the sign ' ⊃ '. *Journal of Symbolic Logic* 18.

Nagel, T. 1974 What is it like to be a bat? *Philosophical Review* 83.

Nelson, J. O. 1966 Is material implication inferentially harmless? *Mind* 75.

Nossal, G. 1978 *Antibodies and immunity*. London, Penguin.

Nozick, R. 1969 Newcomb's problem and two principles of choice. In *Essays in honor of Carl G. Hempel*. ed. N. Rescher. Dordrecht, Reidel.

Parry, W. T. 1957 Reexamination of the problem of counterfactual conditionals. *Journal of Philosophy* 54.

Platts, M. 1979 *Ways of meaning: an introduction to a philosophy of language*. London, Routledge & Kegan Paul.

Pollock, J. L. 1976 *Subjunctive reasoning*. Dordrecht, Reidel.

Popper, K. 1949 A note on natural laws and so-called 'contrary-to-fact conditionals'. *Mind* 58.

1959 On subjunctive conditionals with impossible antecedents. *Mind* 68.

Putnam, H. 1975a *Mind, language and reality*. Cambridge.

1975b The meaning of 'meaning'. In *Mind, language and reality*. Cambridge.

Quine, W. V. O. 1960 *Word and object*. Boston, Technology Press of Massachusetts Institute of Technology, New York, John Wiley & Sons.

1975 Mind and verbal dispositions. In *Mind and language*. ed. S. Guttenplan. Oxford.

Ramsey, F. P. 1978 *Foundations*. ed. D. H. Mellor. Cambridge.

1964 *Hypothetical reasoning*. Amsterdam, North-Holland.

Rescher, N. 1968 A factual analysis of counterfactual conditionals. *Philosophical Studies* 11.

Rescher, N. ed. 1968 Studies in logical theory. *American Philosophical Quarterly Monograph* 2. Oxford, Basil Blackwell.

Ruskin, J. 1865 *Sesame and lilies*. London, Smith, Elder & Company.

Ryle, G. 1950 'If', 'so', 'because'. In *Philosophical analysis*. ed. M. Black. Ithaca, New York, Cornell University Press.

Savage, C. W. ed. 1978 *Perception, cognition and issues in the foundations of psychology*. Minnesota Studies in the Philosophy of Science Volume 9. Minneapolis, University of Minnesota Press.

Schank, R. C. and Abelson, R. 1977 Scripts, plans and knowledge. In *Thinking: readings in cognitive science*. ed. P. N. Johnson-Laird and P. C. Wason. Cambridge.

Schiffer, S. 1972 *Meaning*. Oxford.

Schneider, E. 1953 Recent discussions of subjunctive conditionals. *Review of Metaphysics* 6.

Schwartz, S. P. ed. 1977 *Naming, necessity and natural kinds*. Ithaca, New York, Cornell University Press.

1975 Counterfactuals. In *Causation and conditionals*. ed. E. Sosa. Oxford.

Shoemaker, S. 1982 Some varieties of functionalism. In *Mind, brain and function*. ed. J. I. Biro and R. W. Shahan. Brighton, Harvester Press.

Skorupski, J. 1980 Ramsey on belief. In *Prospects for pragmatism*. ed. D. H. Mellor. Cambridge.

Skyrms, B. 1980a *Causal necessity*. New Haven, Connecticut, Yale University Press.

1980b Higher order degrees of belief. In *Prospects for pragmatism*. ed. D. H. Mellor. Cambridge.

Slote, M. 1978 Time in counterfactuals. *Philosophical Review* 8.

1979 Assertion and belief. In *Papers on language and logic*. ed. J. Dancy. Keele.

Smart, J. J. C. 1959 Sensations and brain processes. *Philosophical Review 68*.

Sosa, E. ed. 1975 *Causation and conditionals*. Oxford.

Stalnaker, R. 1968 A theory of conditionals. In *American Philosophical Quarterly Monograph* 2. ed. N. Rescher. Oxford, Basil Blackwell.

1970 Probabilities and conditionals. *Philosophy of Science* 37.

1975a Indicative conditionals. *Philosophia* 5.

1975b Rev: E. Adams. On the logic of conditionals, E. Adams, Probability and the logic of conditionals. *Journal of Symbolic Logic* 40.

Stalnaker, R. 1976 Propositions. In *Issues in the philosophy of language*. ed. A. McKay and D. Merrill. New Haven, Connecticut, Yale University Press.

Stalnaker, R. and Thomason, R. 1970 A semantic analysis of conditional logic. *Theoria* 36.

Stevenson, C. L. 1970 If-iculties. *Philosophy of Science* 37.

Swain, M. ed. 1970 *Induction, acceptance and rational belief*. Dordrecht, Reidel.

Tarski, A. 1944 The semantic conception of truth. *Philosophy and Phenomenological Research* 4.

Teller, P. 1973 Conditionalization and observation. *Synthese* 26.

Tichy, P. 1975 A counterexample to the Lewis–Stalnaker conditional analysis of counterfactuals. *Philosophical Studies* 29.

Unger, P. 1975 *Ignorance: a case for scepticism*. Oxford.

van Fraassen, B. C. 1976 Probabilities of conditionals. In *Foundations of probability theory, statistical inference and statistical theories of science*. Volume 1. ed. W. L. Harper and C. A. Hooker. Dordrecht, Reidel.

von Neumann, J. and Morgenstern, O. 1947 *Theory of games and economic behaviour*. Princeton, New Jersey.

von Wright, G. H. 1971 *Explanation and understanding*. London, Routledge & Kegan Paul.

1979 *Logical studies*. London, Routledge & Kegan Paul.

Walker, R. C. S. 1975 Conversational implicatures. In *Meaning, reference and necessity*. ed. S. Blackburn. Cambridge.

Wiggins, D. 1971 On sentence-sense, word-sense and difference of word-sense. Towards a philosophical theory of dictionaries. In *Semantics. An interdisciplinary reader in philosophy, linguistics and psychology.* ed. D. D. Steinberg and L. A. Jakobowitz. Cambridge.

Wilson, D. 1975 *Presupposition and the delimitation of semantics.* London, Academic Press.

Wiredu, J. E. 1971 Material implication and 'if . . . then'. *International Logic Review* 3.

Wisdom, J. O. 1952 *Other minds.* Oxford, Basil Blackwell.

Wright, C. 1976 Truth-conditions and criteria. *Proceedings of the Aristotelian Society Supplementary Volume* 50.

Wunderlich, D. 1977 Assertions, conditional speech-acts and practical inferences. *Journal of Pragmatics* 1.

Young, J. J. 1972 Ifs and hooks: a defence of the orthodox view. *Analysis* 33.

Index of names

Index of key terms

This index provides references to pages or sections where key terms are explained.